Perspectives on Social Change

Consulting Editor: Amitai Etzioni

Perspectives on
SOCIAL CHANGE

ROBERT H. LAUER
Southern Illinois University
Edwardsville

Allyn and Bacon, Inc.   Boston

Contents

Preface

James Fenimore Cooper had one of his fictional characters say that the entire country was in "a constant state of mutation." Few would argue that the situation has altered; if anything, the rate of change has accelerated over the past one hundred years. Moreover, much of that change would be defined by many people as undesirable. Over the past few years, for example, we have seen a presidential veto of educational appropriations at the same time as the Senate was approving expansion of the ABM system of defense. And we have seen a continuation of an accelerating arms race while many of our people still agonize in injustice and deprivation.

This book is addressed to all those who are concerned about such change, or who are concerned about change in general. It is not intended to be an exhaustive study of all aspects of change, but rather to indicate the more important issues, problems, and concerns. Some of the topics are of great importance but have been neglected or ignored in other texts—the role of youth in change, the relation of violence to change, and strategies for effecting change. Other topics have been treated more or less adequately by others, but must be understood by any serious student of change—theories of change, mechanisms of change, and patterns of change in the contemporary world.

I hope, then, that the reader of this book will gain a broad understanding of the basic issues, problems, and concerns in the area of social change. Further, I would hope that the reader will be both stimulated and prepared to explore the various facets of change in greater depth. For this important area of sociological study has been neglected, and the opportunities for creative and significant work are manifold.

The value of the book will be maximized if the reader understands its plan of organization. The divisions are obviously arbitrary; one could use any of a number of different schemes. Basically, I have divided the book into sections which are designed to answer important questions: What kinds of assumptions underlie discussions of change (introduction)? How might we explain change (theoretical perspectives)? What is the driving force of change (mechanisms of change)? What form or pattern does change assume (patterns of change)? And what are the important considerations in effecting and guiding change (strategies of change)?

The reader will soon discover that some materials could be placed in two or more of the sections. Ogburn and Veblen could have been discussed as theorists rather than as representatives of the notion that technology is a crucial mechanism of change. But two considerations guided me: 1. I wanted to cover—at least briefly—all the more important thinkers; and 2. I wanted to deal with mechanisms, patterns, and strategies apart from their inclusion in specific theories. The second point should both clarify theories and aid further theoretical development.

But mechanisms, patterns, and strategies are always an implicit or explicit part of theories; and most students of social change have implicit or explicit theoretical perspectives which they employ in their analyses. Consequently, it was necessary to make some arbitrary decisions. My arbitrariness having thus been confessed, I trust it will not distract the reader from seriously digging into the subject of change.

Many minds other than the author's are involved in the writing of a book. I would like to acknowledge my indebtedness to four teachers who have been particularly influential in my own intellectual development: Paul Campisi, Gunter Remmling, Wolf Heydebrand, and Robert Boguslaw.

Finally, in the course of the writing of this book, many people were important to me in terms of their support and encouragement. I am grateful for a family that has been rich in those qualities. They have been an enclave of love in a violent world. To Carol, Jon, Julie, and Jeff, and to a future illuminated by hope, this book is dedicated.

RHL

PART I

Introduction

Sociology emerged out of the turbulence of the nineteenth century as a science of social order and social change. Auguste Comte, who has been called "the sire of sociology," fathered a discipline that would illuminate not only the bases of a viable structure of society but also the course of human development. But the children drifted away from the father's vision; the greater portion of twentieth-century energies were expended on what C. Wright Mills called grand theory and abstracted empiricism. As a result, sociology was in the embarrassing position of confronting a rapidly changing world with a paucity of tools of understanding. There are indications that the second half of the century will be different — works on social change have begun to proliferate.

There are, however, certain impediments that must be cleared away in order for fruitful work to be carried on in the area of social change. I have called these impediments the "myths" of change; they are assumptions that impede our understanding, and the first chapter seeks to dispel them.

CHAPTER 1

The Myths of Change[1]

The world may yet, as T. S. Eliot suggested, end with a whimper rather than a bang. But in the meantime, it plunges breathlessly into a hazy future, convulsed by conflict, writhing in the agony of injustice, and searching with a kind of urgent desperation for a meaningful human existence. Such a world demands an understanding of social change. The perspectives of past thinkers are helpful and are a necessary foundation both for understanding the present and for constructing new perspectives for the future. But some writings on change have been rooted in assumptions which we can now see to be false. Theories of change have been built upon myths about change. These myths hinder our understanding and impede the construction of new perspectives. An understanding of social change, therefore, must begin by shedding the mythical from our thought.

THE MYTH OF DEVIANCE

A considerable amount of sociological thinking has conceived of change as in some sense a violation of the normal.[2] That is, the normal state of affairs in society is persistence; institutions or values or cultural patterns are thought to be quite stable over time. This reflects a conservative strain which has pervaded sociology throughout its history. While Comte, for example, acknowledged the role of human action in social progress, he reduced that role to one of implementing intellectual reform. Utopia, which for Comte was a scientific society, would come when men began to think scientifically. The role of the sociologist was to induce scientific thinking in men.

A variety of theoretical perspectives have appeared in sociology since Comte, but in recent decades the dominant note has been structural-functionalism, which gives primary attention and support to social orders characterized by stability and integration.[3] This focus on stability (and the consequent neglect of change) assumes that static analyses can be made without coming to terms with change, and that an understanding of social change demands a prior and thorough understanding of social statics.[4] Sociologists working within this perspective, then, have been far more concerned with structures than with processes, and even when they have dealt with processes, they have dealt with the latter within structurally limited bounds. Persistence and regularities have been viewed as the normal state of affairs; change has been viewed as a kind of social deviance.

But a thorough understanding of structures is not a guarantee of an understanding of change. This should be clear from the manner in which change has been kept at the periphery of sociological interest during the decades of structural-functionalist dominance. There has been a continuous refinement of structural analysis, rather than a transition to studies of change. Structural understanding has only obscured, not illuminated, the centrality of change in the social system and has discouraged interest in it.

Furthermore, it may be argued that an understanding of change is a prerequisite for the understanding of structures. Those who view society as a system in equilibrium and seek to analyze the structural aspects of that system recognize that equilibrium is maintained only by certain intrasystem changes. These changes occur in response to external forces that impinge upon the system. Both external and internal changes, therefore, are necessary for the equilibrium to be maintained, and there is no logical reason why an understanding of the structure must have priority over an understanding of the changes.

It is more realistic and fruitful, then, to see change as inherent "in the very nature of things," [5] including the very nature of social life. Whether we are talking about the physical world, the history of man, or the human intellect, we find that "nothing remains what, where and as it was, but everything moves, changes, comes into being and passes out of existence." [6] Reality is not static. As the ancient Greek philosopher, Heraclitus, correctly observed, all being is "in flux, is constantly changing, constantly coming into being and passing away." [7]

The ubiquity of change may be easily accepted for transitional societies in the contemporary world. It has, for example, been asserted that change is ubiquitous in modernizing societies, in the United States, and in any society that strives to fulfill human needs.[8] But I am arguing for the ubiquity of change in all societies, including ancient and primitive. With respect to ancient society, we may take China as an example. The Hegelian idea of a China bound by a stagnant social structure is no longer tenable. It has become increasingly clear that China's history was "full of upheavals, abrupt transitions, and gradual changes." [9] In the so-called Axial Period, for example, China was in considerable flux, along with the other major societies of the time. From 900 to 200 B.C., the structure of both Chinese society and Chinese thought was undergoing continual change.[10] The centuries following that period present a marked contrast with the rapidly changing society of the Axial Period but do *not* present a stagnant society which was virtually unchanged over a long span of time. What was unusual about China was not the lack of change but the unusually slow rate of change. And the same argument may be advanced with respect to primitive societies.[11]

Change, in other words, is normal. Whether we are dealing with the individual[12] or social level, change is of the essence, and man must either grow or decay: "The pure conservative is fighting against the essence of the universe." [13] Early evolutionary theory in sociology had many flaws, but one of its central tenets was quite valid — the ubiquity and normality of change. The problem of social change, therefore, becomes one of the *rate* of change rather than of its presence or absence. What demands investigation are such questions as why certain societies and certain times exhibit unusually rapid or unusually slow rates of change; what factors affect rates and how; and whether there is an optimal rate of change for human well-being.

THE MYTH OF TRAUMA

The notion that change is abnormal is often associated with a second idea — change is traumatic. Change has been called an "ordeal," a "crisis," and a "foreign and unwanted agent." [14] And, indeed, it is not difficult to gather evidence that seems to support the myth of trauma.

There is, for example, some evidence that mental illness is related to social change. Not every kind of change is associated with mental illness, however. Rather, certain changes in conjunction with various other social and psychological factors seem to increase mental stress. For example, rates of hospitalization increase for people who migrate from one place to another and for those who are in a state of cultural transition; but lower rates of admission to mental hospitals occur during the change from war to peace and peace to war.[15] Social change *per se*, then, does not lead to mental stress or emotional illness.

But the traumatic nature of change may also be supported by the large number of social and psychological impediments to change which have been identified.[16] These impediments could be seen as defense mechanisms against the trauma of change. And, indeed, there are manifold ways in which people resist change; any change agent faces an incredible array of problems when he seeks to lead people in new directions. In some cases, the value system itself seems to possess built-in resistance to any change. The values may, for example, minimize the importance of material aspirations, or disparage the cultural ways of others, or demand interpersonal and intergroup relationships that are incongruent with a modernized society.

Certain attitudes also impede change. Economic development will lag unless people acquire attitudes of cooperation, the desire for advancement, respect for manual work, and so forth.[17] Even change that promises to fulfill such basic needs as medical care may be resisted because, for example, of traditional attitudes about the propriety of a woman being examined by a male doctor.

Other factors that inhibit change are rigid stratification systems, a high degree of social inequality, community fragmentation, vested interests, and even cultural motor patterns. An example of the latter is provided by the reputedly low efficiency of certain Indian factory workers.[18] The workers service machines and have been far less efficient at the job than their European counterparts. However, the machines require the worker to stand or sit on a high stool. The Indians are able to work efficiently for hours while squatting, but quickly tire when forced to stand or sit. The failure of the Indian workers to adapt to the machines is rooted in a cultural motor pattern rather than in some psychic trauma inherent in change.

Finally, there are social-psychological factors that inhibit change. The government, for example, is generally conceded to be crucial to much change in the contemporary world. The success or failure of the developing nations of the world is crucially linked with actions of the central governments; no nation in the contemporary world is modernizing on the basis of the activities of individual entrepreneurs alone. But the peasants' perception of that government often involves considerable suspicion and distrust. Thus, a Nigerian effort to introduce new fertilizer to the peasants failed, in spite of the fact that the innovation would have greatly increased productivity. But the peasants rejected the fertilizer partly because of past negative experiences with officials, partly because of distrust of the British government, and partly because of a lack of understanding of both the use and the usefulness of the new fertilizer.[19]

All of the above could be interpreted to be social and psychological protective mechanisms that have evolved out of the need to cope with the trauma of change. And the argument could be clinched by citing the numberless concrete instances of resistance to change, including resistance to railroads, the automobile, the typewriter, alternating current, tractors, umbrellas, street lighting, and even potatoes.[20]

But a closer look at the reasons for the ubiquity of resistance to change casts the whole problem in a different light. Spicer[21] points out that people are always changing their ways, but that they will resist change under three circumstances: when the change is perceived to be a threat to basic securities; when the change is not understood; and when the change is imposed upon them. Much of the supposed trauma of change can be accounted for in these terms.

Furthermore, change may be resisted because a rational calculation of the risks involved seems to make the new direction highly foolish. Thus, the apparent conservatism of a peasant community may actually be a weighing of risks, since that community is often one in which people live at the edge of survival, feel compelled to remain within the protection of the group, and must balance risk-taking with the potentially great penalties that may be incurred.[22] From one point of view, it is rational to urge the peasant to opt for cash crops rather than for subsistence farming. As long as the peasant simply grows food for his own consumption, he obviously will remain at the subsistence level. But from the peasant's point of view, it is more rational to insure his subsistence than to risk his minimal security on the altar of a capricious market. Unlike a Western entrepreneur, the peasant is not merely risking money; he is risking his very life.

There are also cases in which change may be resisted because that change would interfere with other, more highly valued, change. For example, Barbadians rejected agricultural diversification as recommended by both British and American experts, because of a high value on another kind of change — upward mobility in their own society. This represents a change in personal life circumstances which, incidentally, may or may not reflect societal change such as economic growth. In any case, the Barbadian who goes into full-time agriculture forfeits his chances for cultural success because of the low prestige attached to agricultural occupations; the potential change in personal status, therefore, was the basis for rejecting a change in agricultural economy.[23] Not all peoples give priority to economic change; the rejection of innovations that would facilitate economic development may, therefore, reflect a higher value on some other kind of change rather than trauma inherent in change.

There are, in sum, numerous bases upon which change is resisted. But none of these is related to any trauma intrinsic to change. Nevertheless, the assumption of trauma has often been made, and that assumption is a negative value judgment about change that is likely to lead to the assertion of persistence and stability as the natural and desired state of affairs for humans. The fallacy of this myth, however, is clearly seen in the obverse side of the question — the changes that are welcomed, initiated, or both, by people themselves. If people clearly resist change at times, they just as clearly value it at other times. For example, it has often been assumed that one of the critical problems of industrializing a traditional society is the securing of commitment of an industrial labor force. People have been known to be frustratingly sporadic in coming to work in the factories. Nevertheless, commitment to industrial work is not always a problem. Lambert has shown that the labor force in Poona, India, was thoroughly committed to working in the factories. Other studies have shown that the integration of factories into traditional communities can be a relatively smooth process.[24] Industrialization is neither inevitably resisted nor inherently inconsistent with a traditional culture. It is only when we assume that a factory in Asia or Africa or Latin America must operate exactly like its American counterpart that we will encounter serious problems of resistance.

Peasant societies do not cling tenaciously to the existing order; the peasant wars of the twentieth century bear ample witness to the peasant's desire for change. One reason that peasants value change is that the peasant community is not often the stable and harmonious society that is depicted in the concept of *Gemeinschaft*, or "folk society." On the contrary, for many peasants, life is a "continual anguish," and change is eagerly sought.[25] Lerner pointed out that in all the Middle Eastern countries he studied, the rural villagers admitted to their unhappiness, while modernizing individuals reported much less unhappiness. Traditional society is receding in the Middle East "because relatively few Middle Easterners still want to live by its rules." [26]

Social change, then, is not inevitably resisted. At times it may be, but at other times people may deliberately initiate change. And the effort may have sufficient intensity to effect radical change within a single generation.[27] At this point, a qualification needs to be introduced. For while change *per se* cannot be viewed as traumatic, the rate of change seems to be related to experienced stress.

Rapid change may generate considerable stress. Thus, the psychologist Kenneth Keniston has maintained that the incessant innovations that characterize American life are part of the "deepest souces of strain" in the nation.[28]   And Toffler has coined the phrase "future shock" to describe the psychic disruption that results from experiencing too much change in too short a time.[29]   One study of health records of military personnel concluded that "a cluster-year of life-changes was seen to occur immediately prior to an illness or to a clustering of illnesses."[30]   That is, when the rate of life-changes (including such changes as death of a wife, divorce, marital problems, a new line of work, a child getting married, personal successes, and new religious patterns) was quite high, with many changes occurring in a short period of time, physical or mental illness tended to follow the changes. The greater the total score of "life-change units" (the various changes were weighted, with death of wife being the most heavily weighted and minor infraction of civilian law the least weighted), the greater the probability of a major health change.

It should be noted that the changes dealt with in the above study were of kinds that would be perceived both as desirable and undesirable. Some of the changes, such as personal successes, would be highly valued; some, such as death of a loved one, would be highly undesirable. It was not merely the kind of a change that the authors found to be related to stress, but the rate of change.

Although the evidence is sparse and more difficult to obtain, a relatively low rate of change may also generate stress. The relationship, in other words, may be curvilinear — both too high and too low rates of change generate stress. This implies an optimal rate of change for human well-being. Such an optimal rate in the organizational context has been suggested by Starbuck, who pointed out that members of organizations will be unhappy in both "an overly stable environment" and "an overly variable one."[31] If rapid change is a source of stress, so may be change that is too slow.

THE MYTH OF UNIDIRECTIONALITY AND UTOPIA APPREHENDED

Some of the first sociologists set forth theories of social evolution that posited a uniform end, and, in some cases, a uniform path to that end, for all societies. Comte, for example, described social evolution in terms of an ineluctable sequence which was leading to a predestined end. Some contemporary thinkers have continued to propagate this notion, while others have admitted to diverse pathways—though still to a predestined end. And in any case, the end is the same—a modern, industrial society that has an obvious Western appearance.

This myth of unidirectionality—the idea that all societies are ultimately heading towards one particular end—is sometimes called the theory of convergence and sometimes the contradiction between tradition and modernity. It is basically a form of technological determinism, although the extent of that determinism varies among theorists. That is, no one argues that each industrial society will be a carbon copy of every other industrial society. But industrialization is often seen as a powerful process that effects a considerable amount of standardization. Consequently, the uniformities of industrial society are perceived to be of far greater significance than any diversity.

Thus, it has been maintained that certain societal patterns (patterns that are similar to those of the West) are inevitable for any society that accepts Western technology.[32] Probably the most noted exponent of this position is the work of Clark Kerr and his associates, who set forth the idea of the "logic" of industrialism.[33] This "logic" does not demand a singular path, but it does insist upon a singular end, namely, "pluralistic industrialism." The pluralistic industrial society is one in which there is a system of checks and balances in the midst of an incessantly changing technology. Conflict between diverse interest groups is regulated by a "web of rules" which are constructed by the State, by managers, and by various associations. The State is very powerful, with considerable economic responsibility. The productive enterprise itself is dominant and possesses "substantial authority" in order to maximize efficiency.

Kerr and his associates argue that a number of factors lead towards uniformity in the pluralistic industrial society. These include the passage of time — the farther the society moves away from the traditional base the more potent the logic of industrialism becomes; technology; the "push of progress"; the imperatives of education and equality; the "omnipresent State"; the dominance of the productive enterprise; and the "compulsion of comparisons" (men in various societies will strive for progress and participation in society upon the basis of their knowledge of the achievements of competing societies).

The idea that all societies are ultimately becoming very similar easily slips over into the myth of utopia apprehended, which is the argument or assumption that a modern, industrial society represents the ultimate in human achievement. The solution for world problems, then, lies in helping the developing nations to modernize (where modernize is equivalent to Westernize) as quickly and painlessly as possible. The sooner they become like the West, it is believed, the sooner will mankind enjoy peace and fulfillment. Utopia has already been apprehended cognitively; it only becomes a matter of time and will until it is apprehended in reality throughout the world. The inherent flaws in modern society are thereby ignored; the modern social structure is held to require only refinement, not radical change.[34]

Undoubtedly there is some truth in the myth of unidirectionality. The dominance of the State for contemporary industrial growth seems to be an imperative for the developing nations. But this is not equivalent to saying that all industrial and industrializing societies are becoming alike with respect to the role of the State. Furthermore, the myths of unidirectionality and utopia apprehended seem contradicted by a substantial amount of evidence. The assumption that industrialization demands particular social forms may be shown to be false in some very basic respects. In the first place, the supposed antithesis between tradition and modernity is false. In his study of Cantel, Guatemala, Nash found that a considerable amount of traditional life can continue and even flourish at a higher level in the process of industrialization.[35] An accommodation was worked out between textile mill and community such that the factory proceeded with its business of production and the community continued with its institutions.

Factory work schedules in Cantel were accommodated to traditional holidays and to the traditional obligations of the people in the civic area. The traditional requirements of male participation in civic affairs sometimes demanded a man's full time for anywhere from a period of weeks to as much as two years. Nevertheless, the men who worked in the factory were allowed to devote the required time to civic duties without penalty. Furthermore, the factory work did not affect the world view of the Cantelenses; the factory and nonfactory workers were found to hold similar beliefs. The traditional modes of thinking were not transferred to the factory, but neither was the rationality implicit in the factory transferred to everyday experience.

The persistence of tradition is particularly evident in the Orient. Scholars generally agree that Japan has modernized while maintaining and utilizing premodern, traditional institutions.[36] Rather than a society that has moved along the path from tradition to modernity, Japan is a nation that employs both tradition and the modern and holds them together in a viable contradiction that has resulted in rapid development. A 1966 study of nearly 1000 Japanese students found that although Japanese political behavior is outwardly similar to that of the West, that behavior has not been truly westernized; traditional Japanese values still persist.[37]

The Japanese pattern is more or less characteristic of the nations of East Asia in general, for those nations have not adopted the Western way in its entirety, but rather have exercised great selectivity. Some aspects of Western society have been accepted, but others have been ignored or rejected outright. And those elements that were borrowed did not have the same effects as they had in the West. A modernized East Asia, therefore, will probably reflect the West neither in its overt cultural patterns nor "in its more fundamental ideals and values." [38]

There is, then, no inherent conflict between tradition and modernity such that the more modern a nation becomes, the more it must necessarily shed its tradition. Traditionalism, the commitment to the past and its ways, can severely hamper change. But tradition itself, as Japan has clearly shown, can be a vehicle for change rather than a barrier. And even traditional ideas that seem, on the surface, to resolutely resist change may actually serve to facilitate it — at least certain kinds of change. An instance of this is the Indian concept of *dharma,* which involves the individual's duty to fulfill his own part of a network of mutual obligations and privileges. On the surface, it would seem that adhering to *dharma* would negate any kind of change, since those obligations and privileges emerge from the past. But in addition to maintaining the social order, the concept admits to flexibility, to modification of duty as the social milieu changes. "The accommodative characteristics of the *dharma* concept has allowed for change without overthrow of basic principles." [39]   Thus, transformation is quite compatible with the concept, and much of the change in India during and since the days of Gandhi may be seen as a working out (rather than a rejection) of *dharma.*

Industrialization does not demand the obliteration of tradition. Nor does it impose a particular social structure upon a people. The logic of industrialism is said to require the priority of the economic. Nevertheless, the relation between the economy and polity in the United States and the Soviet Union, two highly industrialized nations, is obviously not the same. And all efforts at industrialization in Communist China have been marked by the absolute priority of the political. In neither the Soviet Union nor the People's Republic do we find the pluralistic situation supposedly demanded by the logic of industrialism.

A similar argument with respect to the family has been set forth by Goode, who finds a considerable variety of family forms congenial with industrialization; there is no necessary destruction of traditional family patterns.[40]   In an Arab village studied by Tannous, there was an initial conflict between the silk factory with its typical emphasis on individual profit and the traditional Lebanese kinship group which had been the basis of community organization. The problem was resolved not by the disintegration of kinship obligations, but by a new form of factory enterprise. Each factory was the work of an enterprising individual who was supported by the compound family unit. The factories were always referred to in terms that indicated kinship group ownership. And the traditional kinship obligations were transferred to the factory situation.[41]

In general, then, it is not possible to justify the idea of a singular end for modernizing societies. Nor is it possible to justify the idea of a singular path to that end. The study of two Indonesian towns which were in the pre-takeoff period of economic development concluded that the path towards economic takeoff may involve considerable diversity in terms of cultural patterns and social structures. One town was characterized by a highly individualistic, modernized Moslem, economically motivated setting; the other was group-centered, orthodox Hindu, and politically motivated.[42]

Another example is the Arab city of Tripoli, which was changing in the 1960's from an agrarian-commercial to a light industrial economic base. Some of the aspects of the Western industrial nations emerged in Tripoli — trends towards universal education, professionalism, modernized travel and communication, and expanded governmental programs, for example. But these trends became an addition to, rather than a displacement of, the agrarian-commercial patterns. And "when we consider certain values, sentiments, and qualities of interpersonal relationships, we shall find cultural patterns which differ considerably from comparable ones which have been associated with the Western industrial city." [43]

Finally, it has been shown that some of the factors we often associate with modernization on the basis of Western experience may show a negative correlation with sustained growth in the developing nations. At certain levels of development, such factors as degree of literacy, growth of the mass media, formal education, and urbanization may correlate negatively with sustained growth.[44] The reason for this becomes clear if we consider education. When many of the developing nations first gained their independence, they faced a serious shortage of educated personnel to assume positions of responsibility in the polity and economy. But the economy may not expand rapidly enough to absorb an educated elite, particularly if the emphasis has been on universal education. Furthermore, the cost of maintaining a massive public education system may seriously impair the accumulation of capital necessary for economic development. At the same time, education is associated with power and with the material advantages of the West, so that there is a general demand for universal education. The net result may be that the government finds itself in a situation in which it is politically necessary, but economically unfeasible, to maintain large-scale education.

If, then, the idea of unidirectionality is a myth, the question arises as to whether anything can be said about the process of modernization apart from specific situations.   A more realistic view than the unidirectional one is suggested by Black, who foresees a possible "universalization of functions, but not of institutions." [45]   Modernization confronts a society with certain basic problems; but the answers that are given to those problems may vary considerably.   A variety of institutional forms may prove to be adequate.

There are a number of reasons why there will be diverse societal answers to the problem of modernization.   One is that the developing nations of the world have seen both the desirable and the objectionable in industrialized societies.   The ideologies of the leaders of the developing nations always, therefore, have a nationalistic hue that rejects both the Soviet and the American patterns as appropriate *in toto* for their own societies.[46]

Secondly, although I have used the terms "modernization" and "industrialization" interchangeably, modernization may proceed apart from industrialization.   That is, industrialization may be viewed as an essentially economic pattern of development, while modernization refers to the social and political changes that are often, though not necessarily, associated with industrialization.   In the West, industrialization and commercialization were bound up with the process of modernization; but some non-Western development has involved commercialization and bureaucracy without industrialization.[47]

A third reason that developing nations will pursue their own unique courses is that neither modern nor traditional societies are homogeneous entities.   Just as modern, industrial societies exhibit differing systems, so do the traditional societies reveal considerable variations.[48]   The developing nations are starting from diverse bases and aiming at diverse ends.   The myths of unidirectionality and utopia apprehended are just that — myths.   Man's future is not converging towards some social system that is essentially an extrapolation of the contemporary West.   Whatever logic there is in industrialism, it does not foreordain the shape of the future.

THE MYTH OF SEMANTIC ILLUSION

As pointed out above, it has sometimes been assumed that static analyses can be made without coming to terms with change, and that an understanding of social change demands a prior and thorough understanding of social statics.   This error may be compounded by assuming that every static analysis has implications for change, so that ultimately the difference between theories of change and theories of statics is merely a semantic illusion. This position has been argued forcefully by Kim Rodner.[49]

Rodner maintains that change theories are not distinguishable from nonchange theories by the variable of time. Rather, what are called social change theories are characterized by one or both of two properties that are not related to time: (1) the precision in stating the temporal connective and (2) the degree of compoundedness of the theory. As an example of the precision in stating the temporal connective, he refers to the theory of Davies regarding the cause of revolution. That theory can be expressed in terms of increasing temporal precision, from the "folk law" that "thwarted hopes sometimes produce social uprisings" to the more temporally precise law that some exact temporal quantity of an extended increase in expectations and the satisfaction of those expectations, followed by an unexpected reversal of short duration, may cause revolution. What the sociologist means by laws of change, according to Rodner, is the greater temporal precision in the second as opposed to the first formulation.

As to the degree of compoundedness, Rodner is referring to the difference between a single law and a series of laws which can be linked together into an explanatory chain. The greater complexity of the latter would have more obvious temporal implications.

Thus, the myth of semantic illusion concludes that all theories have implications for both change and statics, for all are saying essentially the same thing. The only difference is in the degree of precision with which the theory is formulated. But this conclusion is false. All theories may indeed imply certain dynamics; all may imply movement of some kind; all certainly recognize that social life is not an inert entity. But all theories do not imply change — except, perhaps, in the negative sense that change is some kind of deviance or in the functionalist sense that change is merely an elaboration of a particular system. In addition, some theories regard change as natural, while others view it as that which occurs through some kind of coercion.

Whether change or persistence is seen as the basic reality is quite important. The difference between nonchange and change theories is more than semantic illusion; it is a difference in fundamental attitude towards change and the legitimacy of change. The theorist who works in the context of a "nonchange" theory provides — willingly or not — an ideological basis for the status quo. And the people who operate on the assumption of the normality of persistence rather than of change will tend to inhibit — willingly or not — change in their society.

This latter point is illustrated by the exceedingly slow rate of change in China for hundreds of years prior to the twentieth century. The Chinese viewed persistence as the basic reality.

They valued order, which was derived from the Mandate of Heaven, given to the Emperor that he might "organize a moral system and establish the moral order." [50]   Change in this context was severely limited in scope.   Certain recurrent processes were legitimate and even inevitable.   But the Chinese both perceived and expected the tempo of change to be slow.   As Hsueh Fu-ch'eng, writing in 1879, put it: "According to the way of heaven, there is a small change once every several hundred years, and a great change once every several thousand years." [51]   The difference between the Chinese view of reality and that of those people who held that reality is continual change was not one of mere illusion.   The Chinese expectation of a slow rate of change was matched by the reality of Chinese society.

CONCLUSION

Once we have cleared away the myths about change, we are in a position to begin the task of understanding change. Some of the theories to be discussed in the following chapters will make the assumptions which we have called myths.   This does not mean, however, that nothing can be gained from a study of these theories. Many insights will come through the examination of past perspectives.   The point is, however, that new perspectives on change must be constructed, and these new perspectives will be most fruitful by assuming that change is normal; that change carries with it no intrinsic trauma; that diverse patterns of change and a range of future alternatives are open to any society; and that whether one assumes change or persistence as the basic reality has important practical as well as theoretical consequences.

ENDNOTES TO CHAPTER 1

1.   This chapter is a modified and extended version of my paper, "The Scientific Legitimation of Fallacy: Neutralizing Social Change Theory," which appeared in *American Sociological Review*, XXXVI (Oct., 1971), 881–89.

2.   See, for example, Talcott Parsons, Robert F. Bales, and Edward A. Shils, *Working Papers in the Theory of Action* (Glencoe: The Free Press, 1953), pp. 102–3; Talcott Parsons, "Some Considerations on the Theory of Social Change," *Rural Sociology*, XXVI (Sept., 1961); Richard T. LaPierre, *Social Change* (New York: McGraw-Hill, 1965), pp. 38–39; and

Robert A. Nisbet, *Social Change and History* (New York: Oxford University Press, 1969), p. 270.

3. The debate over whether structural-functionalism adequately deals with social change is dealt with at length in various chapters in N. J. Demerath III and Richard A. Peterson, *System, Change, and Conflict* (New York: The Free Press, 1967).

4. See Talcott Parsons, *The Social System* (Glencoe: The Free Press, 1951), pp. 483–86; and Wilbert E. Moore, "A Reconsideration of Theories of Social Change," *American Sociological Review*, XXV (Dec., 1960), p. 817.

5. Alfred North Whitehead, *Science and the Modern World* (New York: Macmillan, 1925), p. 179.

6. Frederick Engels, *Anti-Duhring*, trans. Emile Burns (New York: International Publishers, 1939), p. 26.

7. *Ibid.*, p. 27.

8. By, respectively, C. E. Black, *The Dynamics of Modernization* (New York: Harper & Row, 1966), p. 47; Daniel Bell, *The End of Ideology* (New York: The Free Press, 1960), pp. 35–36; and Amitai Etzioni, *The Active Society* (New York: The Free Press, 1968).

9. Etienne Balazs, *Chinese Civilization and Bureaucracy*, trans. H. M. Wright, ed. Arthur F. Wright (New Haven: Yale University Press, 1964), p. 15.

10. Don Martindale, *Social Life and Cultural Change* (Princeton: D. Van Nostrand Co., 1962), pp. 93ff.

11. See, for example, R. M. MacIver and Charles H. Page, *Society: An Introductory Analysis* (New York: Rinehart and Co., 1937), p. 512; and Raymond Firth, *Elements of Social Organization* (London: Watts & Co., 1951), pp. 80ff.

12. The Swiss psychiatrist, Paul Tournier, in his *The Meaning of Persons*, trans. Edwin Hudson (New York: Harper & Row, 1957), p. 100, says: "The perfectly stable being is nothing but an automaton, without life — a thing."

13. Alfred North Whitehead, *Adventures of Ideas* (New York: Mentor Books, 1933), p. 273.

14. By, respectively, Eric Hoffer, *The Ordeal of Change* (New York: Harper & Row, 1952); Robert A. Nisbet, *Social Change and History*, p. 282; and Richard T. LaPierre, *Social Change*, p. 39.

15. H. B. M. Murphy, "Social Change and Mental Health," *Milbank Memorial Fund Quarterly*, XXXIX (July, 1961), 385–445.

16. For a brief account of some of these factors, see Philip Hauser, "Cultural and Personal Obstacles to Economic Development in the Less Developed Areas," *Human Organization*, XVIII (Summer, 1959), 78–84. A more extensive

treatment is provided by George Foster, *Traditional Cultures: And the Impact of Technological Change* (New York: Harper & Row, 1962), pp. 64–142.

17. Gunnar Myrdal, *Asian Drama* (New York: Pantheon, 1968), Vol. 3, p. 1873.

18. Bert F. Hoselitz, "Tradition and Economic Growth," in *Tradition, Values, and Socio-Economic Development,* ed. Ralph Braibanti and Joseph Spengler (Durham: Duke University Press, 1961), p. 89.

19. Ronald Cohen, "The Success that Failed: An Experiment in Culture Change in Africa," *Anthropologica,* III (1961), 21–36.

20. See Bernard Barber, *Science and the Social Order* (Glencoe: The Free Press, 1952), p. 213, and W. I. Thomas, *Primitive Behavior: An Introduction to the Social Sciences* (New York: McGraw-Hill, 1937), pp. 726–27.

21. Edward H. Spicer, ed., *Human Problems in Technological Change* (New York: Russell Sage Foundation, 1952), p. 18.

22. Guy Hunter, *Modernizing Peasant Societies* (New York: Oxford University Press, 1969), p. 49.

23. Sidney M. Greenfield, "Stocks, Bonds, and Peasant Canes in Barbados: Some Notes on the Use of Land in an Overdeveloped Economy," in *Explorations in Social Change,* ed. George K. Zollschan and Walter Hirsch (Boston: Houghton Mifflin, 1964), pp. 619–50.

24. Richard T. Lambert, *Workers, Factories, and Social Change in India* (Princeton: Princeton University Press, 1963); Afif I. Tannous, "Social Change in an Arab Village," *American Sociological Review,* VI (Oct., 1941), 651–62; Manning Nash, *Machine Age Maya* (Chicago: The University of Chicago Press, 1967).

25. Joseph Lopreato, *Peasants No More* (San Francisco: Chandler Publishing Co., 1967), p. 65.

26. Daniel Lerner, *The Passing of Traditional Society* (Glencoe: The Free Press, 1958), pp. 398–99.

27. Anthony Wallace, "Revitalization Movements," *American Anthropologist,* LVIII (1956), 264–81.

28. Kenneth Keniston, "Social Change and Youth in America," *Daedalus,* XCI (Winter, 1962), 145–71.

29. Alvin Toffler, *Future Shock* (New York: Random House, 1970).

30. Richard H. Rahe, Joseph D. McKean, Jr., and Ransom J. Arthur, "A Longitudinal Study of Life-Change and Illness Patterns," *Journal of Psychosomatic Research,* X (1967), 366.

31. William H. Starbuck, "Organizational Growth and Development," in *Handbook of Organizations,* ed. James G. March (Chicago: Rand McNally & Co., 1965), p. 472.

32. George A. Theodorson, "Acceptance of Industrialization and its Attendant Consequences for the Social Patterns of Non-Western Societies," *American Sociological Review*, XVIII (Oct., 1953), 477–84.

33. Clark Kerr, John T. Dunlop, Frederick H. Harbison, and Charles A. Myers, *Industrialism and Industrial Man* (Cambridge: Harvard University Press, 1960), pp. 282ff.

34. For a critique of the theory of modernization along these lines, see Michael Walzer, "The Only Revolution: Notes on the Theory of Modernization," *Dissent*, XI (Autumn, 1964), 432–40. For examples of the explicit argument or implicit assumption that a modern, industrial society is utopia apprehended, see Ernest Gellner, *Thought and Change* (Chicago: The University of Chicago Press, 1964), pp. 69ff; C. E. Black, *The Dynamics of Modernization* (New York: Harper & Row, 1966), pp. 129ff; Francis R. Allen, *Socio-Cultural Dynamics* (New York: The Macmillan Company, 1971), pp. 340ff; and Brigitte Berger, *Societies in Change* (New York: Basic Books, 1971), pp. 13–14, 174.

35. Nash, *Machine Age Maya*.

36. A brief summary, some references, and divergent viewpoints regarding the Japanese experience are provided in a number of articles in the *Journal of Social Issues*, XXIV (Oct., 1968).

37. F. Kenneth Berrien, "Japanese Values and the Democratic Process," *Journal of Social Psychology*, LXVIII (1966), 129–38.

38. John K. Fairbank, Edwin O. Reischauer, and Albert M. Craig, *East Asia: The Modern Transformation* (Boston: Houghton Mifflin Co., 1965), p. 9.

39. Joan Bondurant, "Traditional Polity and the Dynamics of Change in India," *Human Organization*, XXII (Spring, 1963), 10.

40. William J. Goode, "Industrialization and Family Change," in *Industrialization and Society*, ed. Bert F. Hoselitz and Wilbert E. Moore (Paris: UNESCO-Mouton, 1963), pp. 239–55.

41. Tannous, *American Sociological Review*, VI, 651–62.

42. Clifford Geertz, *Peddlers and Princes* (Chicago: The University of Chicago Press, 1963).

43. John Gulick, "Old Values and New Institutions in a Lebanese Arab City," *Human Organization*, XXIV (Spring, 1965), 51.

44. S. N. Eisenstadt, ed., *Readings in Social Evolution and Development* (Oxford: Pergamon Press, 1970), p. 23.

45. Black, *The Dynamics of Modernization*, p. 49.

46. Paul E. Sigmund, ed., *The Ideologies of the Developing Nations* (New York: Frederick A. Praeger, 1967).

47. David E. Apter, *The Politics of Modernization* (Chicago: University of Chicago Press, 1965), pp. 43–44.

48. Donald N. Levine, "The Flexibility of Traditional Culture," *The Journal of Social Issues*, XXIV (Oct., 1968), 129–42.

49. Kim Rodner, "Logical Foundations of Social Change Theory," *Sociology and Social Research*, LI (April, 1967), 287–301.

50. Hajime Nakamura, *Ways of Thinking of Eastern Peoples*, ed. Philip P. Wiener (Honolulu: East-West Center Press, 1964), p. 271.

51. Quoted in Ssu-yu Teng and John K. Fairbank, *China's Response to the West* (New York: Atheneum, 1967), p. 142.

PART II

Theoretical Perspectives on Change

"When I even hear the word 'theory,'" an intelligent student said to me, "I go into a panic." A considerable number of students have expressed similar concerns about dealing with theory. But theories need not unsettle us. In fact, we use theories all the time. In simplest terms, a theory is an explanation. We act upon the basis of theories about man, society, and the world in which we live, i.e., ideas that explain what man, society, and the world are all about. Some theories explain problems in society on the basis of the evil nature of man; individuals who relate to other individuals with mistrust may be acting on the basis of such a theory.

In a more formal sense, a theory is a set of logically related propositions that explain some phenomenon. This may be easily illustrated by Durkheim's famous effort to explain suicide.[1] Durkheim argued that one type of suicide, which he called "egoistic," varies inversely with social integration. Specifically, the suicide rate will be less (1) among families in which there are children (domestic integration increases with children in the home), (2) during times of national crisis (an external threat increases political integration), and (3) among Catholics as opposed to Protestants (Catholics form a more integrated religious group than the highly individualistic Protestants).

Durkheim's theory of egoistic suicide can be summed up in

one sentence: the suicide rate of any group varies inversely with the degree of social integration of that group. However, we have said that a theory is a *set* of propositions, and there is such a set of propositions implied in what Durkheim has said. Merton[2] has spelled these out with respect to religious groups:

1. Social cohesion provides psychic support to group members subjected to acute stresses and anxieties.
2. Suicide rates are a function of unrelieved anxieties and stresses to which persons are subjected.
3. Catholics have greater social cohesion than Protestants.
4. Therefore, lower suicide rates should be anticipated among Catholics than among Protestants.

Durkheim's theory, in sum, is an effort to explain the phenomenon of suicide. Likewise, all the theories we shall examine in this part are attempts to explain social change. What causes change? What is the pattern of change? What is it that changes? Why does change occur in the particular direction we observe it to rather than in some other, just as reasonable, alternative way? These are the kinds of questions the various theories attempt to answer. The kinds of answers provided by the theories allow us to categorize them. Thus, some theories are based upon sociohistorical processes (chapters 2 and 3); some emphasize analytical rather than empirical materials (chapter 4); and some stress the importance of social-psychological factors in change (chapter 5).

ENDNOTES TO PART II

1. Emile Durkheim, *Suicide,* trans. John A. Spaulding and George Simpson, ed. George Simpson (New York: The Free Press, 1951).
2. Robert K. Merton, *Social Theory and Social Structure* (Glencoe: The Free Press, 1957), p. 97.

CHAPTER 2

Socio-Historical Theories: Cyclic

Where is mankind heading? Are we plunging recklessly towards the annihilation of civilization, or groping our way with agonizing slowness towards utopia? The question as framed sounds reasonable to modern, Western ears, but to many peoples throughout history it would provide an inadequate number of alternatives. For a more common way of explaining the direction of change has been to conceive of it as cyclic. The Greeks, Romans, and Chinese, among others, thought of human life as enmeshed in vast historical cycles rather than in a particular linear direction.

In the Chinese view, for example, the universe was thought to be in continual flux, but that flux followed a

> fixed and therefore predictable pattern consisting either of eternal oscillation between two poles or of cyclical movement within a closed circuit; in either case the change involved is relative rather than absolute, since all movement serves in the end only to bring the process back to its starting point.[1]

Because of this cyclic pattern, Chinese historians gave world history neither a beginning nor an end. Time was a series of cycles based upon planetary motions, and could therefore be thought of as "extending indefinitely into the past and future for as long as the planets themselves exist." [2]

The difference between this view and that of the modern West was expressed clearly by the scholar Yen Fu, who pointed out that while the Chinese neglected the present because of their love of antiquity, Westerners were struggling in the present in order to overcome the past and transcend it. The Chinese, he observed, believed that a "period of order and a period of disorder, a period of prosperity and a period of decline" was the normal course of human history. By contrast, Westerners believed that "daily progress should be endless." [3]

In contrast with the dominant Western view, then, some theories have tried to explain the course of history by viewing that history in terms of an ongoing series of cycles. In this chapter, we shall examine three such theories; in detail they differ considerably, but each in some fashion stresses a cyclic pattern. And each, thereby, asserts that what may appear as an upward or downward linear direction of change is actually only the phase of a cycle; ultimately, the direction will reverse itself.

NOMADIC AND SEDENTARY MAN: IBN KHALDUN

At a time when most men thought of history in terms of Providence, a remarkably perceptive Arab scholar endeavored to identify causal factors in the historical process.[4] Ibn Khaldun (1332–1406) was born in Tunis, and was a descendant of an aristocratic family that included many prominent political figures and scholars. Khaldun himself spent the greater part of his life in political service, where he was able to observe political turmoil in northwest Africa. For by the fourteenth century, the expanding civilization of Islam had begun to decline. Khaldun was struck by the disintegration of the Islamic world, and he determined to explain it.

For four years, Khaldun retired from political life in order to write his "universal history." To start with, he felt that existing approaches to the writing of history were totally inadequate. For Khaldun perceived that the mere chronicling of events was at best a beginning task of the historian; what was needed was an explanation, an identification of the pattern of changes. This explanation, or pattern, is contained in *The Muqaddimah*, the introduction to his history. And it is this work, rather than the history itself (which he entitled *Book of Lessons and Archive of Early and Subsequent History, Dealing with the Political Events concerning the Arabs, Non-Arabs, and Berbers, and the Supreme Rulers who were Contemporary with Them*), for which he can justly be called one of the world's great thinkers.

The Muqaddimah explores the manifold factors involved in

social change. Khaldun examines the influence of the physical environment on man, the forms of primitive and advanced social organization, intergroup relationships, the nature of leadership, urban life, and various cultural phenomena (arts, crafts, sciences, and so forth). In other words, he not only made a bold new advance in trying to ascertain causal factors in change; he also recognized that those factors would be numerous and diverse.

As a result, Khaldun may be regarded as a pioneer of sociological thought, identifying and utilizing six "basic principles on which sociology must rest." [5] These principles are:

1. Social phenomena follow lawful patterns. These patterns are not as rigid as those operative in the physical world, but they exhibit sufficient regularity to be recognized and described.

2. The laws are operative at the societal level. While the individual, therefore, is not a mere pawn of vast historical forces, neither is he able to escape the limitations imposed upon his behavior by societal laws. Contrary to the American expectation that if all is not well with the social order a change of president may resolve our problems, Khaldun asserted that reformers in corrupt states would be neutralized by overwhelming social forces.

3. The laws of the social process must be discovered through gathering much data and observing relationships among the variables. Both written records of the past and present observation can provide the data.

4. Similar social laws are operative in societies that are structurally similar. Societies may be separate both in time and space, yet be characterized by similar laws because of similar social structures.

5. Societies are characterized by change. The rate of change may vary considerably. Khaldun thought that in some past eras, not many significant changes had occurred for long spans of time. But in his own time, it seemed as though "the entire creation had changed and the whole world been altered, as if it were a new and repeated creation, a world brought into existence anew." [6]

6. The laws that apply to the change are sociological, not biological or physical, in nature. Khaldun considers the impact of the physical environment upon human behavior, noting such things as the effects of heat upon the inhabitants of tropical zones and the effects of air and food. He argues that great civilizations can only arise in the temperate zones, that hot air creates mirth, that heavy, starchy foods make people dull of mind. But these are not crucial factors in understanding history. The thrust of history must be understood in terms of social phenomena such as solidarity, leadership, occupation, and wealth. Social change must be seen in terms of social variables that alone can account for the change.

Furthermore, Khaldun builds his theory of change upon the premise that man is a social creature. "Human social organization is something necessary." [7] This was expressed in the philosophical saying that man is by nature political. That means simply that man must have "the social organization for which the philosophers use the technical term 'town.'" [8] Man's social nature derives from the fact that he must rely upon others to help him in the activities necessary for his existence — cooking, planting, making utensils and tools. No man is self-sufficient. Human needs can be fulfilled only through the cooperative efforts of many.

At the same time, Khaldun believed in the innate aggressiveness of man. Like Hobbes, therefore, he argued that man required strong authority in order to restrain his aggression. A sovereign is required who will have absolute authority over his subjects, and prevent them from attacking each other. This "royal authority is a natural quality of man which is absolutely necessary to mankind." [9] Man is a creature who was made to be ruled by a sovereign.

The importance of these assumptions regarding the social nature and innate aggressiveness of man will become clear as we turn to Khaldun's theory of change. That theory involves two contrasting forms of social organization — the nomadic (Bedouins) and sedentary. The theory is an attempt to explain the Bedouin success in overthrowing a number of North African civilizations.

Both Bedouins and sedentary people are "natural groups," i.e., groups that result from differing ways of making a living. The Bedouins live a Spartan existence, their life is difficult and simple. They subsist in the desert, and make their living through the raising of camels. This distinguishes them from most Berbers and non-Bedouins, who cultivate grain and engage in agriculture, and from a number of other groups who make their living from such animals as sheep and cattle. The Bedouins are unable to secure any but the bare necessities of existence. Their way of life generates in them great courage and a high degree of self-determination. There is also intense solidarity among the Bedouins; indeed, the rigors of existing in the desert demand the cooperative efforts that arise from group solidarity. The net result of all this is that the Bedouins are "the most savage human beings that exist." [10]

Solidarity is a crucial aspect of Bedouin life and a key concept with Khaldun. Those people who possess it are likely to conquer those who lack it; given equal numbers, the antagonist united by a sense of "group feeling" is always stronger than and superior to the opponent that is composed of differing groups. But why do some groups possess solidarity and others lack it? Khaldun identifies a number of sources of Bedouin solidarity, including the exigencies of desert life mentioned above, kinship bonds, and religion.

Kinship ties are important in creating solidarity in that men possess a natural urge to protect their blood relatives from attack or injustice. Religion is important in that it restrains the savage Bedouin nature; religious zeal neutralizes the competitiveness and envy which group members might otherwise feel towards each other and provides shared goals and a common perspective.

In sum, as a religious, kinship-oriented group living under severely demanding environmental conditions, the Bedouins emerge in Khaldun's writing (and, no doubt, did emerge in reality) as a horde of Genghis Khans — ruthless, tough, and both willing and able to overwhelm every opponent.

In spite of this portrait of human ferocity, Khaldun does not mean to disparage the Bedouins. Quite the contrary, in fact, for the Bedouin way of life existed before the sedentary, and the latter represents a process of degeneration in almost every respect except material goods. "Sedentary people" are those who live in cities and countries and make their living either by the crafts or by commerce. And sedentary man presents quite a contrast to nomadic man.

Sedentary man is primarily interested in pleasures of various kinds. He craves luxury and success, and eagerly immerses himself in every kind of "worldly" indulgence. He becomes more and more removed from the goodness that was to be found among the Bedouins; the soul of sedentary man is "coloured with all kinds of blameworthy and evil qualities." [11] His life of indulgence makes him lazy; his life of ease erodes the Bedouin qualities of courage and strength. Energy, fortitude, and vigor are swallowed up in the cesspool of riotous, self-indulgent living.

The qualities that made for survival and triumph melt away from sedentary man. Group solidarity and religion weaken and finally crumple before the onslaught of unrestrained indulgence in pleasure. People who once might have joined together in zestful cooperation become alienated and worse: they are "devoted to lying, gambling, cheating, fraud, theft, perjury, and usury." [12] Like an Arab Savonarola, Khaldun lays bare the utter corruption of sedentary man.

Yet the picture is not totally bleak. For Khaldun does acknowledge that the crafts and sciences are brought to perfection only in a large sedentary civilization. The cultural development of man cannot occur when the individual struggles at the subsistence level. Some measure of luxury and surplus are necessary for science and the crafts to develop beyond very simple levels.

Sedentary man, then, is secular, individualistic, and relatively affluent. He is the obverse of nomadic man in virtually every characteristic.   Morally, spiritually, physically, and culturally, sedentary and nomadic man live in two quite different worlds.

We have, then, been presented with two contrasting forms of social organization and their resulting personality types.   In the description itself, we have already seen hints of Khaldun's theory of change; that theory is based on conflict, the clash between nomadic and sedentary man.   The desert nomads covet the luxuries of the city; "urbanization is found to be the goal to which the Bedouin aspires." [13]   The nomads, therefore, continually attack and conquer cities and towns; the sedentary inhabitants of the urban areas are no match for the fierce Bedouins.   As a result of the conquest of the urban areas, a state or empire is formed.   But once the conquerors settle in the cities, they fall prey to the same degeneration of the sedentary peoples they conquered.   It is only a matter of time before a new horde of nomads sweeps over the empire.   Thus, there is a cycle of change, with empires being established, decaying into a state of vice and impotence, and falling before the power of a new generation of desert nomads.   The state is established and overthrown by conflict.   History is an ongoing cycle of growth and decay, of conquest and collapse.

Khaldun describes the natural history of the empire that is established (and that will sooner or later fall) in terms both of three generations and of five stages.[14]   An empire, like an individual, has a "natural life span," which is generally no more than three generations or about 120 years.   The first generation includes those who swept over the land to conquest; once settled in the cities, they retain the strength and solidarity of their desert existence.   The effects of sedentary living begin to appear, however, in the second generation.   Luxury and royal authority replace rigorous living and solidarity.   There is the remembrance of the qualities of the past, and some hope of recapturing them.   But by the third generation, the very qualities of desert life have been forgotten.   By this point, sedentary living has taken its toll; the empire has become "senile and is worn out," and the fourth generation faces destruction.

Khaldun describes this same process in terms of five stages. In the first, the nomads have succeeded in overthrowing all opposition and establishing a new empire.   In the second, consolidation takes place as the new ruler secures control over his domain.   The third stage is one of "leisure and tranquility"; the quest for more and more experiences of luxury has begun, and there is an expansion of the culture (such as development of governmental functions, erection of buildings and monuments). Peace continues in the fourth stage, which, however, is marked by preservation of what has been obtained in the past rather than by any new expansion of culture.   Traditionalism characterizes the fourth stage.

Finally, the fifth stage is one of degeneration. The ruler wastes money on luxury on himself and his "inner circle." He surrounds himself with those who are incapable of carrying on the affairs of state. He alienates the people, and loses the support of many of the soldiers. The empire has been seized by a social sickness that is relentless and chronic; there is no cure for its illness — it can only await its destruction.

As this summary of Khaldun's thought shows, this great Arab thinker set forth numerous insights about social change that demand that he be ranked among the most perceptive of social theorists. He recognized the complexity of social life and tried to account for the multitude of factors that would bear upon the question of change. Environmental, social, and social-psychological factors are all considered. In the general context of a conflict theory of change, Khaldun looked at the importance of the physical environment, the social structure, the role of leadership and personality, and the crucial importance of group cohesiveness. He perceived the importance of occupation (ways of making a living) in understanding personality types. He examined the roles of religion and leadership in effecting change. We have not discussed the latter in detail, but Khaldun gives considerable attention to it. He points out, for example, that what matters to the subjects is not the ruler's appearance or intellect but the kind of relationships he establishes with his subjects. The ruler who relates to his people in a despotic manner is engaging in an act of self-destruction; the ruler must be concerned for the needs of his subjects and must seek to gain their love. And, in fact, it is the ruler's failure in benevolence and his obsession with luxury and self-indulgence that paves the way for the degeneration and fall of the sedentary civilization.

In sum, writing at a time and place when explanations were likely to be clothed in fatalistic terms, Ibn Khaldun set forth an incisive theory of change. Among the important insights of his work are the following:

1. The historical method offers the best approach to understanding social change.
2. The factors involved in change are many and diverse; no single factor (such as personality and technology) can adequately account for change.
3. Differing forms of social organization create differing personality types.
4. Conflict is the basic mechanism of change.
5. A variety of social-psychological factors — leadership, personality, group cohesiveness — help us to understand both the antecedents and the outcome of intergroup conflict.

6. Change tends to be pervasive, occurring in all the social institutions; religion, the family, the government, and the economy are all alike involved in the process.

CHALLENGE AND RESPONSE: ARNOLD TOYNBEE

Like Khaldun, whom he called an "Arabic genius," Arnold Toynbee
(born 1889) sees a process of birth, growth, stagnation, and disintegration in social life.[15] Toynbee takes as the unit of his study
societies or civilizations rather than nations or periods of time.
The study of any particular nation is unintelligible as a "thing-in-
itself"; it must be seen as part of a larger process. We cannot, for
example, understand England by merely studying the history of
that nation itself; rather, we must see England in terms of its place
in Western Christendom. The focus of study, therefore, is not
England or the United States or any other particular nation, but the
civilizations of which any nation is but a part.

There are, according to Toynbee, twenty-one such civilizations
(e.g., the Egyptian, the Indic, the Sumerian, the Babylonian, the
Western). Six civilizations arose spontaneously from primitive
societies: the Egyptian, the Sumerian, the Chinese, the Mayan,
the Minoan, and the Indic. Each of these arose independently of
the others, and appeared in widely separated areas. All the other
civilizations derive from these original six. In addition, there have
been three abortive (Far Western Christian, Far Eastern Christian,
Scandinavian) and five arrested (Polynesian, Eskimo, Nomadic,
Ottoman, Spartan) civilizations.

What caused a civilization to arise out of a primitive society?
The latter are oriented toward the past, and remain static; societies in the process of civilization, by contrast, are in "dynamic
motion along a course of change and growth."[16] Toynbee first
examines racial and environmental explanations and rejects them.
There is no superior race, and there are no environments which
virtually create civilizations themselves because of their facilitating
characteristics. Rather, civilizations arise out of responses to challenges: the causal mechanism is not an entity but a relation. And
that relation may be one of man-nature or man-man. For example,
the Egyptian civilization arose as the result of an adequate response to the challenge of the swamps and jungles of the Nile Valley, while other civilizations emerged from the challenge of
intergroup conflict.

The point is that it is not easy conditions that cause civilizations to arise, but rather adverse conditions. A civilization emerges
in the throes of struggle; it comes into being only by surmounting

barriers, not by traveling an open, smooth road. A number of different kinds of challenges may comprise the adversity necessary for the rise of a civilization. Toynbee talks about five different stimuli: hard countries, new ground, blows, pressures, and penalizations.[17] Hard country refers to a difficult physical environment, such as that provided by the "watery chaos of the lower valley of the Yellow River." [18] New ground refers to land which has not been settled and tilled. Blows include sudden military defeats, while pressures indicate a situation of continuing external threat. Finally, penalizations refer to those classes and races who have historically been subjected to various forms of oppression, discrimination, and exploitation.

Obviously, if we have a challenge, we do not always have the kind of response that generates a civilization. The challenge may be so severe that no adequate response can be made. There is, therefore, not a direct relation between challenge and response, but a curvilinear one. That is, a broad range of degrees of difficulty can evoke an adequate response; but at the extremes — challenges that are overly weak and overly severe — adequate response is not possible. If the challenge is too severe, a civilization may abort or become arrested in its development; in such cases, the challenge has sufficient force to prevent normal development, though it is not so severe as to cause defeat.

The first criterion, then, of whether or not an adequate response will be made is the severity of the challenge. The second criterion of adequate response is the presence of an elite in charge of the response. The growth of the civilization hinges upon the behavior of a creative minority. "All acts of social creation are the work either of individual creators or, at most, of creative minorities." [19] But the bulk of mankind tends to remain mired in past ways. The task of the minority, therefore, is not simply to create new social forms and processes, but to "contrive some means of carrying this sluggish rear-guard along with them in their eager advance." [20] Led by the elite, the civilization grows through a series of successful responses to continuing challenges.

What is the meaning of the growth of a civilization? Toynbee calls it a process of "etherialization," a "shift of emphasis from some lower sphere of being or of action to a higher." [21] This means the conquest of initial obstacles so that energy is released for responding to challenges which are now internal rather than external and spiritual rather than material in nature. Such growth means increasing self-determination, and it involves continual differentiation between the parts of the society. This differentiation occurs because some parts will respond successfully, while others will succeed through imitating those that make adequate response; and still others will fail to be either creative or imitative and so will succumb. The net result is the development of a unique style in each civilization. The Hellenic civilization, for example, had a "predominantly aesthetic outlook on life as a whole," while the Indic and Hindu civilizations tended "towards an outlook that is predominantly religious." [22]

But no civilization continues to grow indefinitely. Commonly, there is a breakdown, which occurs when the creative elite no longer functions adequately, the majority no longer give their allegiance to and imitate the elite, and social unity disintegrates. The breakdown and disintegration is common, but not inevitable. There may also be a petrifaction, as illustrated by the history of Egypt and the Far East. When breakdown does occur, however, it follows a characteristic pattern: there is a societal fission, with the civilization rupturing into the three opposing groupings of dominant minority, internal proletariat, and external proletariat. Each of the three groupings, in turn, creates a "characteristic institution: universal state, universal church and barbarian warbands." [23] The creation of a universal state means that the elite now imposes itself on the masses by force; it has transformed itself into a ruling class. This is done not deliberately to exploit the masses but as a desperate effort to hold together the crumbling civilization. The internal proletariat, made up of those who are "in" but not "of" the society, turns against the elite and forms a universal church. And the external proletariat, those who were culturally influenced by the growing civilization but who are no longer charmed once the breakdown has occurred, then ceases to imitate and becomes hostile towards the civilization. The boundary between the civilization and the external proletariat becomes a military frontier; "this temporary and precarious balance of forces inevitably tilts, with the passage of time, in favour of the barbarians." [24]

Like Khaldun, Toynbee concerns himself with social-psychological aspects of change. Having portrayed the "schism in the body social," therefore, he proceeds to discuss the "schism in the soul." Societal fission is mirrored in the individual psyche; during the time of disintegration, the varied ways of behaving, feeling, and living that characterized the growing civilization are replaced by "alternative substitutes." For example, rather than being sustained by the sense of exhilaration and vigor that pervaded the growing society, the people struggle with a sense of drift (beyond human control) and a sense of sin.

The stage of disintegration, like the stage of growth, has its creative individuals who fashion a response to the challenges. In the growing stage, they led the masses in making successful responses to the varied challenges. In the disintegration stage, they come as saviors of, or deliverers from, the society. Specifically, there are four types of saviors who appear. The "saviour with the sword" is the founder and upholder of the universal state. The "saviour with the time machine" is the "archaist" or the "futurist." The former is one who saves by restoring a golden era of the past; the latter is one who saves by leaping into the unknown of the future (by revolution that severs the society from the past). The "philosopher masked by a King" represents a solution that employs neither the sword nor the time machine, a solution first proposed by Plato. It demands a union of philosophy and political power; either philosophers must become kings, or kings must become philosophers. But this solution will fail, argues Toynbee, because of the essential contradiction between the detachment of the philosopher and the coercive intervention of the king. Finally, there is the "God incarnate in a man." And it is only those saviors who have presented themselves as gods who offer hope, or, more accurately, it is only Jesus Christ who can deliver us from death. It is for this kind of argument that Toynbee has been accused of burying history in an Anglican churchyard.

The disintegration of a civilization does not proceed at a uniform pace, nor does it equally affect all parts of the civilization. There is a rhythm: "In military language the rhythm may be expressed as rout-rally-rout-rally-rout. . . ." [25] For example, the universal state represents a rally after the rout of a time of distress. Finally, whereas the growing civilization is marked by increasing differentiation, the disintegrating civilization is marked by increasing standardization. Dominant minorities "uniformly" create philosophies and universal states; internal proletariats "uniformly" find a higher religion which is expressed through a universal church; and external proletariats "uniformly" gather in war-bands to launch their assault upon the civilization.

In sum, the picture that Toynbee draws for us of the history of mankind is one of continuing cycles of birth, growth, breakdown, and disintegration of civilizations. At one point, he talks about the rise and fall as a rhythm "in which the successive revolutions of a wheel carry forward the vehicle which the wheel conveys." [26] Toynbee sees this whole process as being intimately tied up with the functioning of elites and their relationships with the masses, both the internal and external proletariats. Further, as he grapples with the complexity of societal change, Toynbee tries to avoid the extremes of determinism and historicism. It is questionable whether he is able to do this. For example, we may ask whether a challenge is of the proper severity to elicit a civilization-building response. There is no way to answer the question except by ex post facto analysis; if a civilization develops, the challenge was of sufficient but not too much severity, while an aborted or arrested civilization points to an overly severe challenge. As

Toynbee himself observed, there are no predetermined outcomes to challenges, which are "therefore intrinsically unpredictable." [27]

Nevertheless, there is value in striving, as Toynbee did, to identify critical factors involved in social change without making those factors either deterministic or capricious. In addition, Toynbee stresses for us again the centrality of conflict in change, the important role of elites and the elite-masses relationship, and the significance of social-psychological factors in understanding change.

OSCILLATING SOCIOCULTURAL MODES: PITIRIM SOROKIN

Pitirim A. Sorokin (1889–1968), our final example of a thinker who sees cyclic variations in the historical process, was born in Russia, sentenced to death by the Communists in 1918 and exiled in 1922. He spent the remainder of his life in the United States, where he wrote several important works in the areas of social mobility, sociological theory, and sociocultural change.[28] A brilliant and prolific scholar, Sorokin covered virtually the whole of Western history in his effort to determine historical patterns of change. In his *Social and Cultural Dynamics*, he analyzed change from 600 B.C. to around 1935 A.D., focusing on Western civilization (including the Graeco-Roman), but bringing in some materials from Chinese, Hindu, and Arabian cultures.

Like Toynbee's, Sorokin's writing covers an immense and impressive span of time and humanity. But Sorokin criticized Toynbee's methodology. Toynbee's "civilizations," argued Sorokin, are arbitrarily defined and of little scientific use; basically, this is because Toynbee fails to distinguish between systems and congeries. The civilizations identified by Toynbee are in reality a "conglomeration of many systems and congeries." [29] As such, they are not the integrated wholes envisioned by Toynbee, and they cannot be treated as units of analysis.

Sorokin himself employed the "logico-meaningful" method; this method involves the discovery of some central principle around which a system is organized and which gives meaning to each of the elements of the system, thereby integrating them into the whole. In such a system, there will be a "logical compatibility and specific dependence or interdependence of each meaning-element upon other meanings-elements," and the same relationship will hold true between the meanings-elements and the overall system.[30]

This method yields, according to Sorokin, three sociocultural systems, or "supersystems," which will be described below. Sorokin endeavored to show how all the elements of one of the supersystems tend to be characterized by the one, pervasive principle of that particular supersystem. To do this, he had to examine such aspects of culture as art, systems of truth, religion, ethics, law, philosophy, and the family. These varied aspects of culture were subjected to both qualitative and quantitative analysis. Qualitatively, the various aspects of culture had to be defined in accord with whether they exhibited the principle of one or the other of the three supersystems. Quantitatively, the rate of occurrence of each of the three principles in each facet of culture had to be estimated for each period of time throughout the centuries covered in the study. For example, the percentage of thinkers who held to an ethics of happiness and those who advocated an "absolute" ethics was computed for each century, and was found to vary from certain periods in which all thinkers held to an absolute ethics to periods in which the distribution was nearly even.

Sorokin, then, finds that sociocultural history is a cyclic variation between three supersystems which represent fairly homogeneous cultures. A great culture is not a "mere dumping place of a multitude of diverse cultural phenomena" but a "unity or individuality whose parts are permeated by the same fundamental principle and articulate the same basic value." [31] The three systems are the ideational, which is pervaded by the principle of God as true reality and value; the sensate, which is pervaded by the principle that the sensory world is the true reality and value; and the idealistic, which is a combination of the other two — that is, reality and value are partially sensory and partially suprasensory.[32] Thus, ideational culture is spiritual and nonmaterial in its emphasis; sensate culture is material and hedonistic in its emphasis; idealistic culture manages a balance between the ideational and the sensate, usually with the former somewhat dominant over the latter. Christian medieval Europe exemplifies the ideational culture; the time around the birth of Christ and the present are sensate cultures; idealistic systems (such as Europe in the thirteenth and fourteenth centuries) tend to emerge during the transition from the ideational to the sensate.

There is, then, no linear pattern in history. Cycles of cultural patterns characterize the social process — history is an oscillation between opposing cultural forms such as materialism-idealism, ethics of absolute principles–ethics of happiness, determinism-indeterminism, and visual (sensate)–formal, symbolic (ideational) emphasis in the fine arts. It should be noted, however, that Sorokin does not claim total homogeneity for any empirical culture; none of the supersystems is actually found "monopolistically without the coexistence, as a minor or equal stream, of the other systems." [33] With only a few exceptions, the art, philosophy, religion, and science of any period will have some segments that differ from the dominant principle of the time. If the great bulk of the fine arts in the tenth to eleventh centuries A.D. was ideational, we must not lose sight of the fact that a small number of works were idealistic and a few were sensate. Even when, for example, most paintings and sculpture were religious in nature, at least a few were secular.

How and why does a culture change from one mode to another? Sorokin noted that there are both quantitative and qualitative aspects to the growth and decline of a sociocultural system. In order to understand those aspects, we must first note the three components of an empirical sociocultural system, namely, the system of meanings, the vehicles, and the human agents. Every empirical system has a system of meanings (based upon the dominant sociocultural principle): the Constitution and laws of the United States are an example of a system of meanings at the core of the American system. Secondly, there is a "system of empirical vehicle that objectify these meanings" [34]; the vehicles that objectify the U.S. Constitution and laws include speech, written documents and literature, ceremonies, and buildings such as courts. Finally, there are the human agents who "bear the system of meanings, who actualize it and realize it through the media of the vehicles. . . ." [35]

Returning to the question of the growth and decline of sociocultural systems, Sorokin maintained that quantitative growth referred primarily to a quantitative increase in either the vehicles or the human agents or both. For example, the legal system may be expanded to include an increased number of courts, lawyers, and lawsuits along with an increase in the number of laws. Qualitative growth, on the other hand, involves some kind of improvement of the system of meanings, its vehicles, its human agents, or all three components. Qualitative growth is "movement toward the optimum integration of the system." [36] Qualitative growth, for Sorokin, seems to imply at the societal level what has been called self-realization or self-actualization at the individual level. Thus, qualitative growth would mean that the legal system would more and more approximate perfect equity among the members of the society and that lawyers would more and more conform to the highest ethical and professional standards.

Is there any relationship between quantitative and qualitative growth? At some points — at earlier stages of development — the two kinds of growth may proceed simultaneously. But at later stages, the relationship between the two may be one of independence or even inverse. Thus, "a fairly uniform symptom of disintegration in any great supersystem of culture is the substitution of quantitative colossalism for a sublime quality." [37] For example, in its most creative period (sixth to fourth centuries, B.C.) Greece produced temples (including the Parthenon), statues, and drawings of relatively modest size, music of relative simplicity, and literature which was moderate in terms of number, size, and production. "Nothing was measured by the number of copies sold or by the size of valuable objects." [38] But in the Hellenic and later Roman periods, quality deteriorated, and greater and greater quantity, in terms both of size and number, became the basis of aesthetic judgment (Sorokin's own judgment, of course, identifies this as deterioration). Whether the art, temples, literature, and other facets of culture of the later period were indeed generally inferior because of the value on "colossalism" may be disputed, of course, but Sorokin saw in the differences clear evidence of a culture declining qualitatively along with an increasing stress on quantity.

Like cultural growth, cultural decline is both quantitative and qualitative. Quantitative decline involves decreasing vehicles or human agents or both. The legal system may decline through a diminishing number of law schools and lawyers, obsolescence, and failure to replace laws and legal literature. Qualitative decline involves some kind of deterioration of the system of meanings or in the interdependence among the system of meanings, vehicles, and human agents. Contradictions may develop between the ideals and actual behavior of lawyers, to continue our example. Or ambiguities and contradictions may increase in the statutes. Or the purpose of the law may be distorted by the behavior of judges.

Finally, a system dies when its system of meanings deteriorates to the point where it is no longer recognizable or when the vehicles, human agents, or both are all lost. The actual "life span" of any system varies enormously — but most are finite. Some small systems — fashions and fads — have rather short life spans. Religious systems may continue for thousands of years. But an individual system of religion, like individual systems of philosophy, law, or art, or like political regimes, tends to come into being, to be articulated by its vehicles and human agents over some period of time, and then pass "into the realm of pure meanings." [39]

Thus, both systems and supersystems pass through the phases of growth and decline. But how does this change occur with respect to the relation between the whole and its parts? Sorokin summed up the answer in a series of propositions. First, in a closely integrated system, the change will occur as a whole; all parts will change together. Second, if the system is not closely integrated, change may occur in some subsystems without occurring in others; only significant change in the more important parts of the system will effect change throughout so that the entire culture will experience change. Third, if a culture is merely a grouping of congeries, any part may change without affecting any other part. Fourth, if the culture is composed of the "coexistence" of a number of systems and of congeries, the culture will change differently in its varied parts; namely, all the important parts will change together, while the congeries will change independently of each other. All of this simply says that various elements will either change concomitantly or independently of each other depending upon the extent to which they are integrated. But even when various elements are changing in the same direction, there may be some leading or lagging; music may change in a particular direction before painting and sculpture at one time and may lag behind the latter at another time. Indeed, regardless of the degree of integration, there has probably never been a culture where all the elements changed together simultaneously.[40]

While our discussion has only touched upon the intricacies of Sorokin's thought, it does show that his thought is truly cyclic: history is the oscillation between the three sociocultural supersystems. An important question arises as to the mechanism of change — what causes the shift from one mode to another? Sorokin suggested three possible explanations of sociocultural change. First, change may be the result of factors external to the sociocultural system. If, for example, we look for explanations of change in the family, we seek factors in the economy (industrialization), or demographic changes, or perhaps even biological factors as causal mechanisms. This assumes that the family is a more or less passive grouping, which will remain as it is unless it is disturbed by outside forces.

A second explanation that has been offered is the theory of immanence. In this theory, change occurs because of internal factors in the system. In other words, it is of the nature of the system to change: "It cannot help changing, even if all its external conditions are constant." [41] And the third explanation seeks for both internal and external causes of change. Sorokin opted for the "principle of immanent change . . . supported by the externalistic principle, within certain conditions and limits." [42] If that sentence sounds like an evasive answer, Sorokin's writing basically supports the principle of immanence. He stressed the fact that any actual sociocultural system must necessarily change by virtue of its activity: any system that exists and that is active in some sense is thereby changing. External factors do have some influence, but internal factors provide the main impetus for change, and any particular change may be initiated via the meanings-components, the vehicles, or the human agents.

In spite of his assertion that change can be initiated in human agents, Sorokin's system of thought implies that man is more the helpless tool of vast, impersonal forces than the manipulator of his own destiny. And at times, this view of man becomes quite explicit. The "crisis" of mankind, he wrote in 1941, was not created by Hitler, Stalin, or Mussolini. Rather, "the already existing crisis made them what they are — its instrumentalities and puppets." [43] Even if we won the war, he predicted, the crisis would remain unchanged. For the basic crisis was not the actions of certain men or nations, but the overly developed sensate culture of the West.

And this leads to one final point of Sorokin's. Like Spengler, Sorokin saw the West as being in a stage of decline (though he did not foresee the same future as Spengler did). Our sensate culture, he argued, is "over-ripe." The future holds only disintegration of that culture, including the degeneration of values, the proliferation of force and fraud, the loss of freedom, the growth of tyranny, the deterioration of the family, and the loss of creativity.[44] This is not to underrate the achievements of sensate culture, for it "wrote truly the most magnificent page in the whole history of mankind and culture." [45] But its mission is now completed; the day of its death has already passed, and it lingers on to torment us. It is "tired and exhausted. It deserves a rest. It should hand on the torch of creativeness to other forms of culture." [46] And, of course, the other form of culture that will succeed our sensate culture must be either an ideational or an idealistic culture.

In sum, Sorokin offers us an imaginative and impressive theory of cyclic change that is supported by an immense amount of data. Any work of this scale is subject to many criticisms and will make numbers of assertions which are debatable. Nevertheless, Sorokin, like our two other cyclic theorists, shows us the utility of a historical approach to the study of change. And he, like the others, treats change as normal rather than as a kind of aberration. In one way he is less pessimistic than Khaldun or Toynbee, for to him the disintegration of a sociocultural system does not mean a return to some level of barbarism and a consequent fresh start. The death of our sensate culture, for example, means that we shall journey towards "the magnificent peaks of the new Ideational or Idealistic culture" and that thereby "the creative mission of Western culture and society will be continued." [47]

One of the main deficiencies in Sorokin is his lack of attention to social-psychological factors. The role of man in shaping his own future is minimal in Sorokin's system. But in his emphasis on understanding the interrelationships of social phenomena undergoing change, his assumption of the normality of change, and his insistence on a proper scientific methodology, Sorokin aids us in our quest of understanding change.

ENDNOTES TO CHAPTER 2

1. Derk Bodde, "Harmony and Conflict in Chinese Philosophy," in *Studies in Chinese Thought*, ed. Arthur F. Wright (Chicago: The American Anthropological Association, 1953), p. 21.

2. Wm. Theodore de Bary, Wing-tsit Chan, and Burton Watson, *Sources of Chinese Tradition* (New York: Columbia University Press, 1960), p. 221.

3. Quoted in Ssu-yu Teng and John K. Fairbank, *China's Response to the West* (New York: Atheneum, 1967), p. 151.

4. For Khaldun's thought, see Ibn Khaldun, *The Muqaddimah: An Introduction to History*, trans. Franz Rosenthal, ed. N. J. Dawood (Princeton: Princeton University Press, 1967) and Charles Issawi, *An Arab Philosophy of History* (London: John Murray, 1950). A clear and concise exposition may be found in Howard Becker and Harry Elmer Barnes, *Social Thought from Lore to Science* (New York: Dover Publications, Inc., 1961).

5. Charles Issawi, *An Arab Philosophy of History*, pp. 7–9.

6. Khaldun, *The Muqaddimah*, p. 30.

7. *Ibid.*, p. 45.

8. *Ibid.*

9. *Ibid.*, p. 47.

10. *Ibid.*, p. 93.

11. *Ibid.*, p. 94.

12. *Ibid.*, p. 286.

13. *Ibid.*, p. 93.

14. *Ibid.*, pp. 136–42.

16. Somervell, *A Study of History, Volumes I–V*, p. 49.

15. Toynbee's system is set forth in twelve volumes. An abridgement of most of his *A Study of History* is provided by D. C. Somervell: *A Study of History, Volumes I–V* (New York: Oxford University Press, 1946) and *A Study of History: Volumes VI–X* (New York: Oxford University Press, 1957). These two abridgements, plus Toynbee's *Reconsiderations* (New York: Oxford University Press, 1961) provides a sufficient account.

17. *Ibid.*, pp. 88–139.

18. *Ibid.*, p. 88.

19. *Ibid.*, p. 214.

20. *Ibid.*, p. 215.

21. *Ibid.*, p. 198.

22. *Ibid.*, p. 242.

23. *Ibid.*, p. 368.

24. *Ibid.*, p. 407.

25. *Ibid.*, p. 548.

26. Somervell, *A Study of History, Volumes VI–X*, p. 88.

27. Toynbee, *Reconsiderations*, p. 256.

28. Sorokin's ideas are fully explicated in his *Social and Cultural Dynamics*, 4 volumes (New York: American Book Company, 1937–1941). Sorokin abridged his own work in a single volume, *Social and Cultural Dynamics* (Boston: Porter Sargent, 1957). Two other sources are his *Society, Culture, and Personality* (New York: Harper & Bros., 1947) and, written in a popular style, *The Crisis of Our Age* (New York: E. P. Dutton & Co., Inc., 1941).

29. Sorokin, *Social and Cultural Dynamics*, Vol. IV, p. 87.

30. *Ibid.*, p. 21.

31. Sorokin, *The Crisis of Our Age*, p. 17.

32. Sorokin, *Social and Cultural Dynamics*, Vol. I, pp. 66–75.

33. Sorokin, *Social and Cultural Dynamics*, Vol. IV, p. 141.

34. *Ibid.*, p. 46.

35. *Ibid.*, p. 47.

36. *Ibid.*, p. 83.

37. Sorokin, *The Crisis of Our Age*, p. 252.

38. *Ibid.*, p. 253.

39. Sorokin, *Social and Cultural Dynamics*, p. 92.

40. *Ibid.*, pp. 145–46.

41. *Ibid.*, p. 590.

42. *Ibid.*, p. 592.

43. Sorokin, *The Crisis of Our Age*, p. 23.

44. Sorokin, *Social and Cultural Dynamics*, Vol. IV, pp. 775–77.

45. Sorokin, *The Crisis of Our Age*, p. 271.

46. *Ibid.*

47. Sorokin, *Social and Cultural Dynamics*, Vol. IV, p. 779.

CHAPTER 3

Socio-Historical Theories:
Developmental

Although the cyclic view of history prevailed among the Chinese, Greeks, and Romans, a number of ancient thinkers saw the course of social change differently — namely, in terms of a linear process. That process might be one either of degeneration or of some kind of progress. Mingled in with Chinese thought about the great cycles, for example, was another perspective which saw the past as a golden age and all history since that time as a process of deterioration. Some thinkers tried to reconcile this with the cyclic view by asserting that they were simply living in the downswing of a cycle.[1]

It has been popular to stress the fact that the notion of progress — one type of linear development — is to be found only as we emerge into the modern era. But neither the linear concept of history nor its variant of progress as the direction of development were unknown to ancient man. The linear concept of history may be seen in St. Augustine, who wrote in detail about the "rise, progress, and appointed end of the two cities, one of which is God's, the other this world's."[2] The two cities represent, of course, the Church and the world outside of the Church. History is the process of interaction between the two cities, in which each suffers evil and enjoys good. But the two cities have different faiths, different hopes, and different love and "they must be separated by the last judgment, and each must receive her own end, of which there is no end."[3]

For Augustine, the end for the City of God was unending bliss, while the end for the earthly city was unending damnation. But not all ancient thinkers were as pessimistic about the "earthly city." If progress is conceived not in terms of continuing progress from the remote past into the eternal future but in terms of "human cultural and intellectual advancement over a very long period of time," then both Greek and Roman thinkers held to an idea of progress.[4]

Nevertheless, it is only in the modern West that the notion of progress became the dominant theme, and only in recent centuries that the idea of progress throughout the whole of history has appeared in men's thought. This latter point was argued by Condorcet, Comte, and Spencer, among others. Condorcet proclaimed the progress of man with an almost lyrical enthusiasm. He announced that no limits inhere in the perfectibility of human faculties, "that the perfectibility of man is truly indefinite; that the progress of this perfectibility . . . has no other limit than the duration of the globe on which nature has placed us."[5] He did recognize that the rate of progress might vary, but neither fixation nor regression were possible.

Thus, some developmental theorists have posited a basically evolutionary pattern — man and society are more or less slowly, but surely, evolving towards a better state. Others, while sometimes seeing the ultimate outcome as preferable to the present, stress conflict, or a dialectical pattern of development. In this chapter, we will look at a few theorists of both kinds.

EVOLUTIONARY DEVELOPMENT

Auguste Comte

In part because he coined the name "sociology," Auguste Comte (1798–1857) has generally been identified as the "father" of the discipline.[6] Comte's own work was primarily not that of the innovator, however, as much as that of the systematizer; he gathered together much of the thought of certain French thinkers, fashioned it into a system, and christened it sociology.

Comte divided sociology into statics and dynamics. The "statical" aspect of sociology is similar to what we would call structure today, while the "dynamical" aspect refers to change. Statical sociology rests upon the philosophical assumption that society is an organism united by consensus, for "there must always be a spontaneous harmony between the whole and the parts of the social system." [7]   The study of dynamics is actually more interesting, but we must "contemplate order, that we may perfect it." [8]

Dynamical sociology is the study of the sequence of man's development, and each step in that sequence is the necessary consequence of the preceding step.   As Leibniz argued, "the present is big with the future." [9]   Social science, therefore, has as its task the discovery of the laws that govern the sequence.   The discovery of those laws, in turn, provides a rational basis for facilitating the progress of mankind.

In his own search for the laws of historical sequence, Comte identified three stages of historical development (which corresponded to three stages of development in the human mind). Thus, he posited a "fundamental law" of the development of human intelligence, namely, that it "passes successively through three different theoretical conditions: the Theological, or fictitious; the Metaphysical, or abstract; and the Scientific, or positive." [10] These three stages are both three successive methods of intellectual functioning and three corresponding types of social orders.

In the theological state, intellectual functioning "supposes all phenomena to be produced by the immediate action of supernatural beings." [11]   Comte subdivided the theological state, however, into three divisions: fetishism, polytheism, and monotheism.   The state of fetishism marked the beginning of the theological era of mankind; in this state, man "conceives of all external bodies as animated by a life analogous to his own, with differences of mere intensity." [12]   Comte goes into great detail in showing how this mode of thinking (and all the modes) relate to the social order. In the state of fetishism, for example, society was characterized by sacerdotal authority, by the beginning of the conquest of nature, and by behavior based more on affect than on the intellect.   And the family unit emerged, along with a permanence of residence that facilitated the subsequent development of the state.

During the polytheistic period, the city emerged, landed property became a social institution, the caste system appeared, and war was waged as "the only means of rendering the political organism durable and progressive." [13]   Finally, in the period of monotheism, a modification of the theological and military character of the theological state began to take place.   The Catholic church failed to provide a viable basis for social life.   Women and laborers were emancipated.   Church and state were ruptured by the universal claims of the church and the local nature of political power.   And war shifted from aggressive to defensive action.

Many of the changes and developments of the theological period were a preparation for the Positive era of humanity.   The worship of Mary, for example, paved the way for the worship of humanity.   But a transitional period — the metaphysical era —

was still necessary. The metaphysical state is a modification of the first, the theological, state; the assumption of the mind is not the existence of supernatural beings but of "abstract forces, veritable entities (that is, personified abstractions) inherent in all beings, and capable of producing all phenomena." [14] Nature, rather than God, becomes the basic causal factor of the universe. And natural, abstract laws, rather than divine laws, become the explanatory tools.

In the social order corresponding to this mode of thinking, the theological philosophy and military polity finally reach their "decline and dissolution . . . in preparation for a new and permanent organic state of society." [15] Comte spoke of the analysis of this period as an "irksome task"; the more pleasant task was the consideration of the emerging Positive state.

In the Positive state, then, the human mind no longer searches for "absolute notions, the origin and destination of the universe, and the causes of phenomena"; instead, it looks for the laws governing phenomena, "that is, their invariable relations of succession and resemblance." [16] Reasoning and observation become the tools of the intellect. The social order which will ultimately emerge from this mode of thinking will be an ideal state in which material, intellectual, and moral factors will be properly combined for the maximum well-being of man.

In the Positive state, the Religion of Humanity will emerge. Sociologists will be the priests of the new religion, and will guide man in his harmonious existence. The priest-sociologists will teach man to think positively (i.e., scientifically) and will relate the doctrines of love, order, and progress to man. Military power will be replaced by industrial power, and men will live harmoniously together as their behavior and social institutions are shaped and directed by their Positive mode of thought.

It is obvious, then, that Comte viewed change in terms of progress. That progress is tied up with scientific development; the latest and most complex of sciences — sociology — will enable man to attain the ideal social order. The disorder of his own day, according to Comte, was rooted in the simultaneous existence of the three incompatible philosophies — theological, metaphysical, and Positive. Any of the three can create a social order, but their coexistence precludes any sort of order. It is necessary, therefore, to ascertain which of the philosophies must ultimately prevail, and once this is ascertained, "every man, whatever may have been his former views, can not but concur in its triumph." [17] It is the task of sociology to show the inevitable triumph of the Positive philosophy, and to teach men to accept and utilize it to create the new order.

Progress, in other words, occurs through the exercise of reason in the Positive stage of history:

It is only through the more and more marked influence of the reason over the general conduct of Man and of society, that the gradual march of our race has attained that regularity and persevering continuity which distinguish it so radically from the desultory and barren expansion of even the highest of the animal orders, which share, and with enhanced strength, the appetites, the passions, and even the primary sentiments of Man.[18]

Indeed, "since the birth of philosophy, the history of society has been regarded as governed by the history of the human mind." [19]

We have already seen that the social order that will be created by the Positive mind is one of intellectual and moral progress towards benevolence among men. In fact, Comte's vision of the future does not, in this respect, differ from that of Marx. In the new order, "our characteristic qualities will find their most perfect respective confirmation, their completest mutual harmony, and the freest expansion for each and all." [20] But Comte goes beyond asking about the direction of change, and inquires into the rate. Given the ultimate end of humanity, what factors affect the pace with which we shall reach that end?

There are three factors, according to Comte, that influence the rate of man's progress. The first of these is ennui. "Man, like other animals, can not be happy without a sufficient exercise of all his faculties, intense and persistent in proportion to the intrinsic activity of each faculty." [21] Like modern, self-actualization theorists, Comte saw a hierarchy of needs in man; once man's lower faculties have been exercised, he will be driven to use the higher. And the greater the exercise of the higher faculties, the greater the rate of progress.

A second factor affecting rate is the duration of human life. Comte, like many other thinkers, assumed that age brings with it an increasing conservatism, while youth is characterized by an "innovating instinct." If man's life span were increased, say tenfold, conservative forces would be considerably more powerful, inhibiting the rate of change. On the other hand, "an ephemeral life would be quite as mischievous as a too protracted one, by giving too much power to the instinct of innovation." [22] There is, therefore, an optimum length of human life for an optimum rate of progress; and any increase or decrease in average life span will affect that rate to some degree.

The third factor affecting rate of change is the demographic one — the natural increase of population. This contributes more than any other factor to the acceleration of progress. By increase, Comte referred not simply to more numbers but to density of population. The higher concentration of humans in a given space will create new wants and new problems, and will therefore generate new means of progress and order "by neutralizing physical inequalities, and affording a growing ascendancy to those intellectual and moral forces which are suppressed among a scanty population." [23] Again, however, Comte was aware that factors influencing the rate of change can be extreme in two directions; not only too slow a rate of population increase, but too rapid a rate, can impede progress, by making the support of human life too difficult and the stability of social phenomena too fragile.

In sum, Comte made a number of contributions to sociology in general and to the study of social change in particular. Among the more important of the latter were his recognition that change is normal, that the problem for sociological investigation is to identify those factors that affect the rate of change, and that sociologists must be involved in using their knowledge to shape the future of mankind. To be sure, he perceived the role of the sociologist in somewhat narrow terms. For the direction of change is foreordained. All that the sociologist can do is facilitate the development of society towards its predetermined end. And the sociologist accomplishes this by education. The individual must be educated so as to reproduce the development of mankind: "In his brief career, he must pass through the three stages which an aggregate of nations has wrought out with infinite comparative slowness; and if any material part of the experience is evaded, his training will be abortive." [24] The primary responsibility of the sociologist is to teach people to think, to function in the Positive mode, so as to facilitate the creation of the Positive society.

Comte, of course, also took some wrong directions. He was too restrictive in identifying factors that affect rate. He accepted the myth of unidirectionality, assuming that all mankind was becoming like the Western European, industrial society he knew. And he minimized the power of man to shape his own future; the only strategy for effecting change was an educative one, and that would merely remove the barriers to progress into the Positive era.

But Comte did have a vision of a more humane social order, and he did acknowledge that man could have a part in bringing that order to pass. For that, and for his effort to identify the variables that affect the rate of change, we can credit him with a significant contribution to the study of social change.

Herbert Spencer

Although he had little formal education, Herbert Spencer (1820–1903) wrote prolifically on subjects covering a wide area of knowledge. [25] His writings include volumes on philosophy, biology, psychology, ethics, and sociology. He was initially interested in biology, then turned to engineering before serving for a time as editor of the *Economist* and, finally, leaving that position to write his work on philosophy. His aim was to unify the totality of human knowledge around the principle of evolution. (It was Spencer, incidentally, rather than Darwin who coined the idea of "survival of the fittest," and he applied it to man rather than to the animal world.)

The principle of evolution which governs all being — the natural world as well as man and society — involves a passage "from an indefinite, incoherent homogeneity to a definite, coherent heterogeneity." [26] Another way of stating this is to say that evolution is a process of successive differentiation and integration. The meaning of this for social change will become clear below.

First, however, we must note another premise upon which Spencer builds his theory of change, namely, that society is an organism. There are a number of reasons for treating society as an organism. First, society experiences continuous growth, and as it grows its parts "become unlike: it exhibits increase of structure." [27] Unlike parts have differing functions, functions which are not merely diverse but which must operate together in order for the whole to exist. That is, the parts are mutually dependent upon each other. For example, the human body is composed of eyes, arms, hands, ears, blood vessels, various internal organs, and so on. Each is separate, yet each is dependent upon the other and must work with the others to form a living whole. In society, the various parts — government, family, economy, and other factors — also are separate but interdependent, and must function together for a viable whole.

Spencer obviously used his knowledge of biology to understand social phenomena. The extent to which he pressed the biological perspective may be seen in his description of social institutions, which he spoke of in terms of the sustaining, distributing, and regulating systems. With respect to the first, "the parts carrying on alimentation in a living body and the parts carrying on productive industries in the body politic, constitute, in either case, a sustaining system." [28] The distributing system of society is necessitated by the increasing complexity of society; it is a system of transfer among the interdependent parts. Just as an annelid (segmented worm) cannot evolve into a crustacean or insect without the growth of a vascular system, so a medieval society cannot evolve into an industrial society without roads and commercial classes. Finally, the regulating system emerges out of warfare between societies; it develops, in other words, as a means of "dealing with surrounding organisms, individual or social — other animals to be caught or escaped from, hostile societies to be conquered or resisted." [29]   In the organism, this is represented by the nervo-motor system, and in society by the governmental-military system.

In speaking of social institutions in terms of systems, then, Spencer was not viewing them in a static manner — as the stable structure of an organism.   He described them in terms of their own evolution, their appearance as survival mechanisms, and their subsequent course of development.   We may trace out the evolution of the digestive system of an animal: "the entire alimentary canal becomes adapted in structure and function to the matters, animal or vegetal, brought in contact with its interior. . . ." [30]   We may also trace out the evolution of the industrial or productive system of a society: "it takes on activities and correlative structures, determined by the minerals, animals, and vegetals, with which its workers are in contact. . . ." [31]   Similarly, the evolution of distributing and regulating systems may be identified, whether those systems are part of an individual or a society.

Since evolution is the basic principle of being, and since societies are organisms, we may understand societal development in terms of human growth: "Societies, like living bodies, begin as germs — originate from masses which are extremely minute in comparison with the masses some of them eventually reach." [32] There are, in fact, numerous parallels between the growths of individual and social organisms.   The process in both cases is one of ongoing differentiation and integration; units multiply, enlarging the group, and groups unite, further enhancing group integration.   This "compounding and re-compounding" occurs in the vegetable and animal worlds, and also in the social.   For example, as a primitive tribe spreads through increase in its numbers, it reaches a point where it separates into a number of tribes which gradually grow distinct from each other.   This may be a continuous, repetitive process; but there may also be the formation of a larger society through the uniting of several tribes.   This latter occurs "without obliterating the divisions previously caused by separations." [33]

Furthermore, societal growth involves not only the multiplication of groups and the union of groups, but also increasing density or solidarity.   The integration that follows differentiation means not merely a "larger mass," but also the "progress of such mass towards that coherence due to closeness of parts." [34]   It is clear that the evolutionary principle that Spencer found in the universe as a whole — indefinite, incoherent homogeneity giving way to a definite coherent heterogeneity — is also true of human societies.

Spencer illustrated the societal transition from homogeneity to heterogeneity by contrasting primitive and modern societies. The primitive tribe, he argued, is "alike in all its parts," while the "civilized nation" is "full of structural and functional unlikenesses." [35]   Furthermore, along with the increasing heterogeneity goes increasing coherence. The nomadic group is held together by no bonds (an assertion Khaldun would have vigorously denied). The tribe has more coherence, for it is held together by subordination to the leader. And this coherence increases, until we get the civilized nation, which is sufficiently integrated to hold together for "a thousand years or more."

Increasing definiteness also characterizes the process of social growth. The initial social organization is vague; with growth, social arrangements become more precise, customs become laws, laws become more specific, and social institutions separate and become distinct. "Thus in all respects is fulfilled the formula of evolution. There is progress towards greater size, coherence, multiformity, and definiteness." [36]

What is the driving mechanism of this growth? It is the struggle for existence between the various societies. The whole process of compounding and re-compounding, of change from homogeneity (primitivism) to heterogeneity (civilization), would have been impossible without conflict between tribes and between nations. For group defense and offense require cooperation among the members of the group. This, in turn, has led to "all kinds of cooperations" which have facilitated the growth of civilization. While admitting the "horrors" resulting from such conflict, Spencer insisted that apart from such conflict "the world would still have been inhabited only by men of feeble types, sheltering in caves and living on wild food." [37]

On the other hand, once civilized society has emerged out of the bloody throes of societal wars, there is no longer a need for conflict between men. War, therefore, will disappear. And this leads us to a consideration of the two types of society for which Spencer is known, and which characterize the general pattern of human evolution. In general, societies may be classified as militant and industrial. These are not, however, mutually exclusive types; in theory and in actuality, characteristics of the two types are mingled. Nevertheless, the trend of evolution is from the militant to the industrial.

The militant society is organized on the basis of compulsory cooperation, while the industrial society rests on voluntary cooperation. The militant society has a despotic central power that exercises absolute authority over individual conduct; the industrial society has a democratic or representative type of government which is limited in its political control of personal conduct. In the militant society, then, "the individual is owned by the State." [38] The preservation of the society is the dominant concern; the individual's preservation must be a secondary matter.

There is a necessary relationship between the structure of a society and the personalities of its members. In a militant society, success in warfare is the source of the highest honor and goodness is equivalent to bravery and strength. Men in a militant society are chauvinistic; the "triumph of their society (is) the supreme end of action." [39] Such men lack initiative; they are utterly subservient to authority, which they regard as inevitable and essential.

In the industrial society, these traits give way to converse ones. The industrial society is one of an enduring peaceful life; the society is organized for production, not for warfare, and the individual member rather than the overall society becomes the focus of concern. Instead of absolute authority governing the relations of men, there is interaction based upon contract. Centralized authority is limited to the negatively regulative; that is, it no longer says both "you shall do this" and "you shall not do that," but only "you shall not do that."

What kind of person will we find in industrial society? The citizenry will be marked by "growing independence, a less-marked loyalty, a small faith in governments, and a more qualified patriotism" as well as by "a growing respect for the individualities of others." [40] Thus, Spencer had a vision of a society in which governmental control was minimal and men pursued their own welfare with relative autonomy; as with Adam Smith, Spencer believed that the ultimate end of a laissez-faire society would be maximum well-being for all.

Spencer was not quite the optimist that Comte was, however. Unlike Comte, he saw the possibility of societal regression as well as progress. If the general direction of evolution is towards the industrial society, it should be noted that it is possible to revert back to a more militant society. International conflict or the reappearance of defensive and offensive activities may thrust a society back towards the militant type. In addition, Spencer departed from Comte at the point of the role of sociology in societal evolution. While admitting that human action was an integral part of the evolutionary process, Spencer denied that such action could in any way accelerate the process. Men or governments, by their interference in the social process, might retard the rate of evolution, but they would be unable to increase it: "the processes of growth and development may be, and very often are, hindered or deranged, though they cannot be artificially bettered." [41] There are no shortcuts to utopia; the role of sociology is to identify the process and help men to accept it and calmly await the appearance of the new age. Man must "see how comparatively little can be done, and yet to find it worth while to do that little: so uniting philanthropic energy with philosophic calm." [42]

What have we learned from Spencer? Again, we find the emphasis, abandoned by succeeding generations to a considerable extent, on the normality of change. And again we see the emphasis on conflict as a driving mechanism of social change. Spencer also shared the tendency of others (before and since) to be ethnocentric in his vision of utopia; he believed that nineteenth-century England provided the best example of evolution towards the industrial society.

But Spencer recognized that societies can experience regression as well as progress. And he insisted upon a relationship between the structure of a society and the nature of and behavior of the people in it. For Comte, the social structure was fashioned by man as a consequence of his mode of thinking; in Spencer, this relationship is changed, and it is the structure that demands a particular mode of thinking and type of personality. While both views are oversimplified, contemporary Western man is prone to adopt the Comtean perspective and to neglect the powerful influence on his thinking and behavior exerted by the social structure.

One final point is the issue raised by both Comte and Spencer regarding the role of sociology and sociologists (and, for that matter, man generally) in social change. This issue has plagued sociology throughout its history and is not yet resolved. Should the sociologist be an academic man, or should he be involved in effecting social change? Can sociology provide us with tools for effecting change, or does it simply make us aware of how helpless we are? When we deal with strategies of change in the last part of this book, we will assume that Comte had the greater insight at this point — man can shape his future. Whether sociologists ought to be part of those men who are shaping the future is still being debated. Or, as some would argue (and I agree), by the very nature of their work, social scientists are accumulating knowledge that will be used to shape the future. The question is not one of whether it shall be used, but in whose behalf it will be used.

Emile Durkheim

Our final example of a development theorist of the evolutionary type is Emile Durkheim (1855–1917).[43] Durkheim was the son of a Jewish rabbi; he studied in both France and Germany, taught philosophy in Paris, and initiated the first course in social science ever given in France.

Nisbet has suggested four major points in Durkheim's theory of change.[44] The first is the problem of origins. What was the original state of the advanced nations of the time? For most nineteenth-century thinkers the answer was plain: contemporary primitive peoples provided the clues to the original condition of civilized nations. Durkheim accepted this perspective. Like Spencer, he searched for human origins among the primitive peoples of the day; comparing those people with the citizens of developed nations would indicate the course of social development.

A second point is Durkheim's description of the stages of development. He shared the interest of his time in identifying stages of evolutionary development, but did not make this the focus of his work. Moreover, he rejected the "reality of developmental continuity in the history of social types. In this he was exceptional in his age." [45] Nevertheless, virtually any student of sociology will connect the name of Durkheim with the two kinds of solidarity — mechanical and organic.

Mechanical solidarity was the early, primitive form of social organization, and could still be seen in existing primitive peoples. Organic solidarity derives from the division of labor accompanying social development. In mechanical solidarity, there is a preponderance of shared ideas and tendencies (rather than individual differences); the social order has great homogeneity. In fact, "the collective conscience completely envelops our whole conscience and coincides in all points with it." [46] Furthermore, this solidarity is maintained by the application of repressive sanctions to those who deviate; such sanctions are the expression of social rage in the face of offenses against "strong and defined states of the collective conscience." [47]

Organic solidarity, by contrast, is rooted in differences rather than likenesses (the similarity with Spencer's evolutionary law of homogeneity-heterogeneity is apparent). The increasing complexity of a society demands that solidarity rest upon differentiation; diverse functions involve the division of labor which is the essence of organic solidarity. This solidarity is characterized by restitutive sanctions; not punishment, but "the return of things as they were, in the reestablishment of troubled relations to their normal state" becomes the purpose of the law. [48]

Durkheim summed up the distinction between mechanical and organic solidarity in three points. [49] The former "binds the individual directly to society without any intermediary," while the latter involves interdependence among individuals. The former is found in a society characterized by shared beliefs and sentiments, while the latter characterizes a differentiated society. And the former can be strong only to the extent that individual personalities and rights are relatively indistinguishable from the whole, while the latter demands unique personalities and personal rights.

A third point in Durkheim's theory of change is his identification of the causal factors in change. What leads to the division of labor and the new type of solidarity? He argued that the division of labor varies directly with "the volume and density of societies." [50] Volume and density do not simply facilitate the division of labor; they cause it. In other words, as the number and rate of interaction of the population increases, there is a necessary increase in the division of labor; the latter, in turn, necessarily leads to organic rather than mechanical solidarity.

Finally, Durkheim discussed the direction of change. Although he was immersed in an intellectual context that reveled in the progress of the human race, Durkheim's own conclusions fell in with the minority who had misgivings if not despair about the future of humanity. He pointed to the suicide rate as one indicator of the crisis of modern civilization, that is, as evidence of the lack of integration of society. Moreover, he noted that neither kinship relations nor religion could be an integrating force for man in the modern era, and he would not accept the state as a substitute for these older means. The only hope which Durkheim could see for man was in occupational organizations. For in the future "our whole social and political organization will have a base exclusively, or almost exclusively, occupational." [51] But occupational organization had not developed adequately to meet the needs of the social order; the future, therefore, was at best precarious.

Social evolution, then, is the increasing dominance of organic over mechanical solidarity. It is a historical law "that mechanical solidarity which first stands alone, or nearly so, progressively loses ground, and that organic solidarity becomes, little by little, preponderant." [52] And when group solidarity changes in form, the social structure changes. The two types of solidarity, therefore, correspond to two different types of societies. Durkheim did not contend, however, that either type of solidarity would be total in any real society. The direction of change is towards organic solidarity and the type of social structure characterized by that solidarity; but remnants of mechanical solidarity will remain.

In sum, Durkheim, like Khaldun, stressed the significance of solidarity. Both considered solidarity necessary for a viable society. And like Comte, Durkheim gave great importance to demographic factors in change — a prime mechanism of change is the increasing density of population. If we compare the three theorists considered in this chapter with respect to the direction of change, we find a continuum: Comte saw increasing advance and progress; Spencer saw a tendency towards progress but also the possibility of regress; and Durkheim painted man's future in rather bleak terms. Durkheim was also an early voice of doubt about the attainments of "civilization." He felt that there is probably an inverse relation between the growth of culture and human happiness. Certainly, a "normal savage can be quite as happy as the normal civilized man." [53]   And man's happiness has probably diminished rather than increased with social development. Durkheim thus reminds us to beware of the fallacy of utopia apprehended; there are flaws in the present, and the salvation of mankind does not consist of helping everyone else to become like us as quickly as possible.

DIALECTICAL DEVELOPMENT

As Spencer showed, conflict may be incorporated into evolutionary development. But for the evolutionary developmentalists, conflict was not the focal process; at most, it had a subsidiary place in the evolutionary process. For another set of developmental theorists, however, conflict is the central fact of social change. Since we shall deal with conflict in more detail in a later chapter, we shall examine here one particular type of conflict — dialectical development. And dialectical development is associated above all with the names of Karl Marx (1818–1883) and Frederick Engels (1820–1895).[54]

Both Marx and Engels were born in Prussia; the former was the son of a Jewish lawyer (who was later converted, with his entire family, to Christianity) and the latter the son of an affluent and conservative manufacturer. They became friends in Paris, and subsequently wrote both in collaboration and singly to produce the foundation works of Marxism.

Two of the pillars upon which Marxist thought rests are the dialectic and materialism. The dialectic asserts that contradiction is the essence of all things; in both the natural and human worlds, contradiction is the central fact of being. Consequently, we must look to the dialectic for the key to change, which is inextricably bound up with the struggle of opposites.

In an early work, Marx described the dialectic of change in terms of the Hegelian trinity of thesis, antithesis, and synthesis. But "to those who are not acquainted with Hegelian language, we would say to them in the sacramental formula, affirmation, negation, and negation of the negation." [55]   Engels elaborated upon the meaning of the dialectic in *Anti-Duhring*.[56] Dialectics, he argued, is "the science of the general laws of motion and development of Nature, human society and thought." [57]   And he identified as two of these general laws the change of quantity into quality and the negation of the negation.

The transformation of quantity into quality may be illustrated at the natural level and at the social level. The law asserts simply that at a certain point quantitative variations become qualitative variations. Water changes to steam at 100° Centigrade; continuing quantitative changes have resulted in a new qualitative state. At the social level, an example is provided by the way in which a "new power" is created by group cooperation; the new power is qualitatively different from the total of individual powers.

The law of the negation of the negation can be illustrated by simple algebra. The quantity a can be negated by making it minus a. If the minus a is multiplied by a minus a, the result is a^2, which is the negation of the negation. At the societal level, the law is illustrated by the development of various modes of the economic structure. The capitalist order is the negation of the feudal order; and the socialist order negates the capitalist order — it is the negation of the negation.

Thus, all social development proceeds in accord with dialectical laws. Incidentally, Marx himself never used the terms "historical materialism" (created by Engels) and "dialectical materialism" (created by Plekhanov); nevertheless, he spoke of the materialist basis of his method, and materialism is the second pillar upon which Marxist thought rests. The meaning of materialism is well expressed in a conclusion once reached by Marx which, he said, continued as a "guiding thread" to subsequent work:

> In the social production which men carry on they enter into definite relations that are indispensable and independent of their will; these relations of production correspond to a definite stage of development of their material powers of production. The totality of these relations of production constitutes the economic structure of society — the real foundation, on which legal and political superstructures arise and to which definite forms of social consciousness correspond. The mode of production of material life determines the general character of the social, political and spiritual processes of life.[58]

Marxism, then, seeks to bring the study of social life down from the fruitless flights of speculation; that study must deal with "real individuals, their activity and the material conditions under which they live, both those which they find already existing and those produced by their activity." [59]

Proceeding from these premises of the dialectical and materialist essence of all being, Marx and Engels constructed an interpretation of history which may be outlined as follows.

1. Men enter into relationships which are independent of their will. We should look for the causes of change in the modes of production rather than in ideas, in the economic rather than

philosophical aspects of any era. Historical understanding can come only through structural analysis; the effort to gain that understanding from studying the minds of men will always be frustrated. It is not the way men think, nor what they think about, that shapes history; it is, rather, the manner in which they relate in production and to production. The reason for this will become clearer in the next point.

2. Every society is characterized by an infrastructure, the economic structure, and a superstructure, which includes ideology, law, the polity, the family, and religion. The superstructure arises out of the infrastructure. That is, the material base of a society is the foundation upon which all the rest is built, so that a change in the mode of production leads to a change in all the social relations of men. In turn, men create "the principles, the ideas, the categories, conformably with their social relations." [60] This is not, however, to assert a simplistic, deterministic relationship. In a letter to Bloch in 1890, Engels pointed out that the productive mode of existence was the "ultimately" determining element, but that the various elements of the superstructure "also exercise their influence upon the course of the historical struggles and in many cases preponderate in determining their *form*." [61] Thus, the infrastructure provides a framework upon which varied forms of the superstructure exert some influence.

3. Change comes about as a result of the contradiction between the forces and relations of production.[62] In the course of the development of the productive forces, a stage is reached at which these forces become destructive. They are destructive because they contradict existing relationships of production. But what does Marx mean by this contradiction? Raymond Aron has suggested two possible interpretations.[63] One is that as the forces of production develop, they reach a point at which "individual right of ownership represents an impediment to their progress." There is, then, a contradiction between continued expansion of the productive forces and individual right of ownership. But if one considers corporate growth (which precludes individual ownership) an integral part of capitalist development, this contradiction disappears (since individual right of ownership is not an integral part of capitalism).

A second interpretation is that the contradiction is between distribution and production: a capitalistic society is unable to absorb its own production because of capitalist appropriation of social production. As Engels put it, production expands more rapidly than the market, with an inevitable collision which is insoluble "so long as it does not burst the capitalist mode of production itself." [64] Although we have not yet seen nor been able to predict the point at which a capitalist society becomes incapable of absorbing its own production, this second interpretation seems to me the most reasonable.

4. Contradiction is of the essence of the social process. That is, the contradiction does not arise out of external forces or factors which impinge upon the society; the contradiction is an integral part of social development. A capitalist society gives birth to the material conditions that will ultimately destroy the society. Dialectical development means that the contradiction emerges out of the essence of the social process. No external challenge, no external proletariat is required for Marx and Engels; slave, feudal, and capitalist societies carry within them the seeds of self-destruction.

5. The contradiction between the forces and relations of production is manifested in class conflict. "The history of all hitherto existing society is the history of class struggles." [65] This occurs because in the course of the development of the productive forces there is a class which must "bear all the burdens of society without enjoying its advantages, which, ousted from society, is forced into the most decided antagonism to all other classes." [66] One class rules — the bourgeoisie — and lives in affluence at the expense of the other class — the proletariat — which is driven into an increasingly wretched state of existence. Thus, the society becomes polarized into two antagonistic groups. The ruling class derives its power from its control of property, and maintains its power, in part, because the state is its tool.

The ruled class, the proletariat, exists in the agony of increasing impoverishment and alienation. Impoverishment is due to capitalist exploitation. Alienation includes man's estrangement from the products of his labor, from himself, from his "species-being," and from other men. [67] Both poverty and alienation are created by the capitalist mode of production which concentrates property and power in the hands of a minority of individuals.

6. The outcome of the contradiction is a revolution. The contradiction between forces and relations of production, the struggle between the classes, is resolved by revolution. Past revolutions were inadequate because "the mode of activity always remained unscathed and it was only a question of a different distribution of this activity." [68] The communist revolution, on the other hand, is directed against the preceding mode of activity; it does away with labor (as a class) and abolishes classes and the rule of classes. Along with this is the withering away of the state, which was an instrument of control of the ruling class.

If the revolution is to succeed, if there is to be a genuine social revolution as well as a political transformation, there must be a large-scale "alteration of men." [69] The revolution, therefore, must take the form of a practical movement. For there is no other way to overthrow the ruling class, and the class overthrowing the ruling elite can only "succeed in ridding itself of all the muck of ages and become fitted to found society anew" in revolution.[70]   And only where classes and class antagonisms have been abolished will man experience social evolution without political revolution.

7. Beyond the communist revolution is the classless society. The society of the future will have, as noted in point 6, no classes and no state.   Without entering into the debate about the possibility of a classless society, we may inquire briefly into the meaning of a stateless society.   Is the withering away of the state realistic in a complex, industrial society?   If "the state" refers to a centralized decision-making apparatus, the disappearance of the state in an industrial society would seem inconceivable (although the anarchists would strongly disagree).   But we have noted that Marx identified the state as a tool of the ruling class; it may be, therefore, that the argument about the disappearance of the state really involves the disappearance of the class character of the state.   In other words, the withering away of the state need not demand the elimination of any centralized administrative apparatus.

In any case, in the society of the future, the seizure of power by the proletariat ends class differences and class antagonisms. "The government of persons is replaced by the administration of things and the direction of the processes of production." [71]   Instead of being dominated by external factors, man will gain control and create a fully human existence.   There will be the "abolition of private property, of human self-alienation, and thus, the real appropriation of human nature, through and for man," and, along with this abolition of alienation, there will be a "return of man from religion, the family, the State, etc., to his human, i.e., social life." [72]   Ultimately, the social order will evolve (rather than emerge through violent struggle) into a condition where every man will give according to his ability and receive according to his needs.

Thus, in Marx and Engels we have a portrayal of the social process as dialectical — contradiction inheres in it and becomes the driving mechanism of change.   All history may be characterized in terms of stages which exhibited different modes of production.   Each mode of production, in turn, was characterized by a particular kind of relationship among men.   Ancient society had slavery; feudal society had serfdom; and bourgeois society has wage earners.   But the communist revolution ushers in a stage of history in which we have a "community of free individuals, carrying on their work with the means of production in common, in which the labour-power of all the different individuals is consciously applied as the combined labour-power of the community." [73]   The agony of history has come to an end.   Contradiction has finally been erased from the human scene. Man lives in peace with himself and with other men. The leap has finally been made "from the realm of necessity into the realm of freedom." [74]

It would require volumes to take note of the numberless expositions, critiques, and modifications of the Marxist view. For our purposes, it will be sufficient to acknowledge the immense influence of Marxism since the middle of the nineteenth century and to point out certain facets that particularly bear upon social change. In Marxist thought, of course, change is normal; dialectical development proceeds continually until the communist revolution, after which there is a social evolution. We could well ask the question, if conflict is central to social development throughout most of man's history, how can we conceive of a period in which desirable development occurs without conflict? For contradiction is the basic driving mechanism of development. And certainly all nations that have experienced a communist revolution have also experienced continuing internal conflict to some degree. Mao handled this problem by distinguishing between antagonistic and nonantagonistic contradictions, the former referring to contradictions between "ourselves and our enemies" and the latter referring to contradictions "among the working people." [75] There are also, Mao asserted, some nonantagonistic contradictions existing among exploiters and exploited. The point is that the two types of contradictions demand very different responses; democratic processes are sufficient to deal with the nonantagonistic contradictions.

Marx and Engels did get caught in a myth of unidirectionality. Their identification of a necessary historical sequence has given subsequent Marxist thinkers the thorny problem of fitting actual historical developments into that sequence. For example, can a communist revolution occur in a nation that is nonindustrial and in which the working class is a minority? If not, then it behooves the orthodox theorist to show that the nation has actually passed through the capitalist stage of development. The only alternative is to revise Marx, as Mao did to explain the revolution in China.

One of the important contributions of Marxism, one that makes it attractive to so many people in both the developed and developing nations of the world, is the humanistic vision of the future which it offers, and its stress on man's role in making that future. It is men who make history. Contrary to Spencer, who narrowed man's role to behaving in such a way as not to impede the slow evolutionary process, and contrary to Comte, who limited the significant efforts at shaping the future to an elite of educators, Marxism places history in the hands of the masses. The point of philosophy, argued Marx, is not merely to understand history, but to change it. And he gave the world a philosophy designed to do precisely that.   His vision of the future is optimistic, humanistic, and activistic.   The Marxist theory of change is not a mere adventure of the mind; it is a directive to action, a tool whereby men can seize control of the historical process in order to gain their freedom.

And if men are to gain their freedom, they must be unified through an awarenes of the reality in which they are enmeshed. The proletariat must make the transition from being a class "in itself" to one "for itself."   The peasants, for example, were not considered a class, in the full sense of the word, by Marx.   For they lacked class consciousness, and lacking that consciousness they were helpless to effect change.   In this, we get echoes of the solidarity which Khaldun said was necessary for any group to triumph.

Another important contribution of Marxist thought is its avoidance of the strict determinism-indeterminism dichotomy. In broad outline, the theory is deterministic; the stages of historical development are identifiable and inevitable.   But, as emphasized in point 2, the economic infrastructure is *ultimately* determining; given any specific economic structure there is some latitude for variation and for interacting effects of the superstructure.

Finally, Marxism stresses the crucial significance of the social structure in understanding human behavior.   It is not consciousness that shapes reality, but reality that determines consciousness. What man is, how he thinks, and what he believes reflect the structure in which he exists.   To the extent that we forget the critical influence of the social structure, we will be prone to accept a myth of utopia apprehended, and we may find ourselves making people culpable (e.g., the poor) for effects of the structure.[76]

ENDNOTES TO CHAPTER 3

1.   Derk Bodde, "Harmony and Conflict in Chinese Philosophy," in *Studies in Chinese Thought*, ed. Arthur F. Wright (Chicago: The American Anthropological Association, 1953), p. 27.

2.   Augustine, *The City of God*, trans. Marcus Dods (New York: The Modern Library, 1950), p. 609.

3.   *Ibid.*, p. 668.

4.   Robert A. Nisbet, *Social Change and History* (New York: Oxford University Press, 1969), p. 47.

5.   Quoted in Howard Becker and Harry Elmer Barnes, *Social Thought from Lore to Science*, 3rd edition (New York: Dover Publications, Inc., 1961), p. 474.

6.   Comte's thought has been well summarized by Raymond Aron, *Main Currents in Sociological Thought I*, trans. Richard

Howard and Helen Weaver (New York: Anchor Books, 1968), pp. 73–143. Selections from Comte's works with extended commentaries on his thought may be found in George Simpson, *Auguste Comte: Sire of Sociology* (New York: Thomas Y. Crowell Company, 1969).

7. Auguste Comte, *The Positive Philosophy*, trans. Harriet Martineau (New York: Calvin Blanchard, 1858), p. 461.

8. *Ibid.*

9. *Ibid.*, p. 464.

10. *Ibid.*, p. 25.

11. *Ibid.*, p. 26.

12. *Ibid.*, p. 545.

13. *Ibid.*, p. 574.

14. *Ibid.*, p. 26.

15. *Ibid.*, p. 637.

16. *Ibid.*, p. 26.

17. *Ibid.*, p. 36.

18. *Ibid.*, p. 521.

19. *Ibid.*

20. *Ibid.*, p. 838.

21. *Ibid.*, p. 517.

22. *Ibid.*, pp. 518–19.

23. *Ibid.*, p. 520.

24. *Ibid.*, p. 798.

25. For Spencer's sociological thought, see Herbert Spencer, *Principles of Sociology*, ed. Stanislav Andreski (London: Macmillan, 1969). A good summary may be found in Becker and Barnes, *Social Thought from Lore to Science*, pp. 664–81.

26. Quoted in Becker and Barnes, *op. cit.*, p. 667.

27. Spencer, *Principles of Sociology*, p. 21.

28. *Ibid.*, p. 58.

29. *Ibid.*, p. 79.

30. *Ibid.*, p. 64.

31. *Ibid.*

32. *Ibid.*, p. 23.

33. *Ibid.*, p. 27.

34. *Ibid.*, p. 29.

35. *Ibid.*, p. 154.

36. *Ibid.*, p. 155.

37. *Ibid.*, p. 178.

38. *Ibid.*, p. 503.

39. *Ibid.*, p. 533.

40. *Ibid.*, pp. 570–71.

41. Herbert Spencer, *The Study of Sociology* (New York: D. Appleton & Company, 1874), p. 401.

42. *Ibid.*, p. 403.

43. The main source of Durkheim's theory of change is *The Division of Labor in Society*, trans. George Simpson (New York: The Free Press, 1933). An excellent survey and critique of this and other aspects of Durkheim's thought may be found in Robert A. Nisbet, *Emile Durkheim* (Englewood Cliffs: Prentice-Hall, Inc., 1965).

44. Nisbet, *Emile Durkheim*, pp. 92–102.

45. *Ibid.*, p. 95.

46. Emile Durkheim, *The Division of Labor in Society*, p. 130.

47. *Ibid.*, p. 80.

48. *Ibid.*, p. 69.

49. *Ibid.*, pp. 129–31.

50. *Ibid.*, p. 262. Durkheim posited an interaction between the two variables, however. Thus, there is a cumulative process, with population volume and density increasing the division of labor, which in turn increases the "concentration" of society.

51. *Ibid.*, p. 190.

52. *Ibid.*, p. 174.

53. *Ibid.*, p. 244.

54. The literature on Marx, Engels, and subsequent Marxist thinkers is voluminous. For some of the more important writings of Marx and Engels, along with brief commentary, see Lewis S. Feuer, ed., *Marx & Engels: Basic Writings on Politics and Philosophy* (Garden City: Anchor Books, 1959), and T. B. Bottomore and Maximilien Rubel, eds., *Karl Marx: Selected Writings in Sociology and Social Philosophy* (New York: McGraw-Hill Book Company, 1956). A valuable and lucid exposition and critique of Marx may be found in Raymond Aron, *Main Currents in Sociological Thought I*, pp. 145–236. For a critique and effort to reformulate Marx, see Ralf Dahrendorf, *Class and Class Conflict in Industrial Society* (Stanford: Stanford University Press, 1959).

55. Karl Marx, *The Poverty of Philosophy*, trans. H. Quelch (Chicago: Charles H. Kerr, 1920), p. 114.

56. Frederick Engels, *Anti-Duhring: Herr Eugen Duhring's Revolution in Science*, trans. Emile Burns (New York: International Publishers, 1939), pp. 131–56.

57. *Ibid.*, p. 155.

58. From the Preface to *A Contribution to the Critique of Political Economy*, in Bottomore and Rubel, *Karl Marx*, p. 51.

59. Karl Marx and Friedrich Engels, *The German Ideology*, ed. R. Pascal (New York: International Publishers, 1947), p. 7.

60. Karl Marx, *The Poverty of Philosophy*, p. 119.

61. Karl Marx and Frederick Engels, *Selected Correspondence* (Moscow: Foreign Languages Publishing House, n.d.), p. 498.

62. By the "forces of production" Marx referred to productive capacity, including instruments, people, and experience and skills. By the "relations of production" Marx meant the mutual relationships that characterize people as they engage in production (including property relations).

63. *Main Currents in Sociological Thought I*, pp. 200–201.

64. Frederick Engels, *Anti-Duhring*, p. 301.

65. From the *Manifesto of the Communist Party*, in Lewis S. Feuer, *Marx & Engels*, p. 7.

66. Karl Marx and Friedrich Engels, *The German Ideology*, p. 69.

67. From the *Economic and Philosophic Manuscripts of 1844*, in Robert Freedman, *Marxist Social Thought* (New York: Harcourt, Brace & World, Inc., 1968), pp. 71–78.

68. Karl Marx and Friedrich Engels, *The German Ideology*, p. 69.

69. *Ibid.*

70. *Ibid.*

71. Frederick Engels, *Anti-Duhring*, p. 307.

72. From the *Economic and Philosophic Manuscripts of 1844*, in Bottomore and Rubel, *Karl Marx*, pp. 243–44.

73. From *Capital*, in Bottomore and Rubel, *Karl Marx*, p. 250.

74. Frederick Engels, *Anti-Duhring*, p. 310.

75. Anne Fremantle, ed., *Mao Tse-tung: An Anthology of His Writings* (New York: Mentor Books, 1954), p. 265.

76. As C. Wright Mills reminded us, if one man in 100,000 is unemployed, he has a personal problem. But when a significant proportion of people are unemployed, we must look to the structure of opportunities. Similar differences between the "personal troubles of milieu" and the "public issues of social structure" may be illustrated in the areas of war, marriage, urban areas, and so forth. See his *The Sociological Imagination* (New York: Grove Press, Inc., 1959), pp. 8–11.

CHAPTER 4

Structural-Functional Theories

To step from Marx into structural-functionalism is to enter a totally different world. It is a world that many critics have called static, a world without radical change. But structural-functionalists have dealt with change, and since they represent the dominant theoretical perspective in sociology, it is necessary to see how change looks from their vantage point.

First, however, let us briefly characterize this theoretical perspective. Van den Berghe has well summarized the general structural-functional approach in terms of seven elements:[1]

1. Societies must be analyzed as wholes, as "systems of interrelated parts";
2. Cause and effect relationships are "multiple and reciprocal";
3. Social systems exist in a state of "dynamic equilibrium" such that adjustment to forces impinging on the system is made with minimal change within the system;
4. Perfect integration is never realized, so that every social system has strains and deviations, but the latter tend to be neutralized through institutionalization;
5. Change is basically a slow, adaptive process rather than a revolutionary shift;
6. Change is the result of adjustment to changes outside the system, growth by differentiation, and internal innovations; and
7. The system is integrated through shared values.

Many of these points will emerge again as we examine the perspectives of two prominent structural-functionalists: Talcott Parsons and Neil Smelser. We shall reserve criticism of them, however, for the final section, where we shall ask to what extent structural-functionalism comes to terms with the problem of change.

SYSTEMS IN CHANGE

Talcott Parsons

Few men in the history of sociology have been as popular targets of emulation, modification, and attack as Talcott Parsons. And one of the most frequent points of attack has been his tortuous style of writing. As we strive to understand his perspective on change in the following paragraphs, we shall stay as close as possible within the confines of his own terminology — as close as is consistent with understanding.

Parsons insists that the study of change must grow out of the prior study of structure. In the study of societal evolution, for example, there is a parallel "between organic and socio-cultural evolution: Structural analysis must take a certain priority over the analysis of process and change." [2] In biology, morphology is the "backbone" of the theory of evolution; and in sociology, the identification and sequential ordering of structural types must be the foundation for an understanding of sociocultural evolution.

This, of course, is not to deny the importance of change, as some of Parsons' critics have charged him with doing. In fact, in an early work he asserted that the "theory of action" was "concerned equally with the conditions of stability and the conditions of change . . . It is impossible to study one without the other." [3] In studying the mechanisms by which stability is maintained, we must also deal with the forces tending to change. The existence of change is not denied, and the importance of change is not slighted. But change can be understood only through a prior understanding of structures.

And what is the nature of the structure which is the essential basis for the analysis of change? We begin with the social system. In broadest terms, a system is two or more interacting units, and the units may be psychological aspects of people, individuals as wholes, or groups (including entire societies). Every system is "embedded in an environing situation," however, so that whether a particular entity is a unit of a system or a system itself depends upon the focus of analysis.[4]   That is, for some purposes an organization such as a university may be viewed as a system itself, while for other purposes it may only be an entity within a larger system.

The social system is a particular kind of system — a group of interacting individuals, each of whom seeks to maximize his own gratification within the context of a particular culture.   Or as Parsons himself put it, a social system is

> a plurality of individual actors interacting with each other in a situation which has at least a physical or environmental aspect, actors who are motivated in terms of a tendency to the "optimization of gratification" and whose relation to their situations, including each other, is defined and mediated in terms of a system of culturally structured and shared symbols.[5]

The system, therefore, may be defined in terms of its units, its patterns, and its boundaries. The minimum unit of the social system is the role, while various kinds of groupings may form "higher-order" units.   The patterns of interaction in the social system are normative; that is, they are culturally defined as appropriate and right. And the boundaries of the system are maintained to the extent that the system remains integrated through shared values.

Furthermore, every system has four functional imperatives. That is, every system must confront and successfully resolve (if it is to survive) the problems of adaptation, goal-attainment, integration, and latent pattern maintenance.   These four imperatives apply to all systems of action — nature, culture, personality, and society.   In fact, they apply at the "general action" level, for adaptation is the function of the behavioral organism, goal-attainment is the function of the personality, integration is the function of the social system, and latent pattern maintenance is the function of the culture.[6]   At the level of the social system, the functions of adaptation, goal-attainment, integration, and latent pattern maintenance are associated with, respectively, the economy, the polity, law, and the family.[7]

By examining the entities that perform each of the functions, we gain some idea of what Parsons means by each.   In brief, adaptation involves response to the demands of the environment. Goal-attainment involves the mobilization of resources.   Integration is important for the regulation of subsystems.   And latent pattern maintenance refers to the problem of maintaining the value pattern of the system.   Two of the functional imperatives focus on problems internal to the system — latent pattern maintenance and integration — while the other two focus on problems that relate to the environment of the system — adaptation and goal-attainment. And two involve what are basically instrumental actions — adaptation and latent pattern maintenance — while the other two involve what are basically consummatory actions—goal-attainment and integration.

Finally, the four functional imperatives are related to four structural categories. Adaptation is the basic function of the role. Goal-attainment is the work of collectivities. Integration depends upon norms which "regulate the great variety of processes that contribute to the implementation of patterned value commitments." [8] And latent pattern maintenance is the function of values.

It is important to understand the nature of the functional imperatives because they are the links between structure and process. When we look at processes in and of social systems, we do so in the light of those four functional imperatives which are also the structural essence of any social system.

A first point is a distinction between process and change. According to Parsons, all processes involve some kind of change, but we may "distinguish from others the processes which change social structures." [9] And he calls those particular kinds of processes "change." Change, in other words, is a particular type of process that involves alteration in social structures. Parsons also distinguishes two kinds of dynamic problems in systems. The first kind is problems of processes of equilibrium, which "go on under the assumption that the structural patterns of institutionalized culture are given, i.e., are assumed to remain constant." [10] The second is problems of structural change, i.e., problems of processes which involve fundamental alterations in the system.

The distinction between two kinds of dynamic problems does not involve an absolute dichotomy, however. For there is a very important "mixed case," which involves structural change in the subsystems but not in the "over-all structural pattern." And the most important type of such a process is structural differentiation, which "involves genuine *reorganization* of the system and, therefore, fundamental structural change of various subsystems and their relations to each other." [11]

In all, we may identify four types of processes in Parsons' thought: equilibrium, which involves processes within the system; structural change, which involves fundamental alterations of the system; structural differentiation, which involves change in the subsystems but not in the overall system; and evolution, which is the process describing the developmental pattern of societies over time. These four kinds of processes are not, of course, mutually exclusive or independent. But they are analytically distinguishable, and we shall examine each in turn in a little more detail.

First, equilibrium refers to processes that serve to maintain the boundaries of the system. The equilibrium may be either static or moving. Processes are continual in both types, but in the latter case there is a patterned process of change. An example is the growth of scientific knowledge. This represents, of course, not a fundamental alteration of the system but change in "the cognitive *content* of the relevant part of the culture." [12]

Equilibrium in social systems may be analyzed in terms of four laws: [13]

1. The "principle of inertia" asserts continuation of rate and direction of a process unless "opposing motivational forces" impinge upon the process;
2. The "principle of action and reaction" asserts that any change of direction of a process will be balanced by another change "which is equal in motivational force and opposite in direction";
3. The "principle of effort" states that changes in the rate of processes are in direct proportion to "the *magnitude* of the motivational force applied or withdrawn";
4. The "principle of system-integration" states that the fate of "pattern" elements hinges upon their value as integrative factors.

The similarity of the laws of equilibrium to classical mechanics is obvious. And the idea of equilibrium is also obvious — it states that strong forces are at work to prevent basic changes in the system.

The second type of process is structural change. Such a change in any social system is, by definition, "a change in its normative culture." [14] This means change in "the paramount value system" at the highest level of the social system. There will also be changes among the subsystems and in the social roles. The interdependence of units within a system means that fundamental change in any unit is likely to involve some kind of change in other units, and changes at a particular level of the system are likely to effect some kind of change at other levels.

Examples of structural change are provided by the developing nations of the world, in which the primary impetus to change has come from outside the society itself. But it is also possible for the source of such change to be internal; this may come about through the work of a charismatic leader. Change that results from a charismatic leader takes place in the religious sphere; that is, the meaning of the individual's life and of the nature of the society are given new definitions.

The third type of process is structural differentiation. As

noted earlier, this process involves alterations in the subsystems but not in the overall system's structure. In other words, in structural differentiation, "the institutionalized values will be assumed to remain constant." [15] This is not to say that there are no changes at the value level. The *content* of the values changes as a result of differentiation, but the *pattern* does not. For example, a pattern of "instrumental activism" may continue to underlie different kinds of families in the United States as the family undergoes structural differentiation. The same pattern will underlie "employing-productive units" which have already, earlier in history, differentiated from the family. One pattern, then, may apply to two quite distinct systems (nuclear family and employing-productive unit) which have emerged by differentiation from an older system (the self-sufficient family of early America). The resulting values must be able to "legitimize the functions of both differentiated units under a single formula which permits it to do what it does and, equally essential, not to do what the other does." [16]

What have we just said? Essentially, the argument is that differentiation is a process that involves those kinds of changes which are congruent with the basic values of the society. Parsons outlines the main stages in this process of differentiation, illustrating them by reference to the family.[17] First, there will be some kind of frustration in goal-attainment. Thus, the family household which performs "occupational" functions as well as those we ordinarily associate with the family may differentiate into two new units — a nuclear family and an employing-productive unit — which separately perform the functions once characteristic of the original unit. The frustration encountered in the initial stage of differentiation may be rooted in the productive or socialization functions, or in both.

The second stage occurs at the boundary between the goal-attainment and other subsystems, and involves problematic relations. In the case of the family, the relations of goal-attainment to markets and to the legitimization of the family's position in society are important. In the third stage, there must be a balance between the two aspects of frustration mentioned above, that is, between "the conditional components of facilities and rewards" and the "normative components of expectation systems." [18] It is, in particular, the building-up of frustrations with the latter, the normative aspects of expectations, that is crucial to differentiation.

The fourth and final type of process that we find in Parsons' work is the evolution of societies. The general direction of societal evolution is toward "the enhancement of adaptive capacity." [19] Parsons analyzes this evolution in terms of a paradigm, which begins with the process of differentiation. In this case, differentiation involves new units "which differ in *both* structure and functional significance for the wider system." [20] If this process has been truly evolutionary in nature, then the new units will perform, or have the adaptive capacity to perform, their functions more effectively than those functions were performed in the original unit. Parsons calls this the "adaptive upgrading aspect" of evolution.

Differentiation raises problems of integration. There is greater complexity to the system; there are more units to co-ordinate. Adaptive upgrading may demand that ascriptive facets of mobilizing resources be abandoned, and that "otherwise excluded elements" be included in order to achieve integration.

Finally, the paradigm for the study of evolution includes the problem of values. A value pattern must be effected which is congruent with the nature of the emerging social system. For the value pattern designates the desired type of social system as well as integrating that system. An appropriate new value pattern is therefore necessary for both the legitimization and the integration of the new social system.

Evolution implies not only direction (which we have seen to be enhanced adaptive capacity), but also stages. Parsons identifies three broad levels of evolutionary development — primitive, intermediate, and modern.[21] The crucial factor in the transition from primitive to intermediate levels was language, particularly written language. The latter increased the differentiation between social and cultural systems and made the cultural system far more potent than it had been. The crucial factor in the transition from the intermediate to the modern level was the institutionalization of norms in the form of a legal system. In both instances, in other words, the transition has been marked by "critical developments in the code elements of the normative structures."[22]

One last question that we may ask with respect to Parsons involves the sources of change. It is already obvious that change is highly problematic. The ideas of equilibrium and inertia suggest that forces of considerable magnitude are necessary to overcome the stability of the system. We have also pointed out the endurance of values; structural change involves change in the value system and the latter is highly resistant to alteration. Furthermore, the equilibrium is maintained by the processes of socialization and social control.

On the other hand, Parsons sees intrinsic potential for change in "the combination of the inherent tendencies to deviation and the imperfections of the integration of value-orientations."[23] Nevertheless, these facets of the social system appear limp in the face of the powerful forces tending to maintain equilibrium. Apart from certain institutionalized processes of change, therefore, "change is never just 'alteration of pattern' but alteration *by the overcoming of resistance*."[24] And considerable strain is required to overcome that resistance.

In fact, "severity of strain is never alone an adequate explanation of change." [25]   Strain may be resolved in a way that leaves the structure intact.   In addition to an excess of strain, therefore, change is facilitated by four factors: [26]

1. Mechanisms which are able to overcome the "inevitable resistances of institutionalized structural patterns";
2. A mode of reaction to the strain that includes "adequate constructive possibilities";
3. The existence of a model of the pattern which is to be institutionalized;
4. The use of sanctions to reward behavior that is in accord with the model, and to do so with sufficient consistency so that values and self-interest will be congruent with each other (the "hallmark of institutionalization").

Finally, the factors leading to change may arise either within (endogenous) or without (exogenous) the social system. [27]   Exogenous sources of change are those that arise from the other systems — organisms, personalities, cultures — with which the social system interacts.   Examples of such sources are genetic changes in populations and changes in the physical environment as these are perceived by people or articulated in technological knowledge.   A major source of exogenous change is the other social systems with which a particular system interacts; intersocietal conflict and war or the threat of war may effect change in the social systems involved.

Endogenous changes are those resulting from internal strains, which are disequilibria between inputs and outputs among subsystems.   That is, strain means that the relation between two or more subsystems is under pressure to change, and to change in a manner which is incongruous with systemic equilibrium.   Such strains may be resolved by the system, may be arrested or isolated, or may result in structural change.

Neil Smelser

Smelser provides us with a good example of the application of Parsonian theory to the study of change.   We shall examine his analysis of the Industrial Revolution after first noting a few general points he makes about theories of change.   For Smelser identifies a number of issues that must be dealt with in any theory of change, some of which have not been attended to with any degree of precision.

For example, one essential element of any theory of change is the specification of the dependent variables.   What is it that changes? In general, theorists have defined or assumed that change is temporal variation in one or more of the following: "aggregated attributes of the population of a social unit"; "rates of behavior in a population over time"; "social structure, or patterns of interaction among individuals"; or "cultural patterns." [28] Examples of each of these would be, respectively, changes in the proportion of age groups in a population; changes in crime rates; changes in authority relations in some social entity; and changes in values.

Specification of the dependent variables, of course, cannot be done properly without a concomitant identification of the independent variables. What are the determinants of change? What is it that causes the changes just noted? According to Smelser, the determinants of change generally are identified as one or more of the following: "the structural setting for change," "the impetus to change," "mobilization for change," and "the operation of social controls." [29]

The "structural setting" involves an examination of the social structure in order to ascertain the implications for change that inhere in that structure. For example, if we wanted to estimate the probability of change through reform in any society, we would search for, among other things, the structural means for the expression of grievances. The greater the number of channels for expressing grievances, the more likely it is that reforms would be implemented.

The "impetus to change" implies that structural conduciveness alone is not adequate, however. There must also be some kind of force tending towards change. That force may be an internal one — demographic changes that exert pressure for other kinds of changes; or it may be an external one — the threat posed by another society, whether the threat is a military or an economic one.

"Mobilization for change" is related to the direction of change. The fact that change is facilitated by the structure, and that there is pressure towards change, does not yet indicate what direction such change will take. The direction depends upon the manner in which resources are mobilized and how they are used to effect the change. And such mobilization, in turn, is crucially tied up with the leadership involved in the change.

Finally, social controls are always present to offer resistance to change. These social controls may be the established authorities, such as the mass media, governmental officials, and church leaders. They may suppress change, or they may have a significant role in determining the direction change takes.

Smelser performs a useful service in reminding us of the importance of specifying the independent and dependent variables. One of the problems of comparing various theorists is that they do not take the same variables as the focus of analysis. The reader might, in fact, find it interesting to reflect back upon the theories we have treated thus far, and ask, with respect to each, what is it that changes and what are the determinants of that change?

As Smelser's list of the determinants of change shows, he works within the Parsonian perspective; and he has applied that perspective to a historical analysis — the Industrial Revolution. Smelser points out that over time we may observe both short-term adjustments and long-run structural changes. The latter, in contrast to the former, involve changes in the roles of the social system, including the "disappearance, re-creation, and reorganization" of those roles.[30] It is the latter kind of change that is the focus of his own study.

Specifically, Smelser investigates structural differentiation, which he says is particularly relevant for a growing social system. Differentiation must be understood in terms of the four functional requisites for any system — adaptation, goal-attainment, integration, and latent pattern maintenance. Further, differentiation implies that there is a definite sequence involved in the change. Smelser identifies seven steps in the sequence:[31]

1. Dissatisfaction deriving from the failure to achieve goals satisfactorily and from the awareness of the possibility of change;
2. Psychic disturbances, taking the form of a variety of emotional reactions and aspirations which are, however, inappropriate in terms of resolving the problems;
3. A more rational use of the energy expended in step 2 in an effort to "realize the implications of the existing value-system";
4. A brain-storming stage, in which ideas are generated in profusion without anyone's being responsible for their implementation or consequences;
5. An effort to specify the particular ideas and institutional patterns to be implemented;
6. The implementation of change by individuals or groups, with their performance subjected to sanctions in accord with the existing system of values;
7. The "routinization" of acceptable changes.

But the above are only "empty boxes," says Smelser, and must be filled in by the specific social system under analysis. For the case of industrial change, the filling in results in the following sequence of change:[32]

1. Dissatisfaction deriving from the failure to achieve satisfactory levels of productivity and from the awareness of potential for attaining higher productive levels;
2. Psychic disturbances, which take the form of inappropriate disjunctive emotional reactions and unrealistic aspirations;
3. "A covert handling of these tensions and a mobilization of motivational resources" in an effort to "realize the implications of the existing value-system";
4. Encouragement of the generation of a profusion of ideas without assignment of responsibility for their implementation or consequences;
5. An effort to specify the particular ideas so that entrepreneurs will commit themselves to them;
6. The implementation of change by entrepreneurs, who are rewarded by profits or punished by their financial failure as the consumers respond to their innovations;
7. Routinization through the acceptance of gains "as part of the standard of living and their incorporation into the routine functions of production."

What is the operation of these seven steps in history? They are not to be regarded as discrete stages. That is, dissatisfaction does not vanish with the appearance of psychic disturbances. Various steps may persist, or may disappear and reappear. Furthermore, there may be regression; the attainment of step 5 may be followed by regression to step 2. The sequence may also be "truncated"; minor dissatisfactions may never lead to further steps. Finally, we may expect to find a number of sequences of differentiation operating simultaneously: "the appearance of the factory system concealed several distinct processes of differentiation." [33]

As noted above, this sequence proceeds in the context of the four functional requisites of any social system. The analysis is too complex to be detailed here, but we should note the way in which Smelser makes use of the four functions. For an industry (Smelser's analysis focuses on the English cotton industry from 1770 to 1840), the "functional dimensions" include the "procurement of capital facilities" (the adaptive subsystem), the "control of production" (the goal-attainment subsystem), the "control of industrial organization" (the integrative subsystem), and "technical production" (the latency subsystem). [34] In addition, of course, each of these may be treated as a system in itself with its own four subsystems. Once the boundary interchanges among the resulting sixteen subsystems have been identified, the industrial process has been sufficiently delineated to proceed to an analysis of change. And the change takes the form of differentiation within the adaptive, goal-attainment, and integrative systems (values remain constant during a sequence of differentiation).

Smelser devotes considerable attention to the family, and we may illustrate his approach by sketching in very broad terms the application of the seven steps outlined above to the family unit affected by the revolution of the English cotton industry. One of the early technological improvements in spinning involved the enlargement of mules (spinning machines) and an increase in the number of mule spindles. Power looms were introduced into weaving in the 1820's. These developments exerted pressure on the traditional family division of labor and became the foci for dissatisfaction. Families felt constrained to differentiate the work of the various members and to separate work roles from other functions of the family unit.

Dissatisfaction, however, is always legitimated by values, in this case the "broad values of personal responsibility, discipline, and the calling." [35]   (These values underlay the pleas of moral leaders for people to be industrious, temperate, and rational with regard to their use of time and money.) The combination of this legitimated dissatisfaction with the inflexibility of the family led to various disturbances, including destruction of property, strikes, and a variety of forms of psychic distress. A number of "stopgap measures" such as police action, public pleas, and some legislative measures were employed to cope with the disturbances (step 3). It was, ultimately, factory legislation that "eased the family economy of the working classes toward a new structure" [36] (steps 3 to 7). That new structure involved the differentiation of the family unit with respect to division of labor and to consumption and savings: the new family was one in which economic roles of adults were segregated from those of children and educational responsibility was shifted out of the family; and a number of innovations, including savings banks and cooperative stores, were developed to ensure the financial welfare of the family.

THE GREAT DEBATE: EXEGESIS OR EISEGESIS?

In the first chapter, we briefly noted that a considerable amount of debate has revolved about the issue of whether the position represented by Parsons and Smelser adequately deals with change. Does a full interpretation of the Parsonian perspective yield a basic concern for understanding change (exegesis), or is the concern for understanding change read into the perspective (eisegesis)?

Let us first acknowledge that the perspective is an imaginative and logical analytical framework.[37]   Furthermore, we have seen that Parsons asserts the importance of understanding change and that he and Smelser have demonstrated the utility of the perspective by applying it to specific analyses of change.   In other words, the Parsonians have not ignored the problem of change to the extent that some critics have charged.

Nevertheless, to assert the importance of understanding change is not necessarily to work for that understanding.   And it seems undeniable that the topic of change was a peripheral matter during the time when structural-functionalism sat on the throne of theoretical sociology.   And this, it would appear, is a natural outgrowth of the perspective.   We have seen that considerable use is made of ideas and concepts that derive from biology and classical mechanics.   Parsons uses the analogy of biological evolution to argue the point that the study of structure is a necessary prerequisite to the study of change.   Without in any sense minimizing the importance of understanding structure, it seems clear that the particular approach taken in structural-functionalism, with its biological and mechanical modes of thought, stifles the study of change.

In sum, it seems to me that the reason for the neglect of the study of change inheres in the perspective.   One has the feeling that the adequate understanding of structure which is necessary for the analysis of change forever eludes the grasp of the intellect. The law of inertia triumphs.   Change is a deviance and a traumatic experience.   The fact that Parsonians have tried to deal with change, therefore, seems to derive from two sources, neither of which is the logic of the perspective itself: one is the reality of the changing world, and the other is the numerous criticisms which have been heaped upon functionalist thought.   We are left with the feeling that the structural-functionalist perspective will not carry us very far in understanding change.

ENDNOTES TO CHAPTER 4

1. Pierre L. van den Berghe, "Dialectic and Functionalism: Toward a Synthesis," in *System, Change, and Conflict,* ed. N. J. Demerath III and Richard A. Peterson (New York: The Free Press, 1967), pp. 294–95.

2. Talcott Parsons, *Societies: Evolutionary and Comparative Perspectives* (Englewood Cliffs: Prentice-Hall, Inc., 1966), p. 111.

3. Talcott Parsons and Edward A. Shils, eds., *Toward a General Theory of Action* (New York: Harper & Row, 1951), pp. 230–31.

4. Talcott Parsons, Robert Bales, and Edward Shils, *Working Papers in the Theory of Action* (Glencoe: The Free Press, 1953), p. 174.

5. Talcott Parsons, *The Social System* (New York: The Free Press, 1951), pp. 5–6.

6. Talcott Parsons, Edward Shils, Kaspar D. Naegele, and Jesse R. Pitts, eds., *Theories of Society* (New York: The Free Press, 1961), p. 61.

7. Talcott Parsons, *Sociological Theory and Modern Society* (New York: The Free Press, 1967), p. 348.

8. Parsons, *Societies*, p. 19.

9. *Ibid.*, p. 21.

10. Parsons, Shils, Naegele, and Pitts, *Theories of Society*, p. 37.

11. *Ibid.*

12. Parsons, *The Social System*, p. 491.

13. Parsons, Bales, and Shils, *Working Papers in the Theory of Action*, pp. 102–103.

14. Parsons, Shils, Naegele, and Pitts, *Theories of Society*, p. 73.

15. Talcott Parsons, "A Functional Theory of Change," in *Social Change*, ed. Amitai Etzioni and Eva Etzioni (New York: Basic Books, Inc., 1964), p. 89.

16. *Ibid.*, p. 96.

17. *Ibid.*, pp. 89–90.

18. *Ibid.*, p. 90.

19. Parsons, *Societies*, p. 21.

20. *Ibid.*, p. 22.

21. *Ibid.*, p. 26.

22. *Ibid.*

23. Parsons and Shils, *Toward a General Theory of Action*, p. 231.

24. Parsons, *The Social System*, p. 491.

25. Parsons, Shils, Naegele, and Pitts, *Theories of Society*, p. 75.

26. *Ibid.*, pp. 75–76.

27. *Ibid.*, pp. 71–72.

28. Neil J. Smelser, *Essays in Sociological Explanation* (Englewood Cliffs: Prentice-Hall, Inc., 1968), pp. 200–201.

29. *Ibid.*, pp. 205–207.

30. Neil J. Smelser, *Social Change in the Industrial Revolution* (Chicago: The University of Chicago Press, 1959), p. 14.

31. *Ibid.*, pp. 15–16.

32. *Ibid.*, p. 29.

33. *Ibid.*, p. 32.
34. *Ibid.*, p. 25.
35. *Ibid.*, p. 210.
36. *Ibid.*, p. 272.
37. The logical consistency of Parsons' thought, however, is not as complete as some have thought.   See Robert R. Blain, "A Critique of Parsons' Four Function Paradigm," *The Sociological Quarterly*, XI (Spring, 1970), 157–68.

CHAPTER 5

Social-Psychological Theories

Although some of the theorists we have examined so far have dealt with social-psychological factors in change, they have generally given the role of the individual as minor. We have seen the effects of broad historical currents, of great impersonal forces, of the nature of the structure in which men carry on their existence, but we have not encountered an approach that focusses on the individual and his personality (Khaldun's theory, it will be remembered, asserted that the personality was a function of the social structure). And even where it is granted that it is men who make history, we are not sure how much latitude those men actually have to shape the direction of change.

Can the actions of individuals alter the direction of development? Is personality a factor in change? Are men the pawns of forces which are beyond their control if not their understanding? Can we do no more than, as Spencer insisted, allow free sway to the inevitable evolutionary process? The two theorists we shall study in this chapter attempt to answer such questions, and they answer them by affirming the critical significance of the individual. More specifically, they assert the critical importance of personality in economic development.

THE CREATIVE PERSONALITY: EVERETT E. HAGEN

Hagen is an economist who has attempted to incorporate principles of psychology into a theory of economic development. He argues that economic development, which may be defined in terms of continuing increase in per capita income arising out of technological advances, must be understood in terms of the creative personality.

There are, of course, other explanations of economic growth, and Hagen deals with a number of them in order to show their inadequacy. Thus, theories based upon race or climate or particular social, religious, or economic conditions have all failed to explain adequately why certain groups became the cutting edge of technological and economic change. These past theories are not wholly wrong; they are simply insufficient (and in some cases irrelevant).

How, then, does economic growth occur? First of all, we must keep in mind that such growth is gradual, encompassing an extended period of time. For one thing, the innovations required are not simply technoeconomic, but social. We are not talking, therefore, about sudden, radical shifts, but long-term processes. And those processes are intimately linked with creative individuals, who themselves emerge out of a particular kind of social context over time. These individuals are not randomly dispersed throughout the society; rather, innovations that generate economic growth are taken "disproportionately by members of some one or more social groups, and not the groups who are in the best position to have contacts abroad or access to new knowledge and to capital." [1]

The task of the theorist, therefore, is to ascertain how the creative personality develops, and, specifically, why it develops in certain groups within the society rather than in others or in the society at large. Note that the creative personality *develops;* that is, as we shall see, the traditional individual is not creative. The question is, what leads to a generation of innovators? We must understand this, for the growth which is the goal of most men will not occur without the development of creativity in personality: ". . . social change will not occur without change in personalities." [2]

But if we are going to study personality, we must know what we mean by it. Hagen says that we may describe personality in terms of "needs, values, and cognitive elements of world view, together with intelligence and energy level." [3] If we can identify the types of needs, values, and cognitions that characterize an individual, and combine this with a knowledge of his intelligence and energy level, "then no important ambiguity remains concerning how he will act in any given situation." [4]

The needs which comprise one important dimension of personality may be classified according to whether they are manipulative, aggressive, passive, or succorant-nurturant. Manipulative needs include the need to achieve, to gain autonomy, and to secure order. Aggressive needs are illustrated by the need to attack, the need to overcome opposition, and the need to dominate. Passive needs include the need for dependence, for affiliation, and for being guided by others. And succorant-nurturant needs include the need to both give and receive such things as support, protection, and love.

Using these dimensions, we may distinguish between innovational and authoritarian personalities. The two personality types do not necessarily differ by intelligence or energy level; highly intelligent and highly energetic individuals may be found among both types. But there are important differences in needs, values, and cognitions. The innovational personality perceives his social milieu as having a logical order to it which he is able to comprehend. Furthermore, he believes that his social milieu values him; such valuation, however, may appear to rest upon his achievements, causing him considerable anxiety. Because the innovational personality has a high need for succorance and for being assured of his value, he is driven to achieve.

Among other characteristics of the innovational personality are high needs for autonomy and order, self-understanding that enables him to empathize with others, a high need for nurturance, and a concern for the welfare of others as well as for his own well-being.

The above qualities not only fit the innovational personality for the work of economic development, but present a rather stark contrast with the authoritarian personality. The latter perceives the social milieu as lacking in any order that is comprehensible to him. He does not believe that he is valued by his social milieu. He perceives power to be a function of one's position rather than of one's achievements.

This cognitive view of the world generates, in the authoritarian personality, a considerable amount of rage which must somehow be contained. Consequently, there is a high need for submission-dominance, a low need for succorance-nurturance, and a low need for both autonomy and achievement. Finally, the authoritarian personality, in contrast to the innovational personality, does not give the same weight to the welfare of others as he does to his own well-being.

It is perhaps already evident how these two personality types are said to lead to two different types of behavior. The innovational personality almost by definition engages in behavior that is creative. At least, he possesses every quality that would facilitate creative behavior. The world must be comprehensible, for example, if man is to make the effort to shape the direction of change. One of the reasons the traditional individual does not innovate, according to Hagen, is that he "perceives the world as an arbitrary place rather than an orderly one amenable to analysis and responsive to his initiative." [5]

We would expect, then, to find any economically stagnant society to be pervaded by authoritarian personalities. The whole society, in fact, will be one that has a rigid hierarchy of authority. Relationships will be structured in accord with authority, and any problematic situation will be dealt with by submission to authority. Hagen sees the experiences of childhood as inevitably generating considerable rage, which can be channeled into creative action. But in the traditional society, "rage can be vented by dominating everyone below one in the social hierarchy . . . it can also be vented in more overt form against outsiders." [6]   In every way, then, the traditional society and the authoritarian individual are structured for uncreative behavior.

Nevertheless, change does occur. Economic growth does begin in some societies. Personality types do change. How can we account for such changes? What is it that impels some groups to break out of the strong bonds of tradition and authoritarianism? Hagen has summarized the answer in terms of five laws: [7]

1. The "law of group subordination," which locates the impetus to change in some group that perceives itself to be subordinated;
2. The "law of rejection of values," which states that the subordinated group will discard the values of those who dominate it;
3. The "law of social blockage," which qualifies the above by pointing out that a subordinated group will discard dominant values and engage in deviant behavior only when traditional avenues for advancement have been blocked;
4. The "law of group protection," which says that individuals engaging in novel behavior gain social support from the subordinated group;
5. The "law of non-alien leadership," which asserts that economic growth will not occur in the whole society unless the deviant group which has begun the process is accepted and followed.

Let us attempt to follow through the process described by these five laws. Because of the stability of a traditional society, something must happen to alter the personalities of some group within that society. The needs, values, and cognitions must change, and that change is effected by "the perception on the part of the members of some social group that their purposes and values in life are not respected by groups in the society whom they respect and whose esteem they value." [8] Hagen calls this the "withdrawal of status respect."

Withdrawal of status respect, in turn, exerts pressure on authoritarian parents, who will respond by structuring a home life that leads to "progressively increasing retreatism over a period of several generations." [9]   Eventually, the creative personality will emerge from this.   The shift from retreatism to the generation of creative personalities is given impetus by changes in parental personalities, which occur gradually over a period of generations.

Hagen focuses in particular on the personality of the father, which he says varies along two dimensions during the time of increasing retreatism.   One dimension is the expectations the father has regarding his position in the family, and the other is the expectations he holds regarding the behavior of his son or sons.   He may remain traditional in one set of expectations while becoming untraditional in the other.   That is, "a stern father may expect high achievement of his sons, and a weak father may expect only that they learn to behave in the traditional manner." [10]

Thus, the father in the retreatist family has a "transitional" personality.   And that personality varies along the two dimensions noted; the father may be stern or weak and he may expect either strong achievement or traditional obedience.   The various combinations of these dimensions leads to a number of different types of transitional personalities.   Hagen selects four for analysis, and says that each of the four will tend to generate creative personalities.   The four are: [11]

1.   The father who is still relatively authoritarian, but who has high expectations for his son's achievement because of his own guilt over his lack of achievement;
2.   The father who is stern, who also senses guilt over his failure to achieve and transfers his expectations for achievement to his son, but who nevertheless shows love towards his son;
3.   The father who is erratic, who tends to dominate his home, who has few expectations for his son's achievement, but who is sufficiently detached from the home or his son to allow the latter to avoid the threat posed by the father;
4.   The father who is weak and who does not impede the "childhood explorations" of his son (although he also does not have high expectations for his son's achievement).

Thus, over several generations, the withdrawal of status respect leads to retreatism, which ultimately leads to creativity due to modifications in personality.   But this does not yet tell us the direction of the creative behavior.   That is, when will the innovational personality direct behavior towards creative economic and technological activities?   This depends upon the values that have been incorporated into the innovational personality, and upon the social recognition which potentially may be gained through economic innovation. With respect to the latter, it will be remembered that creative efforts on the part of members of a status-deprived group will be directed towards regaining social approval. With respect to the former, a number of values are important for technoeconomic innovation, including: merit based upon personal achievements; approval of business; and approval of manual work.

Hagen supports his theory by examining a number of historical examples of economic development, including that which occurred in England prior to the Industrial Revolution, and nineteenth- and twentieth-century development in Japan, Colombia, and Burma. He has provided us with an ambitious attempt to account for the importance of the personality in economic growth. But there are a number of serious problems with the theory.

First, Hagen leaves us with the feeling that economic development is largely a matter of the caprice of history. If some group experiences withdrawal of status respect, and if that status can be regained through entrepreneurial activity that results in technological and economic innovation, then the society will experience development. Change is neither normal nor continuous, but is more like historical mutation. Hagen does, however, present a theory that reveals change as gratifying rather than traumatic; that is, once growth has begun, the process is presumably one that is psychically therapeutic to the status-deprived group.

A second major difficulty with Hagen's theory is one common to any perspective that makes extensive use of psychoanalytic tools, namely, the problem of scientific verification. Many of the concepts Hagen uses, such as the Oedipus complex, various defense mechanisms, rage, guilt, and anxiety, must be inferred from behavior. But the inferences seem valid only if one accepts the basic psychoanalytic theory. For example, to say that the apparent friendliness of the Burmese is a mask for their underlying rage and aggression is highly questionable unless one accepts the psychoanalytic framework. Indeed, the interpretation is problematic even if the framework is accepted; Hagen admits that at points his analysis is necessarily "speculative, or, to use the term loosely, intuitive." [12]

A third difficulty with Hagen's theory is that certain ideas are discordant with some empirical evidence. For example, the Oedipus complex, which assumes hostility on the part of boys towards their fathers due to jealousy over the father's role as lover of the boy's mother, does not appear to be as universal as Freud assumed. In fact, the hostility may not be due at all to jealousy over the father's role as lover, but to the father's role as disciplinarian. Malinowski found, in Trobriand society, that the mother's lover (father) is not the same as the disciplinarian (uncle) and that youthful hostility was directed towards the uncle rather than towards the father.[13]

Hagen also assumes that withdrawal of status respect by the larger society leads to debilitating consequences, at least for some considerable time, for the personalities of members of the deprived group. But this assumption is problematic. Rosenberg found that self-esteem depended upon experience in the neighborhood rather than upon the esteem with which one's group was held by the larger society; his sample of 5,024 New York secondary school students indicated that "the social prestige of a nationality or religious group is generally unrelated to the self-acceptance of its members." [14] What was important was the neighborhood in which the child grew up; if the child had to endure status deprivation there, his self-esteem tended to be lowered.

The implications of such findings may not be quite so clearly in opposition to Hagen's theory as the foregoing brief statements would indicate; nevertheless, the studies cited leave us feeling somewhat uncomfortable with the theory. A Freudian view of man has generated an imaginative theory of change, but we are left unconvinced. Hagen's challenge to social change theorists does not lie in the specifics of his theory; rather, it lies in his coming to terms with the role of the individual and various psychological factors involved in change.

THE ACHIEVEMENT-ORIENTED PERSONALITY: DAVID C. McCLELLAND

More prominent than Hagen's writings is the work of David McClelland, who also focussed upon the personality as a prime mover in change. And, like Hagen, McClelland has been interested primarily in a specific kind of change — economic development. Since, according to McClelland, it is the entrepreneurial spirit that impels development, the task of the theorist is to account for the emergence of that spirit. The spirit is exemplified in businessmen, who, contrary to the popular image, are not driven by any profit motive per se, but rather by "a strong desire for achievement, for doing a good job. Profit is simply one measure among several of how well the job has been done, but it is not necessarily the goal itself." [15]

McClelland's basic thesis, then, is that "a society with a generally high level of n Achievement will produce more energetic entrepreneurs who, in turn, produce more rapid economic development." [16] The need for achievement (symbolized by n Achievement) is one of the basic needs of man, and, as with motives in general, it is the result of the social experiences of childhood. Thus, a variety of social factors influence child-rearing practices, which, in turn, either facilitate or impede the development of a need for achievement. That need is also a function of the kinds of reading materials which the child is exposed to. If the need for achievement is strongly developed, the individual will exhibit appropriate behavior, will manifest the entrepreneurial spirit, and will thereby act in such a way as to promote economic development.

This, in brief, is the thesis. A question now arises as to how we may measure the need for achievement. McClelland notes that Freud has taught us that a variety of motives may lead to any particular behavior. Man's behavior is not always rational, particularly as an observer might conceive of rationality. But Freud showed us how to get at motives in his analysis of dreams and free associations; that is, we may discover irrational motives in fantasy.

Using Freud's insights and the methodology of psychology, McClelland devised a projective technique for measuring the achievement motive. The technique essentially tries to ascertain the extent to which people's thoughts turn naturally to achievement-oriented ideas. For example, if an individual writes a story on the basis of a picture he has been shown, we can count the number of ideas in the story that are related to achievement. This simple count may then be used as a score of n Achievement, representing the individual's achievement drive, or the strength of his motivation for achievement.

The projective technique just described was part of the initial development of the study of achievement. In the effort to explore more fully the relationship between n Achievement and economic development, McClelland and his associates pursued three types of research. First, they sought to get group measures of n Achievement and to relate these to indicators of economic development. Second, they obtained "individual measures of motives, interests, values and performance of both mothers and their sons in various countries." [17] And third, they investigated the behavior, including motives, of business entrepreneurs.

The group measures were based upon the idea that fantasy could as readily be discerned in literature as it could in stories written by ordinary individuals. Folk tales, stories used in elementary schools, and imaginative literature of the past were utilized to provide a group score of n Achievement. Content analysis yielded the extent to which the varied literature reflected high levels of achievement motivation; the literature, in turn, was assumed to influence members of the society and to reveal the "natural" mode of thinking in the society. For example, a children's story might be developed along the theme of children building a boat. In an achievement-oriented society, the emphasis might be on constructing a boat that sails properly. An affiliation-oriented society may prefer the story to stress the enjoyment of shared play in sailing the boat. A power-oriented society might produce a story in which the emphasis was on the way the children organized in order to build the boat.

The second type of research conducted by McClelland and his associates focussed on the sources of n Achievement and on its effects among adolescents. Why do some boys acquire high levels of n Achievement, while others remain at very low levels? How does the level of n Achievement bear upon vocational interests and performance? Answers to these questions were sought in the context of a cross-national study. In Japan, Germany, Brazil, and India, samples of boys were tested, and (except in India) their mothers were interviewed. The mothers were questioned about their views on independence and mastery training. The boys were tested by two projective techniques: story writing and spontaneous drawings. The boys were also given questionnaires relating to their values.

Finally, the third type of research involved testing of living businessmen to ascertain whether their level of n Achievement was higher, and their entrepreneurial activity more extensive, than other men their age. This research was also cross-national, involving businessmen and other professionals in the United States, Turkey, Italy, and Poland.

Obviously, McClelland has tried to identify a factor that is not restricted to any particular culture. In fact, he points out that while there may be some cultural differences, there are also basic similarities — people in all societies seem to strive to perform well according to some standard when their level of achievement motivation is high. And do the data support the cross-cultural validity of the achievement motive? After comparing rates of growth of various nations (based upon increases in electrical production) with levels of n Achievement and then making historical comparisons between rates of growth and achievement-related stories in children's readers, McClelland concludes that the relationship between n Achievement and economic growth is strongly supported. Preponderance of achievement-oriented stories in imaginative literature "is associated in modern times with a more rapid rate of economic development." [18] And this holds true for both Communist and Western nations and for both newly developing and well-developed nations.

Neither stage of development, political structure, nor any other known factor seems to inhibit the relationship; men who have high levels of motivation to achieve will do so: "What people want, they somehow manage to get, in the main and on the average, though as we shall see later other factors can modify the speed with which they get it." [19]

If a high level of achievement motivation can account for economic growth, a low level can explain the lack of such growth. For example, Rosen asked why Brazil has not maintained a rate of growth necessary to meet the needs of its expanding population. The natural resources are certainly sufficient. Rosen's explanation was that the level of achievement motivation and the kind of achievement values possessed by Brazilians are inadequate to the task. When compared to a sample of Americans, Brazilians showed lower levels of achievement motivation, a lower value on activism, less future orientation, and a lower valuation on such things as work and physical mobility.[20]

The careful reader who is familiar with Weber's thesis regarding the Protestant Ethic has probably already discerned some familiar ideas. And McClelland himself points out the similarities, suggesting that the historical development of capitalism detailed by Weber may be understood, in its psychological aspect, by the notion of n Achievement. For "Weber's description of the kind of personality type which the Protestant Reformation produced is startlingly similar to the picture we have drawn of a person with high achievement motivation." [21] Protestants, according to Weber, worked harder and longer, saved money for future goals, and overtook and outdistanced others in the race for business success. And what drove them on? The Calvinist businessmen were prevented by religious convictions from using their success to indulge themselves; consequently, according to Weber, they got little from their wealth except an "irrational sense" of having done their work well. And "this is exactly how we define the achievement motive in coding for it in fantasy." [22] In essence, McClelland says that the effect of the historical factors delineated by Weber was to increase the n Achievement in those Calvinists who facilitated the development of capitalism.

What, specifically, are the sources of n Achievement? In a general way we may say that the motivation to achieve derives from the values, beliefs, and ideologies held by people. More particularly, the studies indicate that three factors are particularly important in creating high n Achievement in boys: "parents' high standards of achievement, warmth and encouragement, and a father who is not dominating and authoritarian." [23]

Thus, the experience of the child is crucial; the need for achievement may be acquired by the time the child is 8 or 10 years old. One important experience for the child involves "early mastery training," which tends to produce high levels of n Achievement. For example, it was found that mothers of boys who had high n Achievement "tended to expect 'self-reliant mastery' at earlier ages than mothers of sons with low n Achievement." [24]   As long as early mastery training is based upon parental concern rather than authoritarianism or rejection, it is likely to generate high n Achievement.

A second important experience, therefore, is the quality of parent-child interaction.   It seems to be important for the mother to react with affection whenever the child achieves and for the father to refrain from domination of his son.   But the inhibiting nature of paternal authoritarianism does not apply to the mother: ". . . the mothers of the 'highs' also show more authoritarianism towards their sons, just as they showed more 'warmth.'   They appeared to be much more actively involved than the mothers of the sons with low n Achievement." [25]

Thus, n Achievement may be inhibited by a number of factors in the child's experience, including paternal authoritarianism, low parental expectations for achievement, and demands for achievement which come too early in the child's life (as the case of the lower-class child who is expected to care for himself at a very young age).   High levels of n Achievement, on the other hand, are most likely to be produced when there are "reasonably high standards of excellence imposed at a time when the sons can attain them, a willingness to let him attain them without interference, and real emotional pleasure in his achievements short of overprotection and indulgence." [26]

Finally, there are certain social background variables that influence the development of the achievement motive.   That is, the patterns of child-rearing just described are less likely to be followed in more traditional Catholic groups.   The emphasis on a ritual rather than on an individual contact with God does not encourage self-reliance.   In addition to religion, McClelland briefly looks at the effects of social class, the individual's physique, family structure, slavery, occupational status, and climate.   These latter exercise at most an indirect influence, however; the crucial factors are those outlined earlier.

An initial reaction to McClelland might be that he has presented a much stronger case than Hagen.   He has operationalized all his variables and provided an abundance of empirical evidence to support his case.   But a closer look raises a number of questions.   McClelland himself discusses the varied measures that can be employed to indicate economic growth.   His own selection of increased electrical production as a particularly useful measure makes his data look far better than would other indicators.   For example, if we use annual growth of gross national product per capita as an indicator of economic development, countries with high n Achievement do not appear to have always fared very well. The 1925 scores, based on children's readers, showed Ireland,

Australia, Canada, and Sweden at the head of the list. Yet, in the period roughly from 1948 to 1960, when the effects of the 1925 stories should be manifesting themselves, Ireland ranked 44.5 out of 68 countries in annual growth of GNP per capita, while Canada ranked 50 and Sweden ranked 31. The same 1925 data put the Soviet Union at the bottom of the list of 30 countries in n Achievement; yet that nation ranked 12 in annual growth of GNP per capita during the decade of the 1950's.

Another problem revolves about the validity of the idea of a group level of n Achievement. The need for achievement was conceived of as a personality variable, as individual motivation. What does it mean to speak of a level of achievement motivation for an entire society? Does that make any more sense than, for example, a group level of wrath? Hagen seems more realistic at this point in his identification of small status-deprived groups within a society who account for development. McClelland himself recognizes that not every member of a society engages in entrepreneurial behavior. How, then, does the societal level of n Achievement translate itself into an individual level? McClelland does not really give an adequate answer to this problem.

Finally, the graphs provided by McClelland raise serious problems with his thesis.[27] We expect a lag between the time children read achievement-oriented stories and the time they engage in entrepreneurial behavior. But the graphs give us little confidence that levels of n Achievement are related in any consistent way to subsequent entrepreneurial activity. In ancient Greece, there seems to be a lag of hundreds of years. In other cases, depending upon the time lag we allow, achievement motivation and entrepreneurial activity appear to change simultaneously or even inversely. In any case, the historical evidence presented does not allow us to anticipate with any confidence that a high level of n Achievement in a nation's literature will result in increased entrepreneurial activity at some more or less specified point in the future.

In sum, both Hagen and McClelland have tried to come to terms with the role of the family, and the consequent personality type developed in children, in economic development. In some cases, their conclusions are similar — authoritarianism inhibits innovational activity, and the irrational facets of human existence are very important in understanding behavior, for example. But two quite different pictures of the entrepreneur emerge: Hagen's entrepreneur is a somewhat grim creature, driven by anxiety, struggling with a stigmatized identity; McClelland's entrepreneur appears far more emotionally stable and healthy, driven by the desire to achieve but deriving his identity from the dominant, approved values of his social milieu.

Neither of the two social-psychological theories, then, is convincing in toto, but both are notable efforts to account for social-psychological variables. That there are individual factors involved in change, both as dependent and independent variables, is undeniable. A particular individual may significantly affect the direction of change.[28] And there are various consequences for the individual who must come to terms with change; as noted in Chapter 1, a high rate of change seems to generate considerable stress in individuals.

But the precise relationships between social structure, culture, and the individual have not yet been fully clarified. Hagen and McClelland have directed our attention to the family and personality development; in addition, the former theorist stresses the importance of the irrational and the latter stresses the importance of motivation. Such factors warrant future study, and perhaps a future theorist will more fully illuminate our understanding.

ENDNOTES TO CHAPTER 5

1. Everett E. Hagen, *On the Theory of Social Change* (Homewood: The Dorsey Press, Inc., 1962), p. 35.
2. *Ibid.*, p. 86. In a later publication, Hagen backs away from this somewhat by saying that change in personality is not "the only possible or important cause" of innovation. But it is, at any rate, the only one with which he is concerned, and he seems to give it major prominence in historical cases of economic growth. For the disclaimer, however, see Everett E. Hagen, "British Personality and the Industrial Revolution: The Historical Evidence," in *Social Theory and Economic Growth*, ed. Tom Burns and S. B. Saul (London: Tavistock Publications Ltd., 1967), p. 35.
3. Hagen, *On the Theory of Social Change*, p. 101.
4. *Ibid.*
5. *Ibid.*, p. 98.
6. *Ibid.*, p. 57.
7. Everett E. Hagen, "How Economic Growth Begins: A General Theory Applied to Japan," *Public Opinion Quarterly*, XXII (Fall, 1958), 380–82.
8. Hagen, *On the Theory of Social Change*, p. 185.
9. *Ibid.*, p. 200.
10. *Ibid.*, p. 217.
11. *Ibid.*, pp. 219–20.
12. *Ibid.*, p. 201.

13. Bronislaw Malinowski, *Crime and Custom in Savage Society* (Totowa: Littlefield, Adams & Co., 1967), pp. 100ff.
14. Morris Rosenberg, *Society and the Adolescent Self-Image* (Princeton: Princeton University Press, 1965), p. 61.
15. David C. McClelland, "Business Drive and National Achievement," in *Social Change*, ed. Amitai Etzioni and Eva Etzioni (New York: Basic Books, Inc., 1964), p. 166.
16. David C. McClelland, *The Achieving Society* (New York: The Free Press, 1961), p. 205.
17. *Ibid.*, p. 57.
18. *Ibid.*, p. 105.
19. *Ibid.*
20. Bernard C. Rosen, "Achievement and Economic Growth in Brazil," *Social Forces*, XLII (March, 1964), 341–54.
21. McClelland, *The Achieving Society*, p. 47.
22. *Ibid.*
23. McClelland, "Business Drive and National Achievement," p. 176.
24. McClelland, *The Achieving Society*, p. 342.
25. *Ibid.*, p. 352.
26. *Ibid.*, p. 356.
27. *Ibid.*, pp. 120, 132, 139, 150, and 155.
28. This has been persuasively argued with respect to Lenin's role in the Russian revolution by Sidney Hook, *The Hero in History* (Boston: Beacon Press, 1955), pp. 184ff.

PART III

Mechanisms of Change

One question that all theories seek to answer is the nature of the driving mechanism of change. And, as we have seen, a great variety of answers have been given. Change has been conceived of as being the result of conflict, of creative elites, of new modes of thinking, of external forces, of individual motivation to achieve, and of a number of other causes.

We have already argued in the first chapter that change should be viewed as normal. In this part, we shall examine in greater detail the mechanisms that may help explain the direction and rate of that change. Some of these mechanisms have already been identified by the theorists we examined in the last part. But now we shall examine them without restricting their influence to a particular theoretical framework. If, for example, we look at technology and try to see its effects in the light of a number of empirical studies that have been made, what conclusions can we draw about technology as a driving mechanism of change? Such an analysis provides materials out of which new theories can be constructed. And new theories should advance our understanding beyond its present level.

CHAPTER 6

The Materialistic Perspective

Marx succinctly captured the materialistic perspective on mechanisms of change in his well-known statement: "The windmill gives you society with the feudal lord; the steam-mill, society with the industrial capitalist."[1]   As Marx himself recognized, the relationship between technology and social change is more complex than a simple reading of the above statement would indicate.   In this chapter, we shall try to clarify the relationship.   First, many writers have stressed the primacy of technology in change; Thorstein Veblen and William F. Ogburn have done so in a way that merits some attention, and we shall begin by examining their ideas.   Then we shall note certain inadequate ideas about the relationship between technology and change, ideas that lead one into an intellectual cul-de-sac.   A third step will be to examine empirical studies and to try, in the light of those studies, to specify the relationship between technology and change.   Finally, we shall look at what has become a burgeoning concern: the potential impact of technology on man's future.

THE TECHNOCRATIC VISION: VEBLEN AND OGBURN

Thorstein Veblen (1857–1929) lived a life of detachment and protest.   Both his private and his professional life were highly unconventional, and his writings portray a man who stood aloof and used a merciless scalpel of criticism on the diseased social order of his day. Veblen, who was greatly influenced by Marx and by evolutionary thinking, saw that social order as crucially shaped by technology:

> The machine process pervades the modern life and dominates it in a mechanical sense . . . the machine has become the master of the man who works with it and an arbiter in the cultural fortunes of the community into whose life it has entered . . . The machine is a leveller, a vulgarizer, whose end seems to be the extirpation of all that is respectable, noble, and dignified in human intercourse and ideals.[2]

In other words, Veblen was particularly concerned with the effects of technology on patterns of thought and behavior. He argued that man's beliefs and conduct are primarily shaped by the way in which man earns his living and gains his wealth, which, in turn, is a function of technology.

The ineluctable link between technology and economic factors on the one hand and social change on the other is seen in Veblen's account of social evolution.[3] That evolution involved the change from savage, neolithic society to "barbarism" in its initial phases. The former society was characterized by smallness, peace, cooperative relations, and industriousness. Property was communally owned for the most part and was shared by the members of the group. Men and women were regarded as equals.

But as the population grew, various groups with diverse ways came into contact with each other. The stage of barbarism emerged, in which the relationships between groups were competitive and warlike. Furthermore, men became oriented towards private gain rather than towards communal ends. Veblen saw the same type of social order as present in his own time; for that reason, he declared that modern society is little more than a latter-day barbarism.

A crucial step in the process of social evolution, according to Veblen, was the emergence of private ownership. With private ownership, the "leisure class" came into being. The first form of ownership was the ownership of women by the stronger men of the community, who captured the women in war. Technological developments in the areas of handicraft and agriculture gave a productive value to the female captives, who initially were taken because of "their usefulness as trophies." [4] The victors found it profitable to marry the women, for they could then receive not only prestige in the eyes of their peers but also the fruit of the woman's work.

Man had evolved to a new point. He now acted not simply on the basis of the instincts of workmanship, idle curiosity, and parental concern but in accord with the "quasi-instinct" of pecuniary emulation. His possessions had come to mean his "prepotence" over other members of his community. Property became the basis both for esteem in the eyes of others and for one's own self-respect.[5] In such a situation, men were driven by the quasi-instinct of pecuniary emulation; that is, they struggled to outdo each other in the acquisition of wealth.

But the question emerges of how, in an expanding society, to demonstrate one's wealth. Women did most of the work in the period of early barbarism, so that labor was a mark of inferiority. "Conspicuous leisure" therefore became the "conventional mark of superior pecuniary achievement and the conventional index of reputability."[6] With the continuing development of society, however, conspicuous leisure as a means of displaying status became more difficult to maintain; conspicuous consumption and conspicuous waste became the common means of demonstrating one's position in society. Moreover, the "leisure class" that employed these means to the fullest (even the poorest engaged in some degree of conspicuous consumption) set the standards of what was right, good, and beautiful. And those standards were all pecuniary in nature. Things are right, good, and beautiful in terms of their relationship to money. The gloss on a gentleman's hat has no more intrinsic beauty than the gloss of worn pants; but the former is beautiful because of its cost, while the latter is repugnant because it indicates lack of wealth.

Thus, for Veblen, man's thinking and behavior reflect technological and economic factors. The standards set by the leisure class infect the entire society; not simply the wealthy, but all people, are driven by pecuniary emulation. Human evolution and human society today are alike the consequence of technoeconomic developments; to understand the direction of change over the course of human history, we must understand first of all the technoeconomic processes.

There are similarities between Veblen's thought and that of William F. Ogburn (1886–1959). Ogburn also gave primacy to technological developments, and he developed and became famous for an idea that pervades Veblen's work — the lag and inevitable adjustment of cultural factors vis-à-vis technology. The "theory of cultural lag" involves the identification of at least two variables which can be shown to have been in adjustment at one time. One of the variables is then shown to have changed before, or to a greater extent, than the other. The consequent adjustment is "less satisfactory" than that which obtained initially.[7]

Even a casual observer can find examples that support the notion of cultural lag. Take, for example, the two variables of family size and religious doctrine. The doctrine may sacralize the large family. Then, with modernization or new techniques of birth control, or both, family size may shrink. But the religious doctrine may oppose this trend and the use of birth control methods, causing maladjustment between church and family.

The theory of cultural lag is only one aspect of Ogburn's thought on change, however. His explanation of cultural evolution focuses on four factors: invention, accumulation, diffusion, and adjustment.[8] Of these, invention stands out as a prime factor, analogous in importance to mutation in biological evolution. Invention refers not only to mechanical inventions but also to social inventions (e.g., international organizations) and cultural innovations (e.g., new religious rituals). Scientific developments are also included, and much of the work of Ogburn and his students has centered on showing the consequences of new technology to the social order.

The second factor, accumulation, results from a greater number of new elements' being added to a culture than old elements lost from it. Diffusion, the third factor, simply refers to the spread of inventions from the area of their origin to other areas. And adjustment, the final factor, refers to problems arising from the interdependence of all aspects of a culture. For example, inventions in the economy will inevitably affect government in some way; the government is constrained to adjust to the new situation posed by the changed economy. Or new technology will have repercussions on the family, compelling it to adjust to a changed environment, even though the technological innovations were not directly related to the family.

Material invention, then, is the main source of progress. The nonmaterial aspects of the culture must adjust to material developments, and the gaps between the two will be areas of social problems. Technology is the driving mechanism of change, according to Ogburn; man seems to be forever gasping to keep up and adapt to the world which technology is ever creating anew.

TECHNOLOGY AND THE INTELLECTUAL CUL-DE-SAC

Because technology is so prominent and potent in the modern world, there is a tendency to take extreme positions, positions that lead into an intellectual cul-de-sac. The result is a blockage of further thought regarding the complexities of change. Veblen and Ogburn make a valuable contribution in demonstrating the compelling effects of technology and the manner in which technological changes create human problems. But has the case been overstated? Can too much be claimed for technology? A number of positions that have been taken on the subject of technology and change seem one-sided and self-defeating: they lead into a cul-de-sac.

One cul-de-sac is the view of technology as *the* prepotent factor in change. This position, represented more by Ogburn than Veblen, seeks to explain change solely in terms of technology as the driving force. But change can also result from political, economic, and social factors quite independently of technological developments. As Andrzejewski has pointed out, there are numerous examples of fundamental changes that have occurred without any significant technological developments.[9] There was little improvement in production methods during the ancient Greek commercial expansion or during the growth and subsequent decline of capitalism in classical antiquity. Or consider the rise and fall of dynasties in the Arab world that formed the basis for Ibn Khaldun's theory; such changes occurred without any technological developments. The position that technology is the prime mechanism of change, therefore, seems refuted by considerable historical evidence.

A second cul-de-sac is the view of technology as an inexorable force in change. As McLuhan put it: "Any technology gradually creates a totally new human environment."[10] According to this view, technology is an irresistible force in change as well as an overwhelming one (in the sense of effecting massive changes). But we need to distinguish between change which did, and that which had to, result from technology. And we need to distinguish between changes which technology made possible and those which it compelled. As we have just pointed out, some change occurs without any particular technological development. Another example of this is provided by Whyte's account of considerable changes that occurred in the social organization of a glass-making factory along with very little technological change.[11] The source of the changes was the influx of a new generation of glassworkers of different ethnic origin from the initial group.

Furthermore, even when there is technological change, it doesn't necessarily lead to other changes. An interesting example of this is provided by a study of two South Indian villages in an area where an irrigation scheme had been introduced twenty-five years previously.[12] One of the villages changed from dry to wet cultivation, since it was in the center of the irrigated area. The other village, however, remained dry. The social order of the wet village was virtually unchanged in spite of the technological change and the new economic opportunities and affluence. The traditional kinship and hereditary nature of politics continued as before.

But the dry village, by contrast, experienced considerable change. There was a diversification of the economy; new job opportunities and entrepreneurial activities opened up for the villagers. Hereditary politics did not completely vanish from the village, but heredity was displaced as the basis for political behavior.

In sum, a technological change resulted in considerable economic, social, and political change in one village. But what happened in the other village refutes the idea of the inexorable force of technology to create massive changes; its social and political life remained essentially as it was prior to the technological change.

A third cul-de-sac is the view of technology as the Savior. Americans have been particularly prone to be awed in the face of technology: "The Big Technology has been for Americans what the Cross was for the Emperor Constantine: *In hoc signo vinces.*" [13] But this perspective was not created by Americans; it has historical roots. The saving power of technology stems from such ideas as the Baconian notion that knowledge is power. Auguste Comte gave impetus to the viewpoint by equating social progress with the development of a scientific mode of thinking. And pragmatic American thought seized the notion with relish and enshrined it. Today, its devotees range from scientists to militarists.[14] Whatever differences those devotees may have among themselves, they share one thing in common: the conviction that the application of technology or the development and application of new technology can resolve all the varied problems of mankind.

But there is abundant evidence that technology creates as many problems as it solves and that technological innovations may generate considerable stress in people. For some people, for example, technological developments mean new opportunities; for others — those displaced by automation — they mean economic and psychological crisis. The invention of the steam locomotive brought prosperity and importance to a community studied by Cottrell; the invention of the diesel made that same community obsolescent, and its stable and comfortable world was shattered.[15]

The same shattering effect has been experienced by many primitive societies into which modern technology has been introduced.[16] Furthermore, modern technology may be of little use to an underdeveloped society, particularly in terms of the human costs of that technology. That is, in an underdeveloped society it is not necessarily better to use machines rather than manpower. A tractor may be of less value than an ox if the problem is one of enormous underemployment. In addition, if the cost of labor is quite low, the use of technology may yield no greater net profit than the use of manpower, and the former compounds the problem of unemployment as well as failing to increase profits.[17]

A fourth cul-de-sac is the idea of technology as the Antichrist. This view carries the previous one to the opposite extreme; technology is the source of man's ills, a modern despot before whom man fawns in helpless adoration. This conception derives in part from thinkers like Rousseau and Thoreau and their ideas of naturalism and in part from the various socialist criticisms of the capitalistic misuse of technology.[18]

Some of the more disturbing critiques of the technologically dominated society have been made in the literary anti-utopias such as Orwell's *1984*. At a more realistic level, thinkers like Jacques Ellul and Theodore Roszak have made trenchant criticisms of the technocracy. Ellul sees modern man losing control over his destiny to a rampant technology. The totality of human life is increasingly shaped by technique: ". . . our civilization is constructed *by* technique . . ., *for* technique (in that everything in this civilization must serve a technical end), and *is* exclusively technique (in that it excludes whatever is not technique or reduces it to technical form)." [19]   Thus, man has become enslaved to that which he thought was his servant. Man has created a monstrosity and is devoured by his own creation. And in the process, his patterns of thought and behavior have become phenomena which are shaped in their totality by technology.

Roszak also paints a grim picture of technology's role in the modern world. He argues that American youth have perceived the fact that the central struggle of the modern world is not with some of the more obvious injustices such as poverty and war but with the more subtle and insidious enemy called technocracy. Technocracy is "that social form in which an industrial society reaches the peak of its organizational integration. It is the ideal men usually have in mind when they speak of modernizing, up-dating, rationalizing, planning." [20]   In a technocracy, the leaders justify their behavior by the technical experts who have, in turn, justified themselves by appealing to scientific thought. "And beyond the authority of science, there is no appeal." [21]   Roszak sees in the youthful rebellion against such a society the hope of a new and better world.

But while it may be true that some modern societies approach the social form which Roszak calls a technocracy, we must distinguish between technology itself as a progenitor of social ills and man's willingness to subject himself to technology's apparent demands. Technology dominates man to the extent that man allows his decisions to be shaped by technological considerations. For example, to invest in a project because it is technologically feasible "is a choice to drop the reins and let technology run itself." [22]

Numbers of people have "died of neglect and malnutrition while a heedless profession ogled at the latest gadget." [23]   But this is a matter of choice and commitment rather than of the irresistible demands of technology itself.

In other words, technology is no more the Antichrist than it is the Savior. To the extent that man exalts technology and willingly enslaves himself to it, the technocracy becomes a frightening reality. But on the other hand, few of those who have enjoyed the fruits of modern technology will wish to join a "back-to-nature" movement. We do well to recognize the potential disjunctive consequences of technology; we would also do well not to forget that modern science and technology have give us new freedom by delivering us "from the bondage of material poverty" and opening up "a great area of choice where vision and will can operate." [24]

HOW TECHNOLOGY CAUSES CHANGE

With the above caveats in mind, we may now look at the impressive evidence that shows technology to be a mechanism of social change and, specifically, at the way in which technology impels that change. There are two approaches which may be, and have been, taken in demonstrating the force of technology: we may either identify specific changes and try to trace them back to technological changes, or we may take a specific technological innovation and try to trace out its ramifications. In either case, the consequences of technological change for social change are seen to be quite extensive.

The former approach was taken by Ogburn and Nimkoff in their effort to account for various changes in the family. [25]   The social changes in the family were first identified by using a panel of experts, and then eight major changes were selected out of the lists supplied by the experts. The eight major familial changes were: a growing emphasis on romance, earlier marriages, smaller families, fewer functions for the family, a greater number of working wives, diminished parental authority, more emphasis on the children, and a greater amount of separation and divorce.

These changes were then traced back to technological innovations. For example, how can we account for the weakening of kinship ties in the modern family? First, there are the effects of rural-urban migration, which causes a spatial and, therefore, social and psychological separation. But such migration is possible only because of innovations in transportation such as the railroad; and the railroad was made possible by the invention of the steam engine. Thus, through the process of sequential causation, we arrive at the steam engine as a causal factor in weakened kinship ties.

The other approach, tracing out the consequences of innovation, is exemplified in Allen's work on the automobile.[26] In addition to the more obvious consequences of the invention of the automobile — such as those for transportation and mobility — Allen points out that the automobile has had an impact on the government (expansion of services and new political influences), on individual health, on sex customs and morality, on attitudes, and so forth. In fact, the effects are "so numerous as to be almost incalculable." [27]

The logic of this approach is easily followed. Consider the logical and similar effects of such technological developments as the automobile, improved refrigeration, and television.[28] With respect to the automobile, a first effect is that extensive travel is facilitated, which means that people are able to travel a greater distance to purchase commodities. This reduces the frequency of contact within the community; an area becomes a mass of strangers who live in relative isolation from each other. People are therefore forced to satisfy psychic needs within the family, and if family members are incapable of meeting such needs there may be sufficient frustration within the family to result in a divorce.

A similar sequence may be traced out with respect to improved refrigeration and television. The former means that food can be kept in the home for a greater length of time, while the latter means that a novel and appealing source of entertainment has entered the home. Consequently, people remain at home more because there is less need to go out for either supplies or entertainment. This means greater isolation; the members of the community are strangers to each other. The family bears the brunt of satisfying psychic needs, and the same consequences result. In other words, all three inventions can be shown (at least logically) to contribute to the breakdown of community life.

As reasonable as the above appears, a little thought will show that there are reasonable alternatives. The same automobile which takes people out of their community can take them to visit other people as well as to shop; the auto can help maintain kinship ties or friendships, thus helping psychic needs to be fulfilled outside of the immediate family. The refrigerator which makes trips to the store less frequent can also mean more time for cultivating interpersonal relationships. And so on. This is not to say that the former interpretation is wrong and the latter right, but only that we must be cautious of accepting arguments that are reasonable but which lack empirical support. Anyone familiar with early 19th-century America would be highly skeptical of any contemporary breakdown of community that has resulted from technological developments. That is, there is little historical evidence that there was any "community" to break down under the impact of the automobile, refrigerator, and television.

Nevertheless, the role of technology in change has been enormous. To exercise some skepticism about some of the statements that have been made regarding the impact of technology is not to deny the potency of that impact. How can we account for the potency of technology? How does technology effect change? There are a number of factors involved.

→   First, technology increases our alternatives. New technology may bring previously unattainable ideals within the realm of possibility, and it may alter the relative difficulty or ease of realizing differing values.[29] Thus, technological innovation means that a society faces a greater range of alternatives, and when it opts for a new alternative it may set off extensive changes in numerous areas.

Even minor technological change may have manifold consequences in this way. Although once again the case is overstated, White has shown that medieval technical inventions had significant consequences both economically and socially in Europe.[30] He argues that the invention of the stirrup, which reached northern Europe by the 8th century A.D., led to a restructuring of medieval society. The stirrup changed warfare; foot soldiers fighting in close order were rendered impotent by the mounted knight. The stirrup enabled the knight to carry his lance rather than to merely throw or thrust it. The knight, horse, and lance became a new entity — a single and powerful weapon.

But considerable capital was required to maintain a knight. A reorganization of land tenure resulted, with each unit of tenure supporting a number of knights. The feudal system, with its knightly class, endowed with fiefs and holding numerous rights and obligations, thus emerged as an alternative which was created by a new military technology.

The stirrup created new alternatives. And once a new alternative is chosen, there are likely to be changes throughout the society. For the choice of the alternative may, in effect, be the choice of a new social order. A society that chooses to industrialize, for example, is also choosing to reorder aspects of its stratification system, its education, and so forth.

→   A second way in which technology effects change is by the alteration of interaction patterns. Once the technological innovation is adopted, there may be certain necessary shifts in interaction patterns, shifts which are demanded by the technology itself. This is most clearly seen in industrial organizations, although we could again refer to changed patterns resulting from the automobile and other innovations which have affected mobility. The latter, however, do not represent a *necessary* shift; in the case of the industrial organization, the changes in interaction are inevitable.

An example of the inexorable changes in interaction patterns is the introduction of automation into an automobile plant.[31]   A number of factors affect the frequency as well as the kind of interaction patterns on the job, including the amount of attention demanded by the job, spatial patterns of the workers, amount of control over the pace of the work, amount of noise, and the number of tasks that involve teamwork.   Automation had considerable effect upon these variables, and, therefore, upon interaction.

In the automated plant, closer and continual attention is required of the worker.   The spatial patterns are altered so that there is greater distance between workers.   The worker tends to have less control over the pace of his work.   The automated machines are perceived by many workers to be noisier than the non-automated ones.   And, finally, fewer tasks require teamwork in the automated plant.   As a result, social interaction within groups of workers is less frequent after automation.   Furthermore, the interaction involves fewer workers, and the quality of the interaction is altered.   There is little sense of teamwork; many workers are social isolates on the automated production line.

Automation also changed supervisor-worker relationships. Because of the closer attention required on the automated line, and because the worker on that line controls a greater proportion of the production process, the worker is subjected to a greater amount of supervision.   There is, therefore, an increased frequency of interaction with superiors.   Unfortunately, because of the changed role of the foreman in an automated plant, this interaction is perceived in more negative terms than the superordinate-subordinate relations in the nonautomated factory.

Similar problems arose with the introduction of computers into insurance companies studied by Whisler.[32]   The computers were a new information technology that effected a number of structural changes in the organization of the companies, including the consolidation of departments, a reduction in the number of levels in the hierarchy of authority, a reduction in the span of control, and a greater centralization of control.   And, as in the automobile plant, a significant alteration in interaction patterns resulted.   The clerks, whose work was computerized, spent a greater proportion of time working alone; there was a significant decrease in interclerk communication, with fully a third of the clerks reporting diminished communication with their peers.

In sum, the net effect on interaction patterns of automation or cybernation in organizations is to increase man-machine interaction and to diminish human interaction.   Whisler quotes an Air Force officer who observed the consequences of the SAGE system on a command-and-control center: "One of the queerest observations that I have made concerns this mass of engineers, technicians, machine operators, and operations people milling around and working almost unaware that anyone else exists." [33] In the old squadron, interpersonal interaction was essential to accomplishing missions; in the new arrangement, the interaction seemed to be basically between humans and the electronic system.

A third way in which technology effects change lies in the tendency for technological developments to create new social problems. These problems elicit some kind of response, which may result in a variety of changes to resolve the problem. For example, in a subsistence economy, poverty may not be defined as a social problem because man's life is perceived to hang precariously by the thread of capricious fate. But in an affluent, technologically sophisticated society, poverty becomes a compelling problem because man's life is a function of the use and misuse of resources. In a primitive society, individual health may rest on the whimsy of the gods or the efficacy of the actions of the witch doctor. In a modern society, individual health becomes a matter of public concern and, to some extent, responsibility. When population density is sparse and the need for sons to help earn a living is great, birth control may be both religiously and pragmatically taboo. But when population threatens to crush every hope for enhanced human well-being, birth control becomes a matter of public concern and responsibility.

In other words, technology has helped to create a highly complex world with numerous new problems, problems which were once either nonexistent (because they were not defined as problems or because they really did not exist) or insoluble. These problems must often be dealt with by the application of technology or the development of new technology (e.g., control of pollution). That means that we are resolving problems by the use of that which has created the problem in the first place — technology. But in using technology to resolve the problems, we are creating new problems. Industrialization resolved for many people the problem of survival; now it has revived the problem in terms of the pollution of the environment. The problems created by the development and use of sophisticated technology for pollution control await us in the future.

It is the combination of the existence of the problems and of the potential for coping with them that creates the pressure for change. For the problems may remain insoluble apart from changes in the polity, or changes in the relative domains of the public and the private, or changes in our hierarchy of values.

Consider medical technology and the health of the aged as an illustration. Developments in medical technology have made good health for the aged feasible.   At the same time, the costs involved are so high that the health of the aged is problematic and a matter of public issue.   The result, in America, has been a continuing struggle involving changes in governmental programs (the initiation of Medicare and Medicaid in 1965), changes in the attitudes of physicians towards the organization of medical care,[34] and public debate over the extent of collective responsibility for the health of the aged and the rest of the nation.   The debate is rooted in, and has the potential for effecting changes in, the relative weight of individualistic versus collective values.   During the first part of 1971, Congress debated the issue of health care along these lines.   President Nixon proposed a plan that was more moderate than a proposal for comprehensive national health coverage but more extensive than a plan favored by the American Medical Association (which merely allowed tax deductions for private insurance plans).

CONTEMPORARY PREPOTENT TECHNOLOGIES

In this final section, we shall briefly examine three contemporary technologies which are "prepotent," [35] and we shall point out some of the implications for change in these technologies.   The three are cybernation, social engineering, and biological engineering. The challenge pointed up earlier in this chapter — for man to seize control of technology rather than allow himself to become subservient to it — becomes particularly acute in the light of the potential changes that could come about through these three technologies.

Cybernation refers to the application of automation and computers.   We have already seen the effects on an industrial organization and on a business concern; cybernation will have considerable impact in any social context into which it is introduced.   Cybernation means that "whole blocks of activity become unnecessary and new ones arise." [36]   It also means an enormous increase in social alternatives.   And in confronting alternatives, we confront our own values.   The decisions that must be made are not simply engineering or business decisions, but moral ones.   Unfortunately, this is not always recognized by those who are planning our computerized utopias of the future.   As Boguslaw points out, "the dominant value orientation of the utopian renaissance can best be described as 'efficiency' rather than 'humanitarianism.' " [37]   The enthusiastic devotees of the computer seem willing to go the way of all apostates from humanitarianism and offer mankind as a sacrifice to the great god Computer.   Thus, the modern "utopian renaissance" threatens as well as encourages us, and its threat "consists precisely in its potential as a means for extending the control of man over man." [38]

The importance of the above considerations is highlighted by some of the alternatives generated by the use of computers. For our purposes, it will suffice to give only a few of the innumerable examples of potential usage and possible consequences.[39] One conceivable development is a central data storage facility which would provide public access to a wide range of specialized and general information. This could lead to: a greater degree of education taking place in the home; an increased tension between traditional teaching techniques and the technique of programmed instruction; the commercialization of information, with extensive changes in business practices; more sophisticated and powerful techniques for combating crime; an enhancement of private proficiency in such areas as law and medicine; and so on. On the other hand, the same technology could obviously be used for a quite different purpose — to create an Orwellian spy system, in which the activities of all citizens were kept accessible to a centralized enforcement agency.

Another possible development is the programmable and self-adaptive robot which can assume many of the duties now carried out by housewives or servants. This would likely increase the demand for various kinds of educational and recreational services; it could bring more women into the labor force; it might create extensive changes in industry, including the creation of new industries; and it might generate a negative reaction that would give more value to tasks (such as cooking) performed by humans than those handled by the robot. On the other hand, for the sake of maximum efficiency, such robots might be linked up with humans, so that a man-robot combination would become a typical work team. And this could complete the process of depersonalization and enhanced stress which we discussed above with reference to the effects of cybernation in the automobile plant.

Social engineering, the second of the prepotent technologies, refers to "the systematic application of knowledge and theory about men and institutions to the guidance-transformation-manipulation of men and institutions." [40] The potential for exercising social control could hardly be more clearly stated. In fact, as Karl Mannheim pointed out long ago, the development of our capacity for social engineering requires us to redefine the meaning of human freedom.[41] Mannheim identified three stages in the development of social techniques and said that freedom means something different in each one. In the stage of chance discovery, freedom may be defined in terms of restrictions on responding to stimuli in the environment; the individual is restricted in his freedom when something intrudes upon his response to environmental stimuli. In the stage of invention, man is involved in conscious modification and direction towards goals, and freedom means the ability to influence the aims of collective action. And in the third stage, which Mannheim felt was imminent, man will be engaged in conscious planning of relationships, and freedom will consist of free zones within a planned structure.

But even if we are willing to redefine freedom to include only free zones, we are faced with the possible loss of that bit of liberty by the potential of social engineering. It is possible, of course, that new methods of behavior manipulation will greatly enhance human capacities and performance; it also is possible that they will greatly encourage dehumanizing totalitarian systems. One way of manipulating human behavior is through chemical and electrical technologies. Drugs may be developed that will produce specific personality changes in individuals. Control is also possible via radio stimulation of the brain. These developments could lead to a new hedonism, or new capacities for learning, or control of criminal behavior and deviance, or the creation of socially desirable attitudes and needs. But what is criminal behavior and deviance? What are socially desirable attitudes and needs? Such questions thrust before us the grim possibility of a tyrannical elite performing a social lobotomy in order to create a servile population.

And if the above sounds like an updated version of a prophet of doom, we might reflect upon the subtle ways in which social engineering has already been utilized. For example, an organization may be restructured to achieve higher productivity and better interpersonal relationships.[42] While such goals may seem laudable on the surface, there is a thin line between aiding human growth and manipulating people for other ends — increased productivity, for example. Another way in which social engineering has been employed is in the field of motivation research. Social scientists who work in this area teach their clientele how to sell their products or market their services in the face of apathy or resistance.[43] And closely related to this is the use of the mass media to create an image of the good life, the meaning of manhood and womanhood and of other social values.[44] The use of social engineering as already with us, and the future potential is enormous.

The last prepotent technology is biological engineering, which is the effort to control man's biological self and environment. And, again, serious moral problems are raised. This is particularly evident in the emerging possibilities for genetic control. The possibility of choosing the kind of progeny we shall have, for example, raises questions regarding a new power elite — namely, those who can afford to utilize the genetic technology. It also raises such questions as the possibility of constructing particular kinds of people who will be predestined to perform particular social roles, and the potential for fads and fashions in human morphology. Something of the latter has already taken place in plastic surgery: a Viennese plastic surgeon discussed changing European fads in nose styles at a 1972 convention in Miami.[45] Even so, choosing one's nose is different from having it chosen by someone else.

Another possible development in biological engineering is the temporal suspension (and, therefore, elongation) of human life through some kind of hibernation or frozen body storage. This could result in, for example, keeping individuals with incurable diseases alive until the discovery of a cure, new industries specializing in maintaining the bodies, and a means of engaging in long-duration travel into space.

Biological engineering also has important implications for population growth. If such developments as genetic control and creation of artificial organs lead to a superior human, relatively free of disease and enjoying increased longevity, what are the consequences for an already overcrowded earth? The moral and social implications of this prepotent technology are complex and compelling.

Technology, then, has always been an important mechanism of change. The wheel, the stirrup, the splitting of the atom, the computer — all have had great impact upon society. Indeed, it is questionable whether the computer has had any greater effects upon the social order of our day than the wheel did upon the social order of antiquity. But there is at least one important difference today: developments are proceeding at an accelerating rate. The pace of technological change leaves us breathless, and the future promises to be even more demanding than the present. Technology will be an increasingly important factor in change and will require numerous agonizing decisions. As such, it demands our studied attention.

ENDNOTES TO CHAPTER 6

1. Karl Marx, *The Poverty of Philosophy*, trans. H. Quelch (Chicago: Charles H. Kerr, 1920), p. 119.

2. Thorstein Veblen, *The Theory of Business Enterprise* (New York: Charles Scribner's Sons, 1904), pp. 306, 323, 358.

3. Thorstein Veblen, *The Theory of the Leisure Class* (New York: Mentor Books, 1953), contains the essential elements of his theory of social evolution.

4. *Ibid.*, p. 34.

5. *Ibid.*, p. 37.

6. *Ibid.*, p. 43.
7. William F. Ogburn, *On Culture and Social Change*, ed. and with an introduction by Otis Dudley Duncan (Chicago: University of Chicago Press, 1964), p. 89.
8. *Ibid.*, p. 23ff.
9. Stanislaw Andrzejewski, "Are Ideas Social Forces?" *American Sociological Review*, XIV (Dec., 1949), 758–63.
10. Marshall McLuhan, *Understanding Media: The Extensions of Man* (New York: Signet Books, 1964), p. viii.
11. William Foote Whyte, *Organizational Behavior: Theory and Application* (Homewood, Ill.: Irwin-Dorsey, 1969), pp. 253ff.
12. T. Scarlett Epstein, *Economic Development and Social Change in South India* (New York: Humanities Press, 1962).
13. Max Lerner, *America As a Civilization* (New York: Simon and Schuster, 1957), p. 227.
14. Emmanuel G. Mesthene, *Technological Change: Its Impact on Man and Society* (Cambridge: Harvard University Press, 1970), p. 16.
15. W. F. Cottrell, "Death by Dieselization: A Case Study in the Reaction to Technological Change," *American Sociological Review*, XVI (June, 1951), 358–65.
16. See the various case studies in Edward H. Spicer, ed., *Human Problems in Technological Change* (New York: Russell Sage Foundation, 1952).
17. Guy Hunter, *Modernizing Peasant Societies* (New York: Oxford University Press, 1969), p. 145.
18. Mesthene, *Technological Change*, p. 17.
19. Jacques Ellul, *The Technological Society* (New York: Alfred A. Knopf, 1964), p. 128.
20. Theodore Roszak, *The Making of a Counter Culture* (Garden City: Anchor Books, 1969), p. 5.
21. *Ibid.*, p. 8.
22. Charles Hampden-Turner, *Radical Man* (Cambridge, Mass.; Schenkman Publishing Company, 1970), p. 308.
23. *Ibid.*, p. 309.
24. Barbara Ward, *The Rich Nations and the Poor Nations* (New York: W. W. Norton & Co., 1962), p. 155.
25. William F. Ogburn and Myer F. Nimkoff, *Technology and the Changing Family* (Boston: Houghton Mifflin Co., 1955).
26. Francis R. Allen, "The Automobile," in *Technology and Social Change*, ed. Francis R. Allen et al. (New York: Appleton-Century-Crofts, 1957), pp. 107–32.
27. *Ibid.*, p. 129.
28. See "The Effects of Technology" in *The Futurist*, December, 1971, pp. 228–29.
29. Emmanuel G. Mesthene, "How Technology Will Shape the Future," *Science*, CLXI (July 12, 1968), pp. 135–43.

30. Lynn White, Jr., *Medieval Technology and Social Change* (New York: Oxford University Press, 1962).

31. William A. Faunce, "Automation in the Automobile Industry: Some Consequences for In-Plant Social Structure," *American Sociological Review*, XXIII (Aug., 1958), 401–407.

32. Thomas L. Whisler, *Information Technology and Organizational Change* (Belmont: Wadsworth Publishing Co., 1970).

33. *Ibid.*, p. 76.

34. John Colombotos, "Physicians and Medicare: A Before-After Study in the Reaction to Technological Change," *American Sociological Review*, XXXIV (June, 1969), 318–34.

35. Donald N. Michael, *The Unprepared Society: Planning for a Precarious Future* (New York: Harper & Row, 1968), pp. 37ff.

36. *Ibid.*, p. 42.

37. Robert Boguslaw, *The New Utopians* (Englewood Cliffs: Prentice-Hall, Inc., 1965), p. 202.

38. *Ibid.*, p. 204.

39. These examples, along with others in the remainder of this chapter, are largely drawn from Theodore J. Gordon and Robert H. Ament, *Forecasts of Some Technological and Scientific Developments and Their Societal Consequences* (Middletown, Conn.: Institute for the Future, 1969).

40. Michael, *The Unprepared Society*, p. 51.

41. Karl Mannheim, *Man and Society in an Age of Reconstruction* (New York: Harcourt, Brace & Co., 1940), pp. 370ff.

42. Rensis Likert, *The Human Organization: Its Management and Value* (New York: McGraw-Hill, 1967).

43. Philip Zimbardo and Ebbe B. Ebbesen, *Influencing Attitudes and Changing Behavior* (Reading, Mass.: Addison-Wesley Publishing Co., 1970), pp. 109–22.

44. Jules Henry, *Culture Against Man* (New York: Random House, 1963).

45. Reported in *Time*, February 21, 1972, p. 44.

CHAPTER 7

The Idealistic Perspective

In contrast to the materialistic perspective, the idealistic approach is reflected in Whitehead's observation that "a general idea is always a danger to the existing order." [1] Whitehead tried to support his thesis by examining the idea of freedom and showing how that idea has been a historical force for change. Not all ideas, of course, are equally effective. It is particularly the ethical ideals of man that have been "the supreme example of consciously formulated ideas acting as a driving force effecting transitions from social state to social state." [2]

Some theorists, then, have stressed the role of ideas, ideologies, or values in effecting change. But this does not necessarily mean that the role of material factors is denied. Nor did the treatment of material factors in the last chapter imply that ideas are of no import. The relationship between material factors, ideas, and social change has been variously conceived, but few, if any, theorists would argue that *either* material factors *or* ideas are wholly the driving mechanisms of change. Our first topic in this chapter, therefore, will be an exploration of the various views on the relationship between materialistic and idealistic forces in change. We shall then examine the way in which ideas effect or affect change, and shall conclude with a look at a few modern, prepotent ideologies.

THE MATERIALISTIC VS. THE IDEALISTIC PERSPECTIVE

Are material factors or ideas more potent in effecting social change? Most thinkers have made neither of these factors completely subservient to the other, but rather have recognized the importance of both. They have, however, emphasized each of the factors differently. Generally, four different positions have been taken: the Marxist, the idealist, the interactionist, and the position of concomitant variation. These positions differ according to the causal weight they give to the two factors.

The Marxist position stresses the ultimate force of material factors. It is important here to emphasize "ultimate," for the Marxist does not neglect the role of ideas. There are many thinkers who battle against "an *imaginary* Marxism, urging against it always the importance of ideological factors that no serious thinker has ever denied." [3]   The Marxist method involves the study of human reality, and that study "leads back to thought" when the point of departure has been material factors, while one is driven to "social and economic reality when one has begun with the history of ideas." [4]   Ideas are important; but the ultimately determining factors of human history are material.

Ideologies are legitimizations of a particular order; they arise out of that order, and they tend to perpetuate it by adorning it with legitimacy. The ideology, then, is part of the superstructure that is erected upon the material base of the society. Nevertheless, as Engels pointed out in one of his letters, elements of the superstructure can react back upon the economic base and thereby influence the course of historical development. Ideas thus acquire, within certain limits, a certain autonomy

> and a possibility of reacting . . . on the functioning of the economic base. Man's creative thought, inventing ever more perfect instruments of production, transforms, gradually and indirectly, the general economic structure, all social relations, and, as a result, the whole of human reality.[5]

In essence, the Marxist position is that ideas arise out of social processes but may then become important in further social development. Ideas are the conscious expressions of changes in material conditions which have already occurred; but once development of those ideas has taken place, they become potent tools in the further realization of the material conditions that gave birth to them. In addition, ideas are able to be communicated through space and over time, so that they may influence other societies and the material conditions of those societies.

The idealist position gives ideas a dominant place in change. We have already noted that the "father" of sociology, Auguste Comte, maintained that man's history must be understood in terms of "the history of the human mind." Comte, then, was basically an idealist in his approach to change, stressing the achievement of a more humane society through the increasing use of reason.

A modern philosophical approach is that of Whitehead, who tried to show how ideas impel men to change their social order. Whitehead argued that Christianity has provided Western man with a set of ideals which have been of enormous importance in the development of Western civilization. In fact, we may understand man's progress in terms of the continual changes effected by men in their effort to make the ideals of Christianity practicable for all people. But Whitehead also recognizes that we are dealing with a case of more-or-less rather than of either-or. For "ideas arise as explanations of customs and they end by founding novel methods and novel institutions." [6] Civilization did not originate in a social contract; men did not come together and agree upon ideas which then shaped the course of history. Rather, the first "effort was the slow introduction of ideas explanatory of modes of behaviour and of inrushes of emotion which already dominated their lives." [7] Ideas did, of course, shape behavior; but practice precedes thought. Thus, Whitehead acknowledged the existential source of ideas but gave primacy to the force of ideas in the evolution of civilization.

But perhaps the most influential advocate and exemplar of the idealist position was Hegel, who conceived of history as the development of Spirit in time. Spirit, according to Hegel, represents the absolute; Spirit is the central principle of all existence. Furthermore, Spirit is a process; its development proceeds by the dialectical process from the "in-itself" of the unconscious stage to the "for-itself" of the conscious stage. This dialectical process involves the continual creation and overcoming of contradictions. An entity creates its opposite and enters into conflict with it. The outcome of the conflict is the partial destruction of both the thesis and the antithesis, and the creation of a new entity which is larger and more differentiated than the original two, and which incorporates into its own being whatever aspects of the original two had a future.

Thus, in the Hegelian dialectic, contradiction is of the essence. Contradiction is

> implicity present in the original products of Understanding, it becomes explicit when these products break down, and start passing into their complements, or being referred to their correlatives, or growing into more "concrete" forms, and it is "preserved" in the result of all such processes.[8]

Furthermore, Hegel held that the dialectic is a universal characteristic of reality. In the *Lesser Logic* he wrote that the dialectic is "the principle of all the movement and of all the activity we find in reality . . . Everything that surrounds us can be treated as an instance of Dialectic." [9] Hegel understood the dialectic both as a method of inquiry and as a pattern of all being. The dialectic is a mode of thinking and the essence of reality, including our experience of reality.

But how does this dialectical development of the Spirit in time relate to concrete history? In simplest terms, individuals and nations become instruments of the Spirit. Spirit comes into being in nature and history; history is "Spirit externalized and emptied into Time." [10] Of particular importance in this process is the state, which is the manifestation of the Divine Idea on earth. The continuing changes in the state result in progress, for the World Spirit is increasingly incarnate in the activities and organization of the state.

This would imply a justification of the existing state, and Hegel was explicit in arguing the point: "The nation to which is ascribed a moment of the Idea in the form of a natural principle is entrusted with giving complete effect to it in the advance of the self-developing self-consciousness of the world mind." [11] This nation would be dominant, because it was the instrument of the Spirit during a particular epoch. Thus, Hegel's objective idealism merges into a worship of the state. Change is the result of the activity of the Spirit in men and nations, and, in particular, in the state; the individual finds his fulfillment as he participates in that state. Few writers have made man any more subservient to an intangible despot as Hegel did in his portrait of the dialectical evolution of Spirit.

The third position on the relationship between material and ideal factors is the interactionist. This position argues that there is interaction between ideas and material factors and gives more or less equal weight to each. It is the latter aspect which distinguishes this position from the first two, which also acknowledgd interaction, but which gave ultimate or dominant consideration to either material or ideal factors.

The interactionist approach is illustrated by Bell's study of Jamaica. [12] A number of changes have occurred in Jamaica with respect to human rights. Various civil, political, economic, and social rights have been extended to a greater number of people. Civil rights include, among others, religious freedom, equality in the process of justice, and the right to assemble and speak freely. Political rights include such matters as voting and equality in receiving public services. Economic rights involve justice in wage scales, decent working conditions, and the right to unionize. And the social rights include a variety of new freedoms such as primary education, choice of one's marriage partner, and adequate material necessities for all.

How did these rights come about? According to Bell, they occurred as a consequence of the playing out of contradictions between ideas and reality.

There has been a demonstrable interplay between ideas and institutions throughout the history of Jamaica. Institutions fostered certain ideas about what is right or wrong, what should or should not be; and ideas, often exogenous to Jamaica itself originally, have led to organized social action which often resulted in changing, eliminating, or creating institutions.[13]

The fourth position is that of concomitant variation. That is, ideas and material factors change together (though not necessarily simultaneously), and it is not possible to identify any causal relationship. This seems to be Brinton's position with respect to revolution.[14] He notes that ideas are always a part of the prerevolutionary situation. Without ideas, there is no revolution. Nevertheless, this does not mean that the ideas cause the revolution nor that a revolution might be nipped in the bud through censorship of ideas. It simply means that ideas are always a part of the set of variables involved in revolutions.

In the prerevolutionary situation, there are always a number of discontents about economic, political, and social conditions. And these discontents are sharpened through the articulation of ideals and of means of realizing those ideals. Thus, the uniformity in revolutions is the *expression* of ideas, rather than particular ideas — which may vary enormously in different revolutions. . . ." [15]

This latter point suggests why ideas must be considered in the study of change. Ideas, as Brinton notes, are *always* expressed in the prerevolutionary situation. Whether one takes one or the other of the four positions we have outlined, it is clear that ideas always form a part of the variables involved in change. And it is not difficult to understand why. Man is a creature who must make sense out of his world. All myths, all religion, all science, all ideologies function to make the world meaningful. The primitive may explain an accident by reference to a demon inhabiting the stone over which he tripped, while the modern will explain it by reference to his inadequate perception of his environment; but both the myth and the science serve the same purpose of making whatever happens have meaning.

It may well be true, therefore, that diverse ideologies may accompany similar patterns of change. This does not mean that ideologies are dispensable elements of change. The fundamental question becomes one of asking about sequence; does the effort to make sense always follow the behavior, or can the behavior itself be shaped by the effort to make reality meaningful? Unless one accepts the position that ideas and material conditions are only matters of concomitant variation, the sequence of the two factors is the basic problem.

HOW IDEOLOGIES AFFECT CHANGE

Advocates of each of the four positions outlined above agree that ideas are factors in change. In this section, we shall examine evidence that shows that ideas, or more particularly, ideologies, are independent variables in change. That is, without asserting that this evidence proves any of the four positions above, it is nevertheless clear that ideas influence the course of change. However much we may argue about their dominance as mechanisms of change, we cannot deny that men do act on the basis of ideas.

An interesting illustration of the difference in behavior that results from differing ideologies is provided by Spengler.[16] He notes that the inhabitants of Lisbon responded in diverse fashion to the catastrophic earthquake of 1775. The king's minister threw himself into the task of rebuilding. Scientists tried to determine natural causes of the disaster. But numbers of the clergy saw it as divine judgment upon an evil city; they resisted the efforts of the king's minister and tried to use the disaster to herd the people more closely into the realm of clerical authority. In other words, there were differing responses based upon differing ideas about the nature of reality. As Lerner put it, "ideas are weapons," and men may either possess the ideas in order to understand and control their existence, or the ideas may possess men "as evil spirits were once said to have entered into witches and possessed them and made them do their bidding." [17]

But granted that ideas or ideologies may be independent variables in change, precisely how do they affect that change? He asked this question with respect to technology and found a variety of ways in which technology affects the course of change. We shall find the same with respect to ideologies. Broadly, ideologies act by preventing, impeding, facilitating, or directing change.

Ideologies as Impediment or Barrier

Karl Mannheim defined ideologies as those systems of ideas which result in behavior that maintains the existing order. The concept of ideology, he said, reflects the idea that "ruling groups can in their thinking become so intensively interest-bound to a situation that they are simply no longer able to see certain facts which would

120

undermine their sense of domination." [18]   We need not restrict ideology to such a definition in order to see the truth of Mannheim's statement.

In particular, a number of religious ideologies have impeded or quelled change. In China, Confucian thought acted as a barrier to change, for it idealized the past. Indeed, it went further and set forth the past to emulate in concrete terms and considerable detail. Mencius wrote about the feudal hierarchy and various facets of economic and political institutions that existed in the golden days of old. And this meant that the Chinese golden age was quite different from the Western myth of Eden. For the latter may have provided innocence and peace, but not a viable social structure. The Chinese image of the past was potentially replicable in the present. Unlike the early Christians, the Chinese could do more than decry a lost innocence; they could work to preserve and restore the past.

This is not to suggest, however, that Christianity has generally been a goad to change in the West. On the contrary, Christian thought as often as not has impeded change. During the Middle Ages, the clergy employed religious ideology as a tool to acquire greater power and thereby inhibited certain changes from occurring. [19]   Economic progress was retarded by the designation of usury as sinful. Whatever surplus wealth developed tended to be channelled into jewels, courtly activities, and the building of religious edifices and palaces. Men focussed their energies and their resources on expiating their guilt through the building of religious monuments. In other words, rather than being invested in trade or commercial development, surplus wealth was sucked into nonproductive religious activities that were believed to bring about the favor of God. One result was that by the late Middle Ages techniques for supplying water and sanitation (which had been developed by the Romans) were still not being used; "towns and cities, while liberally provided with religious edifices, were filthy rabbit warrens of meandering, unpaved streets and haphazard, inconvenient buildings that set the stage for the recurrent plagues of the period." [20]

The large number of religious holidays and festivals served the same purpose of diverting energies and attention from activities that would have enhanced the well-being of the people. The same point has been noted with respect to Eastern religions: ". . . the inhibition to economic growth engendered by religions in Asia lies not in their other-worldly orientation but in their institutional characteristics — especially in their ability to absorb accumulations of wealth that might otherwise be put to more economically productive uses." [21] This was also the point on which Veblen criticized religion, pointing out that all of the trappings and activities associated with religion were essentially "conspicuous waste." From an economic point of view, he asserted, "the consumption of goods and effort in the service of an anthropomorphic divinity means a lowering of the vitality of the community." [22]

A final example of the way in which religious ideology has inhibited change is found in religious efforts at thought control. The Inquisition, the heresy trials, the insistence on pushing all knowledge into an orthodox framework — these are examples of stringent efforts to control the way men think. The history of science abounds in conflict with the religious authorities. From the trial of Galileo to the trial of Scopes in our own country, we may trace out a continuing line of battle. Indeed, we must push the war back beyond the time of Galileo. From earliest times, Christian thought tended to be suspicious of secular learning. A second-century work entitled *Physiologus* pushed all knowledge into an orthodox mold, claiming, among other things, that lion cubs are born dead, but that on the third day they awaken to life when the lion breathes between their eyes. This typifies the resurrection of Christ, the Lion of Judah.[23]

Thought control has not been confined to religious ideologies. Communists have also worked zealously at the task of reshaping men's thinking. In Russia, developments in biology lagged behind the rest of the world because Soviet biology was dominated by Lysenko from the 1940's to the early 1960's. This Russian biologist convinced political leaders that Lamarckian rather than Mendelian genetics was congruent with Marx's thought. At least one of Russia's world-renowned biologists was banished to Siberia, and Mendelian genetics were labelled as nothing more than capitalistic myths. The effort to pursue science only within ideologically legitimate bounds led to the atrophy rather than the development of science.

Thus, not only religious ideologies, but ideologies generally, may inhibit change. In the United States, according to some observers, the ideology of equality of opportunity minimizes the development of class consciousness and class antagonisms. To the extent that this is true, the ideology will impede the change that would result from class antagonisms and class conflict.

Ideologies as Facilitators

One might conclude from the above that ideologies in general and religious ideologies in particular serve only to retard necessary change. But such a conclusion would be false. For ideologies, including religious ideologies, may also facilitate change. This was Weber's thesis in his study of the Protestant Ethic and the spirit of capitalism.[24]

According to Weber, the development of capitalism was greatly facilitated by a particular strain of Protestant thought. That thought shaped the personalities of the entrepreneurs whose activities were responsible for the flowering of capitalism. We may see this by first understanding what is meant by the "spirit of capitalism": "that attitude which seeks profit rationally and systematically" in a way that is exemplified in the writings of Benjamin Franklin.[25] And how did Protestantism, and particularly Calvinism, contribute to this attitude?

Weber pointed to Christian asceticism as the source of the rational, systematic approach that impelled capitalism. A basic element of modern capitalism, "rational conduct on the basis of the idea of the calling," was begotten by Christian asceticism.[26] For in Christian asceticism, the individual is driven by a concern for his own spiritual well-being, and he can assure himself of being in a state of grace through ascetic action. Faith was the gift of God, but a man was able to prove that he possessed that gift through concrete results, namely, "by a type of Christian conduct which served to increase the glory of God." [27] Works never enable a man to gain salvation, but they are indispensable to demonstrating his possession of that salvation.

The Christian ascetic, therefore, systematically and rationally ordered his moral life. He agreed that the waste of time was a deadly sin. He avoided any kind of spontaneous enjoyment or self-indulgence. He saw the achievement of wealth as the result of his labor and his labor as the consequence of his calling from God; success was the sign of God's blessing. And "when the limitation of consumption is combined with this release of acquisitive activity, the inevitable practical result is obvious: accumulation of capital through ascetic compulsion to save." [28] As Wesley observed, religion necessarily produces industry and frugality, which, in turn, necessarily produce wealth.

In sum, Christian asceticism produced precisely those character traits which were conducive to the development of capitalism. Economic growth proceeded as a consequence of the pursuit of assurance of salvation. Men were motivated to behave in particular ways that happened to be the ways needed for the growth of capitalist economy.

But the Protestant Ethic is not peculiar to Protestantism. Elements of that ethic have been found in other religions and the same kind of results attributed to it. Bellah has shown that Tokugawa religion contained the same elements as Weber described in the Protestant Ethic, including admonitions to work hard, to avoid wasting of time, and to be thrifty and honest.[29]   The Tokugawa era preceded the Meiji Restoration which led to the rapid modernization of Japan, and Bellah argues that Tokugawa religion was an important factor in that modernization; for the religion facilitated rational behavior in the economy and polity by securing commitment to core values of the society, motivating and legitimating political innovations, and "reinforcing an ethic of inner-worldly asceticism which stressed diligence and economy." [30]

There are other ways in which religious ideologies have facilitated change.   While Confucianism was a conservative force in China, Taoism and Buddhism provided the ideological foundation for many of the peasant revolts that marked Chinese history.   In contrast to Confucianism, Taoism stressed spontaneity; Laotzu had "no final faith in any authority but the authority of the heart," and he asserted that those who governed human affairs should "act on instinct and conscience." [31]   Buddhism and Christianity, the latter in the Taiping Rebellion, were also linked with revolutionary action in China.   All three religions were employed to fill the void in men's spirits left by Orthodox Confucianism and to justify the rebellion which that same Confucianism found abhorrent.   Thus, "history shows ample evidence of the persistent role of religion in political struggles against ruling dynasties." [32]

At this point, the question of religious ideology and social change may appear quite confusing.   We have seen that the same religion, such as Christianity, can impede some kinds of change and can impel other kinds of change.   Moreover, both an orthodox or a reformed or modernized version of a religion may facilitate change.   Geertz found that a modernized Islam and an orthodox Hinduism were each employed to further economic development in Indonesia.[33]   We might be tempted to conclude that religion is of no importance in change.   But that would be a wrong conclusion. For we have shown that religion is a factor in both impeding and facilitating change.

On the whole, Butterfield is right when he argues that the Christian church has been the "cement of society, the buttress of whatever was the existing order, and the defender of the status quo." [34]   We could expand this to include all other religions.   But on the other hand, there are clearly cases of religious ideologies functioning to facilitate change.   In addition to the cases we have mentioned, one writer has argued that in Tanzania "very nearly a one-to-one correlation exists between mission influence, the cash-crop economy, fertile land, education, and the general desire for progress." [35]

How can these divergent effects of religious commitment be explained?   In his examination of the relationship between religious orientation and civil rights militancy, Gary Marx found the same disparity and suggested an answer to it. He notes that the net effect of religion was to inhibit change by minimizing protest attitudes; at the same time, he found many religious people to be militant. Marx suggests that this can be understood in terms of the multiplicity of themes of any religious perspective, some of which are in tension if not contradiction. One strand of Christianity is the after-life and acceptance of one's lot in this life; but another strand is the realization of religious values in this life.[36]

Recent study of other religions supports this idea of multiple strands of thought that offer people diverse ideological positions and diverse patterns of behavior. Within Hinduism, for example, there are a number of value systems; a comparison of Brahmans and the mercantile bania castes will reveal a good deal of difference in values.[37]

In addition to the multiple strands of thought in all religions, we may briefly note two other reasons why religion facilitates change. One is that some directions of change are congruent with the existing religious ideology. A number of scholars have argued that Christianity provided the value basis upon which modern science developed (in spite of the numerous historical conflicts between the two). And the second reason is that religion changes over time; the relationship between religious ideology and a particular kind of change may be dialectical. Change, then, proceeds out of the context of ongoing resolution of the contradictions between religious ideology and social reality.

Religious ideologies are not, of course, the only kind of ideologies that facilitate change. Economic and political ideologies are also important: in the contemporary world, perhaps more so than religion. In particular, the ideology of nationalism is of central significance in the contemporary world. We will reserve discussion of this ideology, however, for the last section of the chapter.

At this point, we shall explore a little further into the ways ideology can facilitate change. We have seen evidence that it does facilitate change; but precisely how does it affect the direction of change? There are at least five ways.

First, ideology may legitimate the new direction. It does this both by disrupting the old order and by explaining and validating the emerging new order. In other words, the ideology endows the new order with authority. In the United States, the generation of businessmen known as the "robber barons" legitimated their activity through the ideology of social Darwinism. This suggests that an ideology may promote authority to the extent of justifying vicious behavior. As Coser has pointed out, when people engage in conflict as the representatives of groups, and battle for the ideals of those groups rather than for self-interest, the conflict is "likely to be more radical and merciless than those that are fought for personal reasons." [38]   We need only remind ourselves of the Nazi effort to purge Germany of every "undesirable" and inferior element to understand the truth of this statement.

An interesting illustration of the way in which ideology legitimates a new direction is provided by Swift in his study of the ideology of progressive education.   One problem confronting the public school is autonomy; the problem was significant by 1920, when a variety of changes in the nation led to a potentially greater public interference in the schools.   And public interference could mean action contrary to the wishes of school administrators.   To counter this threat, the schools adopted techniques which had spread throughout the business world — methods of human relations.   Certain administrators devoted considerable time to public relations in order to gain public support for policies and financial needs without losing autonomy.   Progressive education ideology included an emphasis on community-centered education, legitimating considerable school-community communication.   Thus, "public relations did not have to remain a marginal activity, operating in the shadows, but instead became a legitimate and even mandatory aspect of the school's program." [39]   The public could not only be informed, but propagandized; and all was legitimate because of the ideology of progressive education.

A second way in which ideology facilitates change is by legitimating or directing behavior that leads to unanticipated change. This was the character of the Protestant Ethic in the development of capitalism.   Economic growth was an unanticipated result of religious devotion.   A similar effect of ideology has been pointed out by Selznick in his study of the Tennessee Valley Authority. The TVA was set up to implement a grass-roots ideology; the administration was to have freedom to make decisions independently of centralized control, and the people of the area would participate in the decision-making process.   The ideology made administrative discretion a legitimate activity; but the administrative discretion, as Selznick shows, led to unanticipated consequences, to changes in the character of the organization. [40]

A third way in which ideology facilitates change is by providing a basis for solidarity.   Ideologies can be integrative mechanisms, neutralizing the conflicting strains that are found in most societies.   This is clear from the differing situations in Mali and Nigeria in the early 1960's.   In the former, solidarity was created and new political forms were implemented on the basis of a Malian brand of Marxism.   But in Nigeria, a number of ideologies competed and conflicted with each other; no single political ideology bound the people together in a common purpose.   As a result, the youth of Mali were "enthusiastic supporters of the regime," while the youth of Nigeria were "estranged from the leadership." [41]

A fourth way that ideology facilitates change is through its power to motivate individuals. A common problem of the developing nations of the world involves convincing the masses that development is possible, that there is purpose to human existence, and that self-sacrifice is a small price to pay for the rewards that shall be theirs in the future. Ideology enters at this point, and becomes a tool of the modernizing elite. But this function of ideology is not limited to the developing nations. Those who participate in social movements in the developed nations are also motivated by ideology. For the ideology of a movement often "includes a concept of personal power and control over one's own destiny or the destiny of the world." [42] To the extent that ideology can infuse members of a movement with the passion to believe and act, the ideology is likely to facilitate the change that is the aim of the movement.

The fifth and final way in which ideology facilitates change is by confronting a society with a contradiction. As mentioned above with respect to religious ideologies, there can be a clear contradiction between ideology and reality which impels people to act in order to resolve the contradiction. One of the problems of the developing nations is the fact that ideology has often surged too far ahead of reality. There is, for example, often a commitment to universal education which is unrealistic in terms of economic resources and limited need for a highly educated citizenry. The gap between the ideology — the right of all people to be educated — and the reality — the underdeveloped economy — can create a revolutionary situation.

Of course all societies have their gaps between reality and ideology. The gap may be rationalized or explained away — particularly by those who have everything to gain by keeping things as they are. But if we glance briefly at social movements again, we find that movement ideologies will generally reject this gap as illegitimate. The ideology of the social movement refuses to allow the society to ignore the gap between the societal ideology and reality. Movement ideology is a relentless message of judgment against the larger society, and, thereby, a continual prod to action for movement members.

Ideologies as Directing Mechanisms

One other way in which ideology affects change is by giving direction to that change, by impelling change in a particular direction that derives from the specifics or the logic of the ideology. Many of the developments in the United States can be related to the ideology that technology will resolve all problems. Rather than in prayer or magic or dependence upon charismatic leaders, Americans have been prone to seek their social salvation in technology. Thus, the way to deal with the problem of war and peace is to insure our superiority in military technology. The American commitment to this technology has resulted in the arms race that all past history indicates can only end in war; but to many Americans, it is a guarantee of peace. And the pursuit of military technology leaves few resources or energies available for considering alternative solutions to the problem of war and peace.

On a broader scale, Polak has argued extensively that the image of the future that prevails in any society will direct the course of change in that society. A similar point was made earlier by Mannheim. As noted above, Mannheim defined ideology as a system of ideas that maintain the existing order. But he recognized that a system of ideas can also initiate change in the existing order. He called the latter utopia rather than ideology, and said that utopian thinking is "incongruous with the state of reality within which it occurs" and tends "to burst the bonds of the existing order." [43]

According to Polak, the future may be shown to be the cause of present behavior in both a positive and a negative sense. In the positive sense, the image of the future functions to direct present behavior in accord with specific values. That is, members of a society are "magnetically *pulled* towards a future fulfillment of their own preceding and prevailing, idealistic images of the future, as well as being pushed from behind by their own realistic past." [44] In a negative sense, the lack of an image of the future implies, in Spengler's terms, happened history rather than willed history.

Polak argues that there is a contemporary aversion to images of the future, with the result that man is left "standing at the edge of a bottomless abyss, facing death, destruction, chaos." [45] Those who speak about the decline of our culture, he argues, have failed to identify the "torn and still" images of the future that characterize our age. These broken and rejected images are the "gaping wound from which the life-blood of the culture is draining away." [46]

Polak devotes considerable attention to delineating the images of the future of various societies — ancient Greece, ancient Israel, ancient Christianity, modern socialism and Marxism, numerous utopian writers, and others — and relating these images of the future to directions of change. With respect to Israel, for example, we must ask how that particular, small group of nomadic people, who were only a minute part of the Arabian Bedouin tribes, attained such great importance in history. And the answer is to be found in Israel's "immortal" image of the future. Israel's image has an imperishable quality to it, involving "the full flowering of human dignity and an indirect *influence-optimism* (as) the common features of all the variations of the *one basic image of the future: the image of a salvation to come through Israel, to Israel, and out of Israel.*" [47]

One of the more striking examples of ideology-directed change in the contemporary world is China. Ideology was employed to mobilize the people during the Great Leap Forward of 1958–1960. This was an effort to attain quick and massive economic growth by decentralizing and mobilizing the masses in intensive work. It was clearly a case of "ideological economics"; the direction of change attempted (decentralization, development of communes in the urban as well as rural areas, and the commitment of the masses to the effort) flowed from the logic of Maoist ideology. [48]

Likewise, the changes effected by the Great Proletarian Cultural Revolution in the late 1960's were directed by ideology. In fact, the Revolution was defined by the Central Committee of the Communist Party as an ideological struggle:

> Although the bourgeoisie has been overthrown, it is still trying to use the old ideas, culture, customs and habits of the exploiting classes to corrupt the masses, capture their minds and endeavour to stage a come-back. The proletariat must do the exact opposite: it must meet head-on every challenge of the bourgeoisie in the ideological field and use the new ideas, culture, customs and habits of the proletariat to change the mental outlook of the whole of society . . . The aim of the Great Proletarian Cultural Revolution is to revolutionize people's ideology and as a consequence to achieve greater, faster, better and more economical results in all fields of work. [49]

Maoist ideology directed the revolt against the bureaucratic tendencies and bourgeois thinking that had crept into Chinese life. Art, education, and other aspects of Chinese society were brought into greater accord with the thought of Mao.

MODERN PREPOTENT IDEOLOGIES

What are the ideologies that are exercising the greatest influence in the contemporary world? In the past, religious ideologies, the ideology of progress, and various political and economic ideologies have been important. In the contemporary world, the most potent ideologies are nationalism and various types of socialism and communism. This is not to say that others are unimportant. In the United States, the ideology of "free enterprise" is a factor in the ongoing conflict over the resolution of various problems. But in the world as a whole, nationalism, socialism, and Marxism are among the most potent, modern ideologies.

Nationalism has been important to all industrializing nations. One of the first great issues in Meiji Japan was that of national unification. The slogan, "Revere the Emperor, Oust the Barbarian," typified the nationalistic hue that characterized the modernization of Japan. In most of the developing nations today, nationalism is linked with some form of socialism. Contemporary ideologies tend to be politico-economic in nature, stressing an indigenous form of economic development that avoids the deficiencies of both the American and the Soviet patterns. With few exceptions, nationalist leaders reject the capitalist and the Communist methods of development (as represented by the United States and the Soviet Union).

Thus, the contemporary ideologies, whether called "communitarian society," "African socialism," "communocracy," or something else, share one element — the need for and the commitment to a type of development that allows for both central direction and coordination and private initiative. As Sigmund has characterized these ideologies:

> At the same time that these theories denounce a stereotyped capitalism for its excessive individualism, its lack of concern with human and social values, and its fostering of the spirit of ruthless competition, they also criticize a stereotyped Communism for its excessive collectivism, its suppression of the individual, its materialism, and its narrow commitment to the national interest of a single country or group of countries.[50]

An example of this perspective is Victor Raul Haya de la Torre of Peru, who writes in both an anti-imperialist (meaning primarily the United States) and an anticommunist vein. He has proposed a social order that rejects the kind of capitalism that leads to imperialism. His society would be one in which the economy is planned scientifically, with production and distribution of wealth controlled by the state. It would be a democratic and representative society, with each of the three major classes of Peru, peasants, workers, and middle-class, participating and working for the common good. Such a society "would be the cornerstone of the Indo-American unity and the effective emancipation of our peoples." [51]

As is already evident from the above, the content of modern nationalistic ideologies varies greatly. Perhaps the only common element is the idea of "the establishment of a fully secular area of life regulated by a social institution before which all men are at least in certain public senses equal." [52] This rather abstract core allows for considerable diversity in content. But as we noted earlier, one way in which ideology facilitates change is by creating solidarity. The nationalistic ideologies have the creation of an integrated society as one of their most important functions. Developing nations may proceed by divergent paths, but certain tools and resources seem necessary to any path. And, among others, one prerequisite for development is the "ideological integration of leaders and followers." [53]

ENDNOTES TO CHAPTER 7

1. Alfred North Whitehead, *Adventures of Ideas* (New York: Mentor Books, 1933), p. 22.

2. *Ibid.*, p. 25.

3. Lucien Goldmann, *The Human Sciences & Philosophy*, trans. Hayden V. White and Robert Anchor (London: Jonathan Cape, 1969), pp. 86–87.

4. *Ibid.*, p. 62.

5. A. Schaff, "The Marxist Theory of Social Development," in *Readings in Social Evolution and Development*, ed. S. N. Eisenstadt (Oxford: Pergamon Press, 1970), p. 82.

6. Whitehead, *Adventures of Ideas*, p. 106.

7. *Ibid.*, p. 114.

8. J. N. Findlay, *Hegel: A Re-Examination* (London: George Allen and Unwin, Ltd., 1958), p. 63.

9. Quoted in *ibid.*, p. 65.

10. G. W. F. Hegel, *The Phenomenology of Mind*, trans. J. B. Baillie (New York: Harper & Row, 1967), p. 807.

11. G. W. F. Hegel, *Philosophy of Right*, trans. T. M. Knox (London: Oxford University Press, 1953), p. 217.

12. Wendell Bell, "Social Change and Elites in an Emergent Nation," in *Social Change in Developing Areas*, ed. Herbert R. Barringer, George I. Blanksten, and Raymond W. Mack (Cambridge, Mass.: Schenkman Publishing Co., 1965), pp. 155–204.

13. *Ibid.*, pp. 165–66.

14. Crane Brinton, *The Anatomy of Revolution* (New York: Prentice-Hall, Inc., 1952), p. 53.

15. *Ibid.*

16. Joseph J. Spengler, "Theory, Ideology, Non-Economic Values, and Politico-Economic Development," in *Tradition, Values, and Socio-Economic Development*, ed. Ralph Braibanti and Joseph Spengler (Durham, N.C.: Duke University Press, 1961), pp. 7–8.

17. Max Lerner, *Ideas Are Weapons* (New York: Viking Press, 1939), p. 3.

18. Karl Mannheim, *Ideology and Utopia*, trans. Louis Wirth and Edward Shils (New York: Harcourt, Brace & World, Inc., 1936), p. 40.

19. This paragraph follows Richard T. LaPiere, *Social Change* (New York: McGraw-Hill, 1965), pp. 305–306.

20. *Ibid.*, p. 306.

21. Richard D. Lambert, "The Social and Psychological Determinants of Savings and Investments in Developing Societies," in *Development and Society*, ed. David E. Novack and Robert Lekachman (New York: St. Martin's Press, 1964), p. 269.

22. Thorstein Veblen, *The Theory of the Leisure Class* (New York: Mentor Books, 1953), p. 201.

23. Sir William Cecil Dampier, *A History of Science* (Cambridge: Cambridge University Press, 1948), p. 66.

24. Weber's thesis has been subjected to considerable debate. See S. N. Eisenstadt, ed., *The Protestant Ethic and Modernization* (New York: Basic Books, 1968) for a recent evaluation.

25. Max Weber, *The Protestant Ethic and the Spirit of Capitalism*, trans. Talcott Parsons (New York: Charles Scribner's Sons, 1958), p. 64.

26. *Ibid.*, p. 180.

27. *Ibid.*, p. 114.

28. *Ibid.*, p. 172.

29. Robert N. Bellah, *Tokugawa Religion* (New York: The Free Press, 1957).

30. *Ibid.*, p. 194.

31. Witter Bynner, *The Way of Life According to Laotzu* (New York: The John Day Company, 1944), p. 19.

32. C. K. Yang, *Religion in Chinese Society* (Berkeley and Los Angeles: University of California Press, 1961), p. 218.

33. Clifford Geertz, *Peddlers and Princes* (Chicago: University of Chicago Press, 1963), pp. 127–28.

34. Herbert Butterfield, *Christianity and History* (London: Fontana Books, 1949), p. 176.

35. Gwendolen Carter, ed., *African One-Party States* (Ithaca: Cornell University Press, 1962), p. 434.

36. Gary T. Marx, *Protest and Prejudice* (New York: Harper & Row, 1967), p. 104. See pp. 94–105.

37. Myron Weiner, ed., *Modernization: The Dynamics of Growth* (New York: Basic Books, Inc., 1966), p. 6.

38. Lewis Coser, *The Functions of Social Conflict* (New York: The Free Press, 1956), p. 118.

39. David W. Swift, *Ideology and Change in the Public Schools* (Columbus: Charles E. Merrill Publishing Company, 1971), p. 123.

40. Philip Selznick, *TVA and the Grass Roots* (New York: Harper Torchbooks, 1966), pp. 262–64.

41. David E. Apter, ed., *Ideology and Discontent* (New York: The Free Press, 1964), p. 23.

42. Luther P. Gerlach and Virginia H. Hine, *People, Power, Change: Movements of Social Transformation* (Indianapolis: The Bobbs-Merrill Company, Inc., 1970), p. 163.

43. Mannheim, *Ideology and Utopia*, pp. 192, 193.

44. Fred L. Polak, *The Image of the Future*, Vol. I (New York: Oceana Publications, 1961), p. 15.

45. *Ibid.*, Vol. 2, p. 14.

46. *Ibid.*

47. *Ibid.*, Vol. 1, p. 132.

48. A brief description of the Great Leap Forward may be found in Franz Schurmann and Orville Schell, eds., *Communist China* (New York: Vintage Books, 1967), pp. 401ff.

49. From the August 8, 1966 "Decision of the Central Committee of The Chinese Communist Party Concerning the Great Proletarian Cultural Revolution," in Joan Robinson, *The Cultural Revolution in China* (London: Penguin Books, 1970), pp. 85 and 95. This book is a good and brief summary of the Revolution.

50. Paul E. Sigmund, ed., *The Ideologies of the Developing Nations*, revised edition (New York: Frederick A. Praeger, 1967), pp. 12–13.

51. Quoted in *ibid.*, p. 352.

52. K. H. Silvert, ed., *Expectant Peoples: Nationalism and Development* (New York: Random House, 1963), p. 19.

53. Leonard Binder, "Ideology and Political Development," in *Modernization: The Dynamics of Growth*, ed. Myron Weiner, p. 204.

CHAPTER 8

Interactional Mechanisms

It is man who makes history. But man never acts in a vacuum; the history he makes always occurs in the context of his interaction with other men. Man is a social animal, whose existence is fashioned in the matrix of social interaction. Many thinkers, therefore, have looked to social interaction as the driving mechanism of change and, in particular, to a specific kind of interaction — conflict. Like Khaldun and Marx, numerous thinkers have seen the course of history as prodded forward by human conflict.

In this chapter we shall examine the interactional perspective. To what extent are competition, conflict, and the extreme form of conflict — violence and war — responsible for change? Does conflict always result in change? What kind of change follows when men enter into conflict? Can change occur without conflict? These are some of the questions to which the following sections are addressed.

COMPETITION AND CONFLICT: PERVASIVE FORCES

Conflict: Thought and Theory

Throughout his recorded history, man has probed into the nature of reality and found conflict there. Man's concern with conflict is reflected in ancient religious literature. Weber has pointed out that the ancient war gods not only protected the "undoubted values of everyday routine" but also "had to fight other gods like themselves, just as their communities fought, and they had to prove their divine powers in this very struggle." [1] Greek mythology had Ares, god of war, who was hated by the other divinities because of his savage nature. His sister, Eris, was goddess of strife and delighted in discord and warfare. Their Roman counterparts were Mars and Discordia.

Among the Babylonians, conflict was an eternal, cosmic struggle. The god Marduk had an annual battle against the powers of chaos, represented by the goddess Tiamat. It was an endless extension of the struggle that took place before the creation of the world.

None of the world's great religions omit the theme. In Buddhism, it is primarily an intra-individual struggle with desire. The Hindu classic, *Bhagavad-Gita,* deals with the problem of war and the goals for which man must struggle upon earth. In Islam, warfare was ordained by Allah, and whoever battled the infidel was to be richly rewarded. And, as we have already seen, in the Christian tradition there is, among others, the work of Augustine on the conflict between the City of God and the earthly city, a conflict that characterizes the whole of human history.

In addition to religious thought, concern with conflict is deeply rooted in the thinking of men actively engaged in political and social affairs. As Martindale notes, "conflict theory is the creation of men of affairs." [2] Heraclitus, whose family had political and priestly claims, saw conflict inextricably woven into the structure of the universe: ". . . all things come into being and pass away through strife." [3] The Indian statesman, Kautilya, delineated a theory of warfare and diplomacy that makes Machiavelli sound gentle; Kautilya wrote his work around 300 B.C. And the Chinese critic and essayist, Han Fei (died 233 B.C.), taught that war is the arbiter of nations, for human nature demands the exercise of power.

Numerous other political and social observers stressed the importance of conflict in human affairs, among them the Greek historian of Rome, Polybius; Khaldun; Machiavelli; the French publicist, Jean Bodin; and Thomas Hobbes. By the eighteenth century, thinkers in economics and biology were making conflict central to their theories. The conflict of self-interest and social interest pervades the work of Adam Smith. Thomas Malthus portrayed the struggle for existence in grim terms. And it was while reading Malthus that Charles Darwin was struck by the insight that the struggle for existence and the survival of the fittest are crucial to evolution.

Darwin's ideas were applied to the social order in the ideology of social Darwinism, the first phase of which was represented by Herbert Spencer and William Graham Sumner. They gave what was purported to be a scientific justification for the ruthless business tactics of the captains of industry of the nineteenth century. The business leaders were the "fittest" members of society, and the underprivileged, the "unfit," had to accept their fate in the name of the well-being of society. How could such ideas be accepted and promoted? Hofstadter suggested that "the answer is that American society saw its own image in the tooth-and-claw version of natural selection, and that its dominant groups were thus able to dramatize this vision of competition as a thing good in itself." [4]

Thus, social evolution was conceived of in terms analogous to biological evolution. Those who survived proved thereby that they were the fittest. And in nineteenth-century America, the captains of industry were the fittest, the victors in the harsh struggle for existence in the business world.

A series of sociologists in Europe and America, working primarily in the latter half of the nineteenth and first quarter of the twentieth century, rapidly developed conflict theory and used it to explain certain kinds of change. The major European sociologists include Gumplowicz, who argued that social and cultural evolution is totally the result of group conflict. Intergroup war is the social analogy of the struggle for existence and survival of the fittest. An inherent and deadly hatred prevails between diverse groups, people, and races, making conflict inevitable. Thus, "conquest and the satisfaction of needs through the labor of the conquered . . . is the great theme of human history." [5]

Another European, Pareto, characterized history in terms of "an interminable struggle for control." [6] The dominating group seeks to maintain and defend its position; force is the most important factor in maintaining stability. Violence may be necessary to restore social equilibrium when that equilibrium is upset. Such violence needs no moral justification, because it has the quality of regeneration, freeing man to follow the irrational dictates of his own nature.

Among the Americans, conflict was of central concern, and as Coser says, any view of social change "that did not include concern with conflict phenomena appeared to them seriously deficient." [7] Among these Americans was Sumner, whose social Darwinism modified as his thought developed. He veered away from his explicit bias in favor of the triumphant businessman. In *Folkways*, he saw the struggle for existence as

> a process in which an individual and nature are the parties . . . In the competition of life the parties are men and other organisms . . . The competition of life is the rivalry, antagonism, and mutual displacement in which the individual is involved with other organisms by his efforts to carry on the struggle for existence for himself.[8]

Albion Small and Lester Ward also stressed the role of conflict. The latter developed a theory similar to that of Gumplowicz. Ward asserted that every kind of structure, whether inorganic, organic, or social, is created by the interaction of antagonistic forces. Such interaction is a universal law, and the law means that structures continually change, passing from "a primordial stage of great simplicity into a more complex secondary stage." [9]

Unlike Gumplowicz, Ward does not attribute intergroup conflict to inherent hatred, but rather to inevitable encroachments by one group upon the rights and territory of the other. Out of intergroup conflict the state arises, and "to conflict between states is due the march forward to greater social efficiency and higher civilization. . . . ." [10]

More recently, change has been inextricably linked with conflict by Dahrendorf:

> I would suggest . . . that all that is creativity, innovation, and development in the life of the individual, his group, and his society is due, to no small extent, to the operation of conflicts between group and group, individual and individual, emotion and emotion within one individual.[11]

Dahrendorf argues that social conflict has a structural origin, namely, the dominance relations that prevail in all social organization. In other words, group conflict is to be "understood as a conflict about the legitimacy of relations of authority." [12]

Dahrendorf's perspective is more intricate than this brief examination can show, but the essence of his thought is contained in four propositions:

1. Every society is at every point subject to processes of change; social change is ubiquitous.
2. Every society displays at every point dissensus and conflict; social conflict is ubiquitous.
3. Every element in a society renders a contribution to its disintegration and change.
4. Every society is based on the coercion of some of its members by others.[13]

In sum, Dahrendorf argues that class conflict (conflict over or arising out of authority relations) leads to structure change (change in values or institutions). Such conflict is pervasive because authority relationships are pervasive. Consequently, change is ubiquitous.

We hardly need to be convinced that conflict is a pervasive fact of life in our own time. And as our historical survey shows, it has apparently characterized social life throughout recorded history. And the linkage that these thinkers make between conflict and change is a reasonable one. But is there evidence to support the relationship between conflict and change? Reasonable hypotheses are constructed to be examined in the light of empirical evidence; let us look at some of the evidence about competition, conflict, and change.

Competition, Conflict, and Change

Competition does not characterize all societies, but it is a prominent feature of most developed nations, particularly the capitalist nations. What are the effects of that competition? This section makes no pretense of being a complete study of competition and its effects. Various scholars have argued that cooperation is more natural than competition, that competition is dehumanizing, that competition within an organization may lower productivity, and that competition may diminish satisfaction with group participation. But the only question raised here is, can competition (which I am assuming is a variant of conflict) lead to change? And the answer is yes. This is not to say that competition always leads to change, nor that it leads to desired change, but only that change can result. The precise conditions under which competition produces change, and the kind of change that results, are matters for future investigation.

But there is little doubt that competition may lead to social change. In their study of change in organizations, Hage and Aiken identified competition as one factor that led to a high rate of program change. They defined program change "as the addition of new services or products." [14] They point out that in our society complex organizations of many kinds — universities, hospitals, schools, and profit-making organizations — are in the competitive arena. Universities, for example, compete with each other for quality instructors. And competition compels an organization towards a "dynamic style," forcing the organization to increase its rate of program change and its degree of complexity. And these changes, in turn, ultimately lead to change in various other characteristics of the organization.

Competition is also a factor in creativity and innovation. In his extensive study of innovation, Barnett identified competition as a "potent incentive when mutually desirable rewards are allocated on the basis of performance." [15] This potency is exemplified in the difference in scientific productivity in medicine in the United States, England, France, and Germany during the nineteenth century. [16] Ben-David used the number of scientific discoveries and the number of scientists making the discoveries as measures of productivity. He found that the number of discoveries continued to rise in the United States during the latter part of the century and in Germany during the middle part. During the same period, scientific medical creativity in England and France declined rather consistently. He also found "relatively smaller fluctuations" in the number of individuals entering scientific careers in Germany and in the United States as compared to other countries.

What accounted for these differences? Why did the science of medicine make its greatest advances in Germany and the United States from the middle of the century on, whereas England and France had shown clear leadership in the earlier part of the century? Ben-David argues that the difference must be sought in the organization of science in the various nations. The situation faced by the medical sciences at the beginning of the nineteenth century required the French and Germans to discover appropriate measures of evaluation and adequate support. Crucial decisions had to be made about scientific facilities, scientific roles, and scientific training, and the Germans made all the right decisions. But this was not due to the peculiar insight of individuals; rather, it resulted from the organization of science in the two nations.

Specifically, the German academic system was decentralized as a result of the "political dismemberment" of the Germans. The French possessed a unified academic system, with the greater part of it located in Paris. This decentralization in Germany seems to account for the difference in scientific productivity in the two nations, for it created academic competition, "and competition forced upon the individual institutions decisions which would not have been made otherwise, or at least not made at that time." [17]

Similarly, competition in the United States stimulated creative efforts and led to decisions that facilitated those efforts. In both the United States and Germany during their creative periods, valued rewards awaited the successful scientist. And the success of some stimulated others to pursue scientific careers. There was also pressure to expand facilities and training and to abandon outmoded techniques and structures. Increased opportunities for careers in research attracted increasing numbers of students (the number entering such careers in France and Britain fluctuated over the period). And underlying and prodding the whole development was competition among the varied segments of the medical world. The field of medicine was changing rapidly, and the driving mechanism of the change was competition.

It is equally clear that conflict leads to change. The Wilsons stressed this in their study of Central Africa.[18] In brief, they argue that numerous contradictions existed in Africa at the time of their study. The primary one was the ongoing conflict between races, with the Africans being subjected to discrimination and at the same time being the object of efforts at education and other improvements. The conflict between the Africans and Europeans was pervasive, occurring

> over land and erosion, over markets, over wages, over the training and employment of Africans in skilled work; and in the obvious inefficiencies of "over-production" and unemployment, together with hunger and preventable ill-health among the Africans.[19]

In addition, conflict occurred over the competition for African women, over various cultural matters such as beer-brewing and witchcraft, and between Europeans who feared and those who supported Africans.

In sum, the Wilsons found Central Africa convulsed by pervasive conflict, and the focal point of that conflict was the confrontation of the races. They called this conflict "radical" because "the existing social structure is inconsistent with itself, i.e., social pressure operates in contrary directions, and continues to do so however much particular partners may be changed." [20]   The Europeans despised and discriminated against the Africans on the one hand, and on the other they apparently strove to educate and "civilize" them.

The contradictions in Central Africa, the radical opposition that existed, could be resolved only through change: "The oppositions and maladjustments of Central Africa are . . . intolerable, and are compelling change." [21]   Needed were changes in the "material relations" among the people, religious changes, increased importance of impersonal relations, increased mobility, and so on. In other words, the traditional society of Central Africa was being transformed into a new kind of social order, and that transformation was being impelled by conflict.

Numerous other scholars have linked conflict with change, including creative change. Martindale described societal creativity that lasted for centuries; but the creative age was neither stable nor peaceful. Rather, such an age was generally experienced by the participants as one of unrest and tension.[22] The Renaissance stands out as a period of striking and creative change in contrast to the bleak age that preceded it. Durant has identified conflict as a factor in the flowering of creativity in Florence.[23] Finally, Coser points out that innovation was discouraged by the medieval guild system; individuals were not allowed to employ methods that gave them a productive advantage over others. By contrast, technological change in the modern West is rooted in the institutionalization of science as a tool for shaping man's existence; and the continual invention and technological change we now experience "was made possible with the gradual emergence of a pluralistic and hence conflict-charged structure of human relations." [24]

Clearly, conflict is a driving mechanism of change. But this is not to say that the change is always desirable from the point of view of those subjected to it. Furthermore, conflict may impede change as well as impel it, and some change may occur without conflict. The former point is made by Eisenstadt, who notes a number of cases of "breakdown of modernization" — in Indonesia, Pakistan, Burma, and Sudan, among others. [25] Specifically, constitutional governments seemed unable to cope with the problems and demands of the modern era, and they yielded to autocratic, authoritarian, or semiauthoritarian regimes. One "basic characteristic" in each case of the breakdown of modernization was the emergence of continuing intergroup conflict which was marked by intense antagonism. The groups involved were unable to create "any continuous and viable *modus vivendi*," [26] so that the conflict stifled development towards a modern, constitutional state.

The other point, that change can occur without conflict, is documented by the Andersons in their study of a Danish village. [27] The village had been a harbor community for two centuries. Then it changed, and the change was rapid and pervasive: "few aspects of the village's cultural inventory emerged without profound alteration." [28] But more striking perhaps than even the tempo and pervasiveness of the change was the fact that "the adjustment from maritime village to urban annex . . . has been embraced by an entire population *virtually without sociocultural conflict*." [29]

The Andersons attribute this to a number of factors. Initially, technological developments affected the village's industry, making that industry obsolete and creating an economic crisis. But the same technological progress resolved the problem, for the village was soon a suburb of Copenhagen. The population grew as workers from Copenhagen settled in the village. Transportation facilities developed to allow these new residents to commute; they also allowed native villagers to find employment in Copenhagen. Within a single generation, the village experienced a social and cultural revolution.

One factor that allowed this change to occur without conflict was the nature of the change; cultural patterns were not rooted up and discarded, but the new patterns were either created out of or conjoined with the old ones. A second factor was the absence of cultural lag; for example, the economic crisis created by the obsolescence of traditional village work was quickly resolved by opportunities for employment in Copenhagen.

A third factor was the absence of groups committed to "the exclusive adoption of either the old or the new cultural forms as symbols of a superior evaluation of culture choice." [30]   Finally, the change that occurred involved an increase in prestige.   Socially and economically, the prestige of the village was greatly enhanced through its new attachment with Copenhagen.

Thus, while conflict is a most important incentive to change, change may occur without conflict.   And when conflict does lead to change, that change may not be defined as desirable by those experiencing it.   The exact conditions under which conflict impels or impedes change, and those under which it impels change in a socially desirable direction, have yet to be specified.

GUN BARREL CHANGE: THE EFFECTS OF VIOLENCE

"Anything can grow out of the barrel of a gun."   So goes a well-known saying of Chairman Mao.   And there are those who would amend Mao slightly to say, "Any meaningful change must grow out of the barrel of a gun."   A 1969 cover of the *New Left Notes* depicted two urban guerillas along with the caption: ". . . war can only be abolished through war, and in order to get rid of the gun it is necessary to take up the gun." [31]   A 1971 Gallup Poll reported that 42 percent of college students surveyed believed that change in America would come through revolution in the next twenty-five years, and 44 percent felt that violence is sometimes justified in order to effect change (78 percent said they had pride in being an American, so the students apparently reflected a viewpoint about the difficulty of change rather than a general discontent with American life).[32]

Can violence bring about meaningful change?   What are the consequences of violence?   What evidence do we have to enable us to appraise intelligently the relationship between violence and change?   Before looking at the evidence and attempting a general appraisal, let us look at the diverse thinking about violence and change.

Violence in Thought and Theory

Some thinkers have argued that violence does little if anything to effect change, and that the change it does bring about is not the kind desired or anticipated.   A survey of violence associated with the American labor movement concluded: "The effect of labor violence was almost always harmful to the union.   There is little evidence that violence succeeded in gaining advantages for strikers." [33]   Hofstadter agreed with this general conclusion.   He noted that one quite effective tactic employed by labor was the series of sit-down strikes in the 1930's.   But in that case, while the workers were using "illegal force," they were acting "to avert rather than precipitate acts of outright violence." [34]

Hofstadter also made the point, as have others, that violence has often been employed to maintain the status quo and has seemed to be more effective for that purpose than for effecting change.   On the other hand, those who use violence to maintain the status quo may find their efforts to be counter-productive.   In the American labor movement, employers used more violence than the workers did, and employer violence served only to gain sympathy for workers and, ultimately, the legitimization of the union.

Finally, it has been argued that violence is but one alternative for effecting change.   Granted, the change may have come about through the agony of violence, but it could have been effected by other means.   In his study of agrarian reform in Colombia, Hirschman argued that sporadic and decentralized violence rather than revolution was sufficient to gain the reforms.   Contrary to Latin American practice, wholesale revolution was not necessary to bring about the change.[35]

This general perspective on the relationship between violence and change has been well summed up by Bienen, who reviewed the literature and offers us three propositions:

(1) Most social and political change does not result from violent revolution.   (2) Where violent revolutions have occurred they constitute much more of a watershed in a slower process than an immediate and radical reordering of society.   Moreover, watersheds can be found in nonrevolutionary societies too. . . .   (3) Large-scale violence can be associated with "the more things change, the more they remain the same," as Mosca pointed out with reference to violence in the Italian communes and the Greek states.[36]

A quite different argument is advanced by other thinkers, who see violence as a chief means of social reform.   In the United States, violence has been associated with the race problem from the days of slave insurrection to the present civil rights struggle; violence has also characterized the labor and woman suffrage movements. In each case, according to Drake, "it is clear that violence has been an important factor in accelerating the movement toward goals. . . ." [37]   He argues that the goals could not have been achieved by any less violent means.

A similar point has been made with reference to problems of change in countries with feudal-type social structures.   Flores, for example, has written that we must accept the need for revolutionary change in Latin America, and that sometimes the change must be violent. For a "harsh fact" of political action in Latin America is that "would-be reformers have faced the determined opposition of the landed elite, the armed forces, and the Catholic Church, as well as . . . the almost inevitable and generally decisive interference of the United States on the side of all three." [38] Even Hofstadter conceded that violence may successfully implement needed change in the special case of "backward" people who have "a firm territorial base and a history of colonial exploitation." [39]

This latter point emphasizes the fact that the utility of violence depends upon the context. And none of the thinkers we are discussing has a moral commitment to violence per se. Those who assert the need of violence do so out of their hatred of oppression rather than from love of violence. And they do so because they see no other way to effect change.

As we have seen, Marx made this point in his theory of change. Revolution, he argued, is necessary both to shatter the existing irrational social order and to cleanse those who have been oppressed by that order. Violence may be abhorrent to those who are comfortable and satisfied, but to those who have been oppressed, violence is the hammer that shatters their chains.

A modification of the argument that violence is necessary involves the utility, as a stimulus to change, of the threat or fear of violence. This, of course, probably demands at least occasional actual violence; but it also means that violence itself is not always necessary. For example, the threat of violence posed by White Citizens Councils in the American South "strengthened the hand of southern moderates in trying to restrain civil rights action from Washington," but the threat posed by the Black Muslims and CORE "strengthens the position of the NAACP in seeking concessions from Southern Whites and action by the Justice Department." [40]

A concrete example is provided by the black struggle for equal public accommodations in Maryland in the early 1960's. Public facilities were segregated in 1960, and nothing seemed able to move the legislature to enact a public accommodation bill. Then groups of blacks led by CORE and a local civil rights group began a series of sit-ins, wade-ins at beaches, marches, and picketing of offices of officials. By 1963, Baltimore and the state of Maryland had passed the public accommodation bills. In this case, violence came from those opposing the blacks and elicited sympathy for their cause. And the success of the effort seems to stem from something other than its own power (relatively few people were ever involved). One factor, in addition to the broader base of support the blacks gained through being the objects of violence, was the fear of violence and civil disorder that was based upon other situations (including the state's own example at Cambridge).[41]

Thus, we have concrete examples of how the fear or threat of violence can effect change. Let us turn now to some of the evidence about the effects of violence itself. Then we shall try to draw some general conclusions about the relation of violence to change.

Violence and Change

As with conflict, if we ask the question: can violence effect change? the answer is clearly yes. And it can do so in more than the counter-productive sense noted above. That is, violence brings about change desired by those who employ it as well as change that the violence was designed to quell. Many revolutions have been nothing more than a "change of the palace guard." But many revolutions have effected radical change in the social structure and social life of nations. The Mexican Revolution of 1910 shattered the old social order and marked the beginning of Mexico's emergence into the modern era. In the ensuing years, land reform, new educational opportunities, economic growth, and significant changes in the stratification system were among the altered aspects of Mexican society.[42]

We could delineate similar effects of the revolutions in such countries as Bolivia, Cuba, and China. The extent to which revolution effects change in a nation varies enormously, of course. But the point is that revolution is one form of violence that clearly can effect radical change. The change may be minimal; the American Revolution was little more than a minor political change. Or it may be massive. The Communist Revolution in China radically changed that nation. In fact, it is impossible to fully capture the nature of the change in a few paragraphs, but Edgar Snow has expressed for us something of the spirit of the new China:

> Collective life in new China was above all change and movement. Elements carried over from the past were engaged in dynamic combination and recombination, with new elements of the time-present which was itself always becoming a future something-else . . . China was not simply a different country; its obsessive haste to catch up with history and to become the world's greatest nation . . . was positively awesome to those who could remember a passive China in which time meant nothing.[43]

There are ways other than revolution in which violence may effect change. War between nations has historically been a stimulant to technological change. From Archimedes' work on trajectories and machines to repulse the Roman attack on Syracuse to the American scientists who fashioned the atomic bomb in order to conquer Japan, technological developments have historically been prodded on by wars.

There is also a strong correlation between violence within a nation and the level of socioeconomic development. The relationship seems to be curvilinear. That is, as the nation begins to develop, internal conflict increases. But with the attainment of full modernization, defined in terms of near-universal adult literacy, and as the GNP per capita rises well above subsistence level, internal conflict subsides.[44] This, however, does not tell us about any causal relation. It is an open question to what extent the development is impelled by the internal violence of the modernizing nations.

Finally, violence may effect change in the context of social movements within a nation. As noted earlier, this is disputed by some, but there seems to be clear evidence that violence has, as Drake has argued, enabled various movements to attain at least some of their goals. Even if the violence itself does not lead directly to change, it may produce the fear or threat that stimulates change in another situation.

Furthermore, violence may have a psychological function for the members of a social movement in that an act of violence seals the commitment of the individual to the movement. Commitment to the Black Power Movement was found to involve "bridge-burning" acts, acts of violence that insured as well as symbolized the individual's commitment to the movement.[45] And since commitment of members is indispensable to the success of a movement, the violence was an important factor in securing change.

What conclusions can we draw about the relation of violence to change? The first is obvious: violence can effect change. Numerous studies indicate that change follows both directly and indirectly in the wake of violence.

But a second conclusion is to qualify the above by noting the cases of violence without change or without much significant change. The American and French Revolutions effected certain political changes, but had little consequence for the social and cultural life of the masses of people in those nations. Such revolutions have been of practically no effect in comparison with the mercantile and industrial revolutions. That is, changes generated by technological developments may have far greater consequences for the lives of most people than those that follow from violence. And in a developed nation like the United States, the major effect of violence on change may be either the indirect effect (producing fear or threat and gaining commitment of individuals to a move-

146

ment) or the counter-productive effect (violence produces precisely the opposite of what those who employed it desired). The report of the Riot Commission supports this, for the survey of twenty disorders in 1967 concluded that little had changed and that in some cases the situation seemed to have worsened.[46]

Third, not only is there violence without change, but there is also change without violence. This was Hofstadter's point about violence in America. Social reforms in the United States, he argued, are primarily the result of intensive and long-term campaigns of reformers, who make much use of education and propaganda but little if any use of violence:

> The entire apparatus of the welfare state, from child labor laws, wage-hour regulation, industrial safety laws, and workmen's compensation to legally regulated collective bargaining, social security, and medical care for the aged is the achievement of active minorities which, while sometimes militant and always persistent, were also patient and nonviolent.[47]

Fourth, violence may be one alternative among others for effecting any specific kind of change. To recognize that certain changes followed from the exercise of violence is not to say that the change could not have occurred without the violence. The work of Gandhi, Martin Luther King, Jr., the Rev. Jesse Jackson, and others illustrates how change may be effected in the context of an insistence on nonviolence. For nonviolence does not mean lack of force. On the contrary, the method of Satyagraha developed by Gandhi involved "the Force which is born of Truth and Love."[48] The "force" is applied by a series of increasingly stronger means of gaining one's objective, ranging from an initial effort to persuade through reason to nonviolent coercion, which involves such things as refusal to cooperate and civil disobedience.

In other words, violence is not the only behavior that fits into the category of "coercive." Another tactic that has been employed is disruption of services, an effort to alter national priorities by tactics that intensify tension in urban areas.[49]   Rent strikes and the organizing of the poor to claim welfare benefits are among the tactics that have been used. The effects of these tactics have yet to be determined, but national concern with the problem of welfare in the 1970's indicates that at least the political leaders have been compelled to examine the situation. And many of those political leaders have spoken about the need to reorder national priorities.

A fifth conclusion is that violence may be counter-productive. This is a difficult point, for how does one assess the consequences of violent versus nonviolent approaches? How does one determine when violence pays off in terms of meaningful change, and when the costs of violence are greater than any benefits which may be gained? We cannot decide this simply on the basis of the cost of the violence, for we must also take into account the cost of not changing (assuming that violence is necessary to effect the change). For example, Moore notes that a reasonable estimate of those who died as a result of revolutionary repression in France would be around 35,000 to 40,000; but he also points out that in all probability the "death rate of the *ancien régime* from such factors as preventable starvation and injustice" would have been at least as high if not higher.[50]

In other words, the use of violence is risky in terms of costs and benefits, but so is the willingness to tolerate a repressive status quo. Furthermore, as we have shown above, the use of violence may impede the change desired or even lead to the opposite of that which is desired. In May, 1886, the movement to gain an eight-hour day for workers was reaching its peak, and many people were optimistic about the outcome. Then a bomb was thrown in Haymarket Square in Chicago on May 4, killing seven policemen and wounding dozens more. The eight-hour day movement was brought to a screeching halt. Gatherings of strikers were broken up by the police, who claimed to have discovered anarchist plots. Workers themselves were confused and divided about the violence. Some people, including some writing in the press, connected the bombing with the agitation for the eight-hour day.

The events of the time have not yet been completely untangled, but one thing is clear. Two social movements intersected in Chicago, and the violence of the one killed the hopes of the other: "As a mass movement, eight-hour agitation was stopped in its tracks."[51]

One final conclusion that comes from our examination of violence and change is that whether violence is necessary seems to depend upon whether there are structural means for effecting change. That is, the very rigid social structure that exercises a feudal type of control over people may be broken by nothing less than violent revolution. One could seriously doubt that China or the Latin American nations that have begun to develop would have progressed without revolution. The only nation in Spanish America to escape civil war during the eighteenth and nineteenth centuries was Paraguay. But the cost of this stability was despotism. And one of the despots, Francisco Lopez, was responsible for leading his nation into a disastrous war with Argentina, Brazil, and Uruguay. It was the "most savage and sanguinary war in all the records of Latin America," and for Paraguay it meant "virtual extinction. Cautious estimate suggests her population was reduced from 525,000 in 1865 to 221,000 in 1871," and only 28,746 men were among those surviving the havoc.[52] A rigid social structure culminated in greater violence for the nation than any civil war would have been likely to produce.

Thus, violence does produce change. But change occurs without violence, and violence occurs without change. In some cases, violence may be necessary in order to break down a rigid social order. For the most part, violence seems to be only one alternative among others for effecting particular change. And it is an alternative that is increasingly perilous. As Martin Luther King, Jr., has eloquently written:

> If we assume that mankind has a right to survive then we must find an alternative to war and destruction. In a day when sputniks dash through outer space and guided ballistic missiles are carving highways of death through the stratosphere, nobody can win a war. The choice today is no longer between violence and nonviolence. It is either nonviolence or nonexistence.[53]

ENDNOTES TO CHAPTER 8

1. Max Weber, *From Max Weber: Essays in Sociology*, trans. and ed. H. H. Gerth and C. Wright Mills (New York: Oxford University Press, 1958), p. 333.
2. Don Martindale, *The Nature and Types of Sociological Theory* (Boston: Houghton Mifflin Company, 1960), p. 142.
3. Quoted in Howard Becker and Harry Elmer Barnes, *Social Thought from Lore to Science*, Vol. 2, 3rd edition (New York: Dover Publications, Inc., 1961), p. 705.
4. Richard Hofstadter, *Social Darwinism in American Thought: 1860–1915* (Philadelphia: University of Pennsylvania Press, 1944), p. 174.
5. Ludwig Gumplowicz, *Outlines of Sociology*, ed. Irving L. Horowitz (New York: Paine-Whitman, 1963), p. 203.
6. James H. Meisel, ed., *Pareto & Mosca* (Englewood Cliffs: Prentice-Hall, Inc., 1965), p. 13.
7. Lewis A. Coser, *The Functions of Social Conflict* (Glencoe: The Free Press, 1956), p. 18.
8. William Graham Sumner, *Folkways* (Boston: Ginn and Company, 1906), p. 16.
9. Becker and Barnes, *Social Thought from Lore to Science*, p. 719.
10. *Ibid.*, p. 721.
11. Ralf Dahrendorf, *Class and Class Conflict in Industrial Society* (Stanford: Stanford University Press, 1959), p. 208.
12. *Ibid.*, p. 176.

13. *Ibid.*, p. 162.
14. Jerald Hage and Michael Aiken, *Social Change in Complex Organizations* (New York: Random House, 1970), p. 13.
15. H. G. Barnett, *Innovation: The Basis of Cultural Change* (New York: McGraw-Hill, 1953), p. 72.
16. Joseph Ben-David, "Scientific Productivity and Academic Organization in Nineteenth-Century Medicine," in *Comparative Perspectives on Formal Organization*, ed. Henry A. Landsberger (Boston: Little, Brown and Company, 1970), pp. 195–214.
17. *Ibid.*, p. 206. See also Donald C. Pelz and Frank M. Andrews, *Scientists In Organizations* (New York: John Wiley & Sons, 1966), pp. 7, 151, 259ff. The authors provide evidence that scientists in organizations are more effective under conditions of competition and intellectual rivalry.
18. Godfrey Wilson and Monica Wilson, *The Analysis of Social Change* (Cambridge: Cambridge University Press, 1968). This work was first published in 1945.
19. *Ibid.*, p. 136.
20. *Ibid.*, p. 126.
21. *Ibid.*, p. 153.
22. Don Martindale, *Social Life and Cultural Change* (Princeton: D. Van Nostrand Co., Inc., 1962), pp. 71–72.
23. Will Durant, *The Renaissance* (New York: Simon and Schuster, 1953), p. 73.
24. Lewis A. Coser, "Social Conflict and the Theory of Social Change," *The British Journal of Sociology*, VIII (Sept., 1957), 199.
25. S. N. Eisenstadt, "Breakdowns of Modernization," in *Readings in Social Evolution and Development*, ed. S. N. Eisenstadt (Oxford: Pergamon Press, 1970). Eisenstadt wrote this paper in 1962–63.
26. *Ibid.*, p. 427.
27. Robert T. Anderson and Barbara Gallatin Anderson, *The Vanishing Village: A Danish Maritime Community* (Seattle: University of Washington Press, 1964).
28. *Ibid.*, p. 138.
29. *Ibid.*
30. *Ibid.*, p. 143.
31. Richard Hofstadter, "Reflections on Violence in the United States," in *American Violence: A Documentary History*, ed. Richard Hofstadter and Michael Wallace (New York: Vintage Books, 1970), p. 29.
32. *St. Louis Post-Dispatch*, Jan. 21, 1971, pp. 1D and 7D.
33. Philip Taft and Philip Ross, "American Labor Violence: Its Causes, Character, and Outcome," in *The History of Violence in America*, ed. Hugh Davis Graham and Ted Robert Gurr (New York: Bantam Books, 1969), p. 382.

34. Hofstadter, "Reflection on Violence," p. 37.
35. Albert O. Hirschman, "Revolution by Stealth! The Case for Sequential Reforms," in *Economic Development: Evolution or Revolution?* ed. Laura Randall (Boston: D. C. Heath and Company, 1964), pp. 76–106.
36. Henry Bienen, *Violence and Social Change* (Chicago: The University of Chicago Press, 1968), p. 78.
37. St. Clair Drake, "Urban Violence and American Social Movements," in *Urban Riots: Violence and Social Change* (New York: Vintage Books, 1968), p. 23.
38. Edmundo Flores, "Land Reform and the Alliance for Progress," in *Economic Development*, ed. Laura Randall, p. 42.
39. Hofstadter, "Reflections on Violence," p. 34.
40. H. L. Nieburg, "The Threat of Violence and Social Change," *American Political Science Review*, LVI (1962), 872.
41. Donald Von Eschen, Jerome Kirk, and Maurice Pinard, "The Conditions of Direct Action in a Democratic Society," *The Western Political Quarterly*, XXII (June, 1969), 309–25.
42. See, for example, Joseph A. Kahl, *Comparative Perspectives on Stratification: Mexico, Great Britain, Japan* (Boston: Little, Brown and Company, 1968), pp. 1–30.
43. Edgar Snow, *Red China Today* (New York: Vintage Books, 1970), p. 185.
44. Ivo K. Feierabend, Rosalind L. Feierabend, and Betty A. Nesvold, "Social Change and Political Violence: Cross-National Patterns," in Graham and Gurr, *The History of Violence in America*, pp. 653–68.
45. Luther P. Gerlach and Virginia H. Hine, *People, Power, Change: Movements of Social Transformation* (Indianapolis: The Bobbs-Merrill Company, Inc., 1970), pp. 142ff.
46. *Report of the National Advisory Commission on Civil Disorders* (New York: Bantam Books, 1968), p. 151.
47. Hofstadter, "Reflections on Violence," p. 38.
48. Joan V. Bondurant, *Conquest of Violence* (Berkeley and Los Angeles: University of California Press, 1969), p. 8.
49. Frances Pivan and Richard Cloward, "Disrupting City Services to Change National Priorities," in *Where It's At: Radical Perspectives in Sociology*, ed. Steven E. Deutsch and John Howard (New York: Harper & Row, 1970), pp. 471–80.
50. Barrington Moore, Jr., *Social Origins of Dictatorship and Democracy* (Boston: Beacon Press, 1966), pp. 103–104.
51. Kurt Lang and Gladys Engel Lang, *Collective Dynamics* (New York: Thomas Y. Crowell Co., 1961), p. 516.
52. Hubert Herring, *A History of Latin America* (New York: Alfred A. Knopf, 1957), pp. 674–75.
53. Martin Luther King, Jr., "Pilgrimage to Nonviolence," in *Instead of Violence*, ed. Arthur and Lila Weinberg (New York: Grossman Publishers, 1963), p. 74.

CHAPTER 9

Structural Sources: Government and Status Anguish

A girl sat alone in a small room, taking part in an experiment designed to discover the kinds of personal problems faced by college students. She was part of a group, each other member of which was also in a small room in order to assure anonymity. They conversed with each other by intercom. One of the students discussed his problem of seizures. When it was his turn to talk again, he suddenly became loud, grew increasingly incoherent, choked, then became silent. Apparently he had had one of his seizures.

What would the girl do under such circumstances? What do you suppose you would do? The situation just described was actually created by two psychologists in an effort to determine how people react to emergencies. They found that different girls responded quite differently. Some would leave their cubicles to try to find help for the student who had apparently had the seizure (the seizure was feigned). But others did not. What made the difference? Were some simply more concerned about human beings than others? Were there significant personality differences that explained the different responses? The experimenters found that personality differences did not account for the different responses. Rather, a most significant variable was group size. If the girl thought that the "group" was composed of only herself and the victim of the seizure, she was far more likely to go for help than if she thought there were six in the group! And she was likely to respond far more quickly than if she thought there were six in the group.

To sum up the results of the experiment, 85 percent of sub-jects in two-person groups, 62 percent in three-person groups, and 31 percent in six-person groups reported the emergency before the victim's voice was cut off. All subjects in the two-person groups eventually reported it, but only 62 percent of those in the six-person groups went for help.[1]

What this experiment stresses is a major point made by sociologists: much human behavior can be understood in terms of the structure in which it takes place rather than in terms of the personalities of those involved. This same point is made by Hage and Aiken in their study of program change in welfare agencies. They reported that structural properties such as centralization, formalization, and stratification "were much more highly as-sociated with the rate of program change than attitudes toward change."[2] And this implies, they note, that an organization's structure may be far more significant in effecting change than the particular mix of personalities in the organization.

In this and the next chapter, therefore, we shall look at some aspects of the social structure that might account for the direction of change. In every society, there is a government, a group of people who have problems with status (who are, that is, structur-ally marginal), a group of elites, and youth. These two chapters will show the effect on change of each of these facets of the social structure.

CHANGE FROM THE CENTER: GOVERNMENT

Government today is pervasive. As Peter Drucker has pointed out, "the most despotic government of 1900 would not have dared probe into the private affairs of its citizens as income-tax collectors now do routinely in the freest society."[3] Drucker also emphasizes the great size of government: "There is no country in the world today where the entire government establishment of 1910 could not comfortably be housed in the smallest of the new government buildings now going up, with room to spare for a grand-opera house and a skating rink."[4] Every local, state, and federal govern-ment agency that existed in the time of Theodore Roosevelt in the United States could easily be put into the regional federal building in Denver.

In other words, both the massiveness and the pervasiveness of government indicate that we ought to examine its effects on change. But books on change generally have little to say about the effect of government, unless the focus is on political change or modernization. Government is indeed an extraordinarily important factor in modernization in the contemporary world; but it is important also in the developed nations — either as a barrier or as a leader of change.

Government as a Barrier to Change

In the Marxist view, the state is a reactionary organization that serves the interests of the propertied class and, thereby, impedes necessary change. As Engels put it, the state generally is "the state of the most powerful, economically dominant class, which, through the medium of the state, becomes also the politically dominant class, and thus acquires new means of holding down and exploiting the oppressed class." [5]

This, of course, is completely contrary to the view of government which many American students have acquired in civics courses. Those courses often teach that the government exists to serve us, that it reflects the interests of all of us. But it seems historically obvious that the government has hardly served the interests of blacks, or American Indians, or the impoverished. Indeed, the composition of the government should lead us to doubt that it could effectively serve such groups, for the government has always been composed for the most part of the middle and upper strata of society. In his study of the American political elite, Mills said: "The first big fact about elite American politicians as a whole is that they have never been representative of a cross-section of the American people." [6] Nearly 60 percent have come from prosperous backgrounds; only about 18 percent have had lower-class origins, and only 5 percent have come from the very lowest class.

Government in the United States has sometimes been described in terms of "creeping socialism." But whatever degree of socialism has entered American life, it has not benefited the lowest groups. In 1910, the 20 percent of the American population receiving the lowest personal income got 8 percent of the total income; by 1964, the lowest 20 percent was receiving only 4 percent.[7] The great heap of legislation that presumably redistributed income during the intervening years helped the middle strata rather than the lower groups.

In terms of helping people's quality of life, the government has often been a barrier for at least some segments of the population. This is evident not only in the United States, but perhaps even more so in some foreign nations. In Latin America, as we noted in the last chapter, the combination of the Church, the military, the landed elite, and the United States government has often proved decisive in maintaining the peasant in a state of oppression.

And the government of many a nation has traditionally been

an oppressive factor for the majority of the people of that nation. This has created a problem for government-directed contemporary change. For the peasants have come to see government agents as little more than their enemies. With justification, they regard government and government agents with extreme suspicion, hampering the work of contemporary governments that sincerely desire to improve the lot of the people.[8]

Govenment as a Force for Change

In spite of government's role as a barrier to certain kinds of changes, it has directed many other kinds. In the United States, the government has been an important factor in change throughout our history, despite the popular ideology that upholds "free enterprise." Even in the days when the ideology of social Darwinism sat upon the throne of men's thought, the government played an important part in the changes that were occurring in the country. But the changes were primarily for the benefit of the business elite, and were defined therefore in terms that made the government's role seem negligible. As someone has said, many Americans feel that what the government does for them is progress, while what it does for others is socialism.

Our ignorance of history blinds us to the present as well. Never has government been quite the disinterested bystander that some ideologies have portrayed it as being. The initial exploration of America resulted from governmental financing, and the first colonists came because of English corporations that were subsidized by the crown. In the days of our early growth, the government seized more and more land away from the Indians and employed the military to "protect" the western-bound pioneers; many early farmers were subsidized in terms of the lives of Indians.

The Homestead Act of 1862 gave farmers great tracts of land. Business was stimulated by the building of canals, subsidies to railroads, and the tolerance of the ruthlessness of the robber barons. Aid to science began at an early date with such things as the Lewis and Clark expedition and the federal grant to Samuel Morse for the building of a telegraph line between Baltimore and Washington, D.C.

The government has been prominent in stimulating education. Before the Constitutional Convention, the government designated large tracts of public land for educational use. The Morrill Act of 1862 gave to each state an amount of public land that was proportionate to its number of Representatives. Money received from the sale of the land could be used for practical education (such as agriculture and engineering).

Thus, the American government has been active in all the

major changes that have occurred in our history. The industrialization of the nation, the growth of education and science, the pattern of land usage, and other large new developments have all been given impetus by government action and government aid. In all this, the government has acted in behalf of particular interests; certain groups in the nation have benefited very little from these activities. But the point is that the direction of change in America must be understood at least in part in terms of government.

A similar situation obtained in Japan, where the government was, if anything, even more actively involved in the modernization of the nation. The government involved, of course, was a new government created by the Meiji Restoration of 1868. "The new government was in essence an oligarchy in the hands of fewer than one hundred young men." [9] This government embarked upon a program to bring Japan swiftly into the modern world. Various tools of modernization were quickly borrowed from the West, including administrative techniques, the Western calendar, religious toleration, a civil service, a national banking system, a modernized currency, a Cabinet, and a Constitution. The Ministry of Education was instituted in 1871, and Japan quickly headed for universal education; it became the first nation in Asia to have a literate population. The government stimulated the industrialization of the nation by creating and controlling such services as railways, the telegraph, and public utilities, and by stimulating enterprise through loans or other methods. The few private capitalists of the early days of development were given government aid and patronage.

In sum, the core of Japanese modernization was government activity. This may be seen clearly by examining a particular facet of change — the development of science and technology. The Japanese quickly saw science and technology as essential to modernization, and the government took the lead in introducing and developing them. "At huge costs to the national treasury, foreign teachers, specialists, and technology were imported, students sent abroad, foreign books translated." [10] Many of the educational institutions that would further scientific development were established in the Meiji era. Tokyo University was founded in 1877 and was reorganized with the College of Technology in 1886, becoming Tokyo Imperial University.

In 1870 the government set up a Ministry of Engineering which guided the development of railways, telegraphic services, and modern techniques of industrial management. Although foreign advisers were important initially, Japanese scholars and technicians were quickly trained. The aim of the whole process was to create a strong nation, so that military development was also pursued avidly.

The government had a practical end, the building of a great nation, and the swiftness of change towards that end was impressive. Before the end of the Meiji era, the Japanese had developed "an important capacity in heavy industry, with obvious military implications. Facilities for shipbuilding, iron and steel production, coal mining, machine production, and electric power were all given government support for the development of military and industrial power." [11]

Thus, the government is a potent source of change, and much of the direction of change in any society with a strong central government must be understood in terms of the activity of that government. Much government activity will be seen to benefit particular segments of the population — generally those segments which are already fairly well off. But some government action benefits the lower strata; such action is likely to result from the perception of threat.

An interesting example of the latter is reform in Iran.[12] In January, 1963, the Shah launched a "White Revolution" that offered six points of reform. Six additional points were later added to the Revolution. The points included land reform, nationalization of forests and pastures, profit sharing in the industrial sector, inclusion of women in the electoral laws, efforts to improve health and increase literacy, educational reform, and others.

The threat that impelled this program came not from the peasants but from the new middle class, who rejected the traditional sociopolitical arrangements. The Shah's program, therefore, was aimed at maintaining traditional power patterns by gaining the support of the peasants; and the support of the peasants was to be gained through the various reform measures. Iranian modernization, like all modernization in the contemporary world, was centered around the government as the government responded to the threat posed by the new middle class. And this leads us to our final topic about government — its role in modernization.

Government and Modernization

It is generally conceded that a strong state is the sine qua non of contemporary modernization.[13] But to some scholars a "strong" state is equivalent to an authoritarian state, while others argue that a democratic state may achieve the same things and do so more humanely.[14] Some point out that democracy will impede economic growth, because that growth necessarily requires the direction of experts and the willingness of the people to sacrifice current consumption for long-term economic gains. Others argue that authoritarian regimes exact their own cost in both economic and social terms, and that a pluralistic or democratic system provides a creative base for building the economy.

The issue is muddied by the fact that both sides can marshal evidence; both authoritarian and democratic nations have had both low and high rates of growth. One possible way of resolving the question is to say that in the contemporary world there is a need for authoritarianism in the early stages of development and for increasing participation of the citizenry as growth proceeds.[15]

Another possible way of resolving the problem is to distinguish between the form and the activity of the government. We saw with respect to ideology that we could distinguish between function and content; that is, diverse ideologists could create solidarity among people and so facilitate change. We can make the same distinction with government: diverse forms of government can provide the same essential functions that facilitate modernization. Those functions, according to Staley, fall into three broad categories: "(1) creating the physical and social foundations for development; (2) overall planning and integration of development; (3) bringing about larger and more efficient production and distribution of goods and services."[16]

There seems to be little inherent reason why such functions could not be handled by either a democratic or an authoritarian government. A slightly different approach to the necessary functions of government has been taken by Eckstein, who specifies five conditions under which the government is likely to play a lesser or greater role in economic growth. Specifically, the role of the government is likely to be greater

1. the greater the "range of ends" and the higher the aspirations for attainment;
2. the more rapidly the growth is to be achieved;
3. the "more unfavorable the factor and resource endowments";
4. the stronger the institutional impediments to economic growth; and
5. "the more backward the economy in relative terms."[17]

These conditions require governmental intervention if the society is to modernize. But, again, there seems to be no inherent reason why different forms of government could not intervene equally well under the above conditions.

In sum, I would not dispute the point that government is essential to modernization among the developing nations today. And the government must be a strong one in order to provide the requisite social, political, and economic conditions for modernization to proceed. But whether we opt for an authoritarian or a democratic government must be decided on other grounds than their relative efficiency in economic growth. At least in view of what we now know about modernization, including economic growth, the functions of government appear far more crucial than its form.

CHANGE FROM THE PERIPHERY: STATUS ANGUISH

Imagine a psychiatrist, a respected and wealthy man, who is hailed by a policeman one day. The policeman calls the psychiatrist "boy" and treats him with obvious contempt. Nor is this an isolated incident, for many people with whom the psychiatrist comes in contact relate to him as though he were their inferior.

The psychiatrist is not really an imaginary character. He is black, and he lives in the American South. And the treatment he received from the policeman and from numerous other whites happened in the recent past. How does he respond to this? He has education, a prestigious occupation, and wealth. But his social milieu does not accord him the prestige that is rightfully his. He suffers from what I have called "status anguish," a psychic distress that arises when there is contradiction in the individual's status set.

Status Anguish and Consistency

It has often been argued that man strives for consistency. Social psychologists have developed a number of theories that explain behavior on the basis of man's drive to attain cognitive consistency. Sociologists have pointed to man's drive to attain status consistency, congruence between various aspects of a status or between differing statuses. As the example of the black psychiatrist illustrates, however, man often faces situations and perhaps even an entire existence in which consistency eludes him. He must come to terms then with status anguish. Status anguish includes marginality, status inconsistency, and status withdrawal. We shall now explain these and look at their relation to social change.

Marginality

One type of status anguish that has been identified is marginality. An early essay by Hughes linked marginality with social change.[18] Marginality, or the "marginal man," was first defined by Robert Park in 1928. According to Park, a marginal man is one who is

living and sharing intimately in the cultural life and traditions of two distinct peoples; never quite willing to break,
even if he were permitted to do so, with his past and his
traditions, and not quite accepted, because of racial prejudice, in the new society in which he now sought to find
a place.[19]

In other words, marginality is existence in two or more social
worlds without being fully a part of any of them.

Marginality generates psychic distress, and Hughes noted five
different ways in which an individual might strive to reduce his
marginality.   One would be to give up the struggle and return to
an earlier status (the black psychiatrist would simply accept his
inferior position and identify fully with his own people).   A second
would be to let one of the statuses disappear as a status (being
black would have no relationship per se to status).   A third course
would be to "resign from the status which interferes with . . . other
status aims." [20]   If he used this alternative, the black psychiatrist
would have to renounce his own people.   Fourth, the individual
might find one or more of his statuses redefined in such a manner
as to resolve the contradiction (psychiatry might degenerate in
prestige to the point where the psychiatrist is like a fortune teller in
status).   Finally, the social system might change or be changed so
that the marginal group would become an integral part of the
whole (black professionals might be defined differently from other
blacks and given a position of prestige within the society).   Thus,
in Hughes' formulation, some kind of change — at either the individual or the societal level — is required for the reduction of
marginality.

Status Inconsistency

A second type of status anguish arises from the lack of what
has been variously called status crystallization, status congruency,
or status consistency.   As Lenski has argued, this is a "non-
vertical dimension" of status.[21]   That is, status is not a unidimen-
sional phenomenon but a "series of positions in a series of related
hierarchies."   An individual might rank consistently or inconsis-
tently in four hierarchies — income, occupation, education, and
ethnicity.   Furthermore, Lenski asserted that the more people
there were who suffered from acute status inconsistency, the more
people there would be who would support programs of social
change.

Lenski's thesis has been subjected to considerable debate and
study.   Some researchers report findings that dispute the thesis,

while others have reported that individuals suffering status inconsistency may react in a variety of ways, including the development of psychophysiological symptoms.[22]

Status Withdrawal

A third type of status anguish was identified by Hagen in his description of economic development. As we have seen, he placed strong emphasis on the fact that a group in a society may undergo status withdrawal. We need not accept all of the dynamics of Hagen's analysis to see the applicability of his idea in certain historical cases, and we shall examine one of these cases — Japan — in the next section.

In sum, we have examined briefly three types of status anguish that have been identified as forces of change. The first, marginality, was developed with specific reference to second-generation immigrants. As members of the second generation tried to move from the ethnic community into the mainstream of American life, they commonly found themselves in a marginal position with respect to both. They were involved in two different social worlds but were not fully a part of either, and they endured considerable psychic stress as a result of their marginal status. Hughes argued that such a status was a factor in change as well as a result of rapid change.

The second type, status inconsistency, was formulated by Lenski in an effort to see if political behavior could be illuminated by relating such behavior to inconsistencies in the societal stratification system. Such inconsistency would presumably be applicable to diverse groups and individuals within a society. And the inconsistency could be rooted in religious affiliation, ethnic background, changes in occupational prestige without a concomitant change in income, and in a number of other factors.

The third type, status withdrawal, would involve the loss of status by a particular group that once possessed it. In effect, this group would be downwardly mobile over time. This kind of status anguish differs from the first type, marginality, which implies efforts at upward mobility, and the second type, status inconsistency, which has no *necessary* reference to mobility (though mobility along one dimension could easily create the inconsistency).

While there are differences in them, therefore, all three indicate problematic status, and all three have been identified with change. I use the term "status anguish" to include the three types of problematic status that may impel a group to strive for change.

We shall now examine some evidence that supports the notion that status anguish is a driving mechanism of change.

Status Anguish and Change

The thesis that status anguish leads to change is based upon the assumption that a moral order prevails with respect to status; that is, people expect consistency between various facets of their status and between various statuses. The business executive does not expect to be, and probably would not be asked to be, an envelope stuffer for a charity drive; rather, he might be the honorary chairman of the drive. Thus, our experience as well as our intuition tells us that the assumption of a moral order is correct.

But there is more. We could fill pages with examples from the literature that support the notion that status consistency is generally conceived of in terms of a moral order. Let us take note of just two. In an experiment, subjects who considered themselves equal in ability were given different voting weights. Another set of subjects in the experiment were given voting weights in accordance with their supposed ability. The former was a case of status inconsistency, and the latter one of consistency. The researchers found that inconsistency tended to lead to interpersonal conflict.[23]

A second example comes from the organizational context. Middle-class girls were found to be far more dissatisfied with their jobs in a French clerical agency than were working-class girls. In fact, a knowledge of status on the job and status outside the work context made it possible to predict work satisfaction in 85 percent of the cases: ". . . status discrepancies between the role on the job and that outside the job are so important that they obliterate all other influences."[24]

When we turn to historical evidence, we find many instances of groups at the cutting edge of change which are characterized by some form of status anguish. The industrialization of England was driven forward by a disproportionate number of religious nonconformists. In Colombia, where three valleys were settled by the Spanish conquerors, only one of the groups of settlers, the Antioquenos, failed to develop landed estates. In modern times, this group became leaders of the economic and political modernization of Colombia; significantly, this group was also viewed with disdain by the other two during the eighteenth and nineteenth centuries. In India, various minority social groups have led the development of business. The examples could be multiplied, but, in general, a traditional society has tended to modernize more quickly "if there was any articulate group of men in it with reason to be unhappy about their position."[25]

This thesis becomes even clearer when we examine in somewhat more detail the leaders of the Meiji Restoration and subsequent modernization of Japan. And at this point it is evident that the categories in this chapter overlap; that is, we have already indicated the centrality of the government in Japan's modernization, and now we find it relevant to indicate just who it was that composed that government.

First, it is important to recognize that the moral order has been even stronger in Japan than in the United States. As Ruth Benedict has pointed out:

> The Japanese . . . order their world with constant reference to hierarchy. In the family and in personal relations, age, generation, sex, and class dictate proper behavior. In government, religion, the Army, and industry, areas are carefully separated into hierarchies where neither the higher nor the lower may without penalty overstep their prerogatives.[26]

Furthermore, the samurai have traditionally occupied a high place in that hierarchy. The sword that symbolized the status of the samurai was not mere decoration; it could be used on the "common" people, the farmers, artisans, and merchants.

The samurai were the warrior class of feudal Japan. But unlike the European knights, the samurai existed on a pension; they were not owners of land or of serfs. And the pension was a fixed amount that had been established for the family lines at the beginning of the Tokugawa era.[27] The Tokugawa era (1600–1868) was one of peace, which made a warrior class problematic. Consequently, the samurai "became increasingly the stewards of their overlords' estates and specialists in peaceful arts like the classical drama and the tea ceremony." [28]

In addition to this demilitarization of the functions of the samurai, a number of other important changes occurred during the Tokugawa era. Three of these have been discussed by Smith: the relationships of the samurai to the land, to political power, and to their feudal lords all changed. Specifically, the first became "purely administrative," the second became bureaucratic, and the third "became distant and impersonal." [29] The samurai possessed certain juridical and social bonds with the land at the beginning of the Tokugawa era, but these gradually disappeared as the lords consolidated their own power. Associated with this was the exercise of a new kind of power by the samurai, whose function became bureaucratic in contrast to the personal and territorial nature of their power in earlier times. And linked with these changes was the third:

The relationship between vassal and lord was slowly, silently, and profoundly transformed. It had been an intimate, intensely emotional relationship . . . which existed between men who had fought side by side, grieved together at the loss of comrades, whose safety and families' safety depended on their keeping faith. . . . It became distant and formal . . . the vassal came to look on his lord less as a leader in war (for there was no war) than as an administrative head.[30]

But there was one additional change which was of great significance. The samurai became poorer. In fact, the distribution of wealth in Tokugawa Japan was clearly discordant with the status hierarchy. The merchants, who occupied a low position, became increasingly wealthy even as the samurai — or that group of them known as the "lower samurai" — were becoming increasingly impoverished. And that impoverishment resulted from the fact that their pensions were insufficient to support them. It is not surprising, then, that "it was the lower *samurai* more than any other group which was responsible for the Restoration of 1868." [31]

Forces had been impinging upon the Tokugawa regime for some time prior to 1868; the legitimacy of the government was already being challenged when the Western intrusion confronted the nation. The additional challenge of a foreign nation was used to hasten the demise of the Tokugawa government. The powerful Satsuma and Choshu clans called for measures to keep foreigners out of Japan. The shogun, the military ruler of feudal Japan, could satisfy neither the internal opposition nor cope with the external threat. The samurai were able to depose him and establish an imperial government in 1868. This government acted with dispatch to dissolve the feudal system and centralize power. The government also implemented an aggressive, innovative policy of reform that would maintain Japanese independence through economic development, military superiority, and Westernization of vital facets of Japanese life.

In concluding our examination of status anguish and change, we ought to reflect on two points. One is that while we have seen that status anguish is a mechanism of change, it is not the only mechanism. Indeed, none of the mechanisms we have studied can account for all change, though sometimes scholars write about a particular one as though it could explain nearly everything. But obviously change can be effected by people who are not subjected to status anguish. And people who are free of status anguish engage in strenuous activities designed to facilitate or encourage change.

For example, it would be hard to argue that status anguish was a factor in the white, prosperous physician who risked reputation and career in order to participate intensively in the antiwar movement. Nor does status anguish seem to play a role in the life of the white, prosperous lawyer who opts for the radical perspective and who devotes his legal efforts to the defense of radicals. There are innumerable individuals throughout history — some, like St. Francis of Assisi or Gandhi, men of note, while others are nameless — who have been motivated by something other than status anguish.

The second point is that, given status anguish, the direction of change is uncertain when change results, and other outcomes are possible besides change. With respect to the first, Malewski argued that while status inconsistency did tend to lead people to support change, the change would not necessarily be of the liberal or leftist type envisioned by Lenski. Rightist causes may also offer promise of a change in the problematic status, as the example of political extremists in Iran has shown.[32]

The Rightist solution is also exemplified in Nazi Germany. A study of the Nazi leadership concludes that "the movement was led and followed by marginal men." [33] For example, a sample of the Nazi propagandists showed 77.4 percent of them to be marginal. Similarly, 82.1 percent of a sample of administrators and 77.1 percent of a sample of police were identified as marginal men.

Finally, with respect to the alternative outcomes of status anguish, we have already noted one study that found an increased incidence of psychophysiological symptoms among people characterized by status inconsistency. In some cases, then, status anguish simply increases psychic disorders rather than leading to change. Further, those who endure status anguish may capitulate to anomie and "become carriers of trends leading towards social disorganization rather than to innovations of a creative type." [34] The consequences of status anguish continue to be a point of debate. While status anguish clearly can result in change, it is not at all clear what circumstances lead to change rather than to psychic disturbance or social disorganization.

ENDNOTES TO CHAPTER 9

1. John M. Darley and Bibb Latane, "Bystander Intervention in Emergencies: Diffusion of Responsibility," in *Confrontation: Psychology and the Problems of Today,* ed. Michael Wertheimer (Glenview: Scott, Foresman and Company, 1970), pp. 71–76.

2. Jerald Hage and Michael Aiken, *Social Change in Complex Organizations* (New York: Random House, 1970), p. 122.

3. Peter F. Drucker, *The Age of Discontinuity* (New York: Harper & Row, 1968), p. 212.

4. *Ibid.*, p. 172.

5. From "The Origin of the Family, Private Property and the State," in Robert Freedman, ed., *Marxist Social Thought* (New York: Harcourt, Brace & World, Inc., 1968), p. 222.

6. C. Wright Mills, *Power, Politics & People*, ed. Irving Louis Horowitz (London: Oxford University Press, 1963), p. 198.

7. Kurt B. Mayer and Walter Buckley, *Class & Society*, 3rd edition (New York: Random House, 1970), p. 70.

8. George Foster, *Traditional Cultures: And the Impact of Technological Change* (New York: Harper & Row, 1962), p. 125.

9. Edwin O. Reischauer, *Japan: Past and Present*, 3rd edition (Tokyo: Charles E. Tuttle Company, Inc., 1964), p. 123. This paragraph follows this work, pp. 123–132.

10. F. Roy Lockheimer, "Prerequisites, Receptivity, and Change: Government and the Development of Science in Japan," in *The Social Reality of Scientific Myth: Science and Social Change*, ed. Kalman H. Silvert (New York: American Universities Field Staff, Inc., 1969), p. 163.

11. *Ibid.*, p. 165.

12. James A. Bill, "Modernization and Reform from Above: The Case of Iran," *Journal of Politics*, XXXII (Feb., 1970), 19–40.

13. As LaPalombara put it: "It scarcely requires exhaustive documentation to demonstrate that major changes in both the developed and developing nations are inconceivable today without the massive intervention of government." See Joseph LaPalombara, "An Overview of Bureaucracy and Political Development," in *Bureaucracy and Political Development*, ed. Joseph LaPalombara (Princeton: Princeton University Press, 1963), p. 4.

14. The authoritarian argument is presented in LaPalombara, *Bureaucracy and Political Development*, pp. 10, 233–300, and Robert Heilbroner, *The Future as History* (New York: Harper & Row, 1959), pp. 80ff. The democratic argument is the substance of William McCord, *The Springtime of Freedom* (New York: Oxford University Press, 1965).

15. See, for example, Frederick F. Clairmonte, *Economic Liberalism and Underdevelopment* (New York: Asia Publishing House, 1960), and Robert E. Ward, "Authoritarianism as a Factor in Japanese Modernization," in *Political Development and Social Change*, ed. Jason L. Finkle and Richard W. Gable (New York: John Wiley & Sons, 1966), pp. 478ff.

16. Eugene Staley, "The Role of the State in Economic Development," in *Modernization: The Dynamics of Growth*, ed. Myron Weiner (New York: Basic Books, Inc., 1966), p. 301.

17. Alexander Eckstein, "Individualism and the Role of the State in Economic Growth," *Economic Development and Cultural Change*, VI (Jan., 1958), 83.

18. Everett C. Hughes, "Social Change and Status Protest: An Essay on the Marginal Man," *Phylon*, X (1949), 58–65.

19. *Ibid.*, p. 59.

20. *Ibid.*, p. 61.

21. Gerhard E. Lenski, "Status Crystallization: A Non-Vertical Dimension," *American Sociological Review*, XIX (1954), 405–13.

22. Elton Jackson, "Status Consistency and Symptoms of Stress," *American Sociological Review*, XXVII (1962), 469–80.

23. Ralph V. Exline and Robert C. Ziller, "Status Congruency and Interpersonal Conflict in Decision-Making Groups," *Human Relations*, XII (1959), 147–62.

24. Michel Crozier, *The Bureaucratic Phenomenon* (Chicago: The University of Chicago Press, 1964), p. 29.

25. Max F. Millikan and Donald L. M. Blackmer, eds., *The Emerging Nations: Their Growth and United States Policy* (Boston: Little, Brown and Co., 1961), pp. 9–10. The examples in this paragraph are from these pages.

26. Ruth Benedict, *The Chrysanthemum and the Sword* (Cleveland and New York: The World Publishing Company, 1946), pp. 95–6.

27. *Ibid.*, p. 63.

28. *Ibid.*, p. 64.

29. Thomas C. Smith, "Japan's Aristocratic Revolution," in *Class, Status, and Power*, 2nd edition, ed. Reinhard Bendix and Seymour Martin Lipset (New York: The Free Press, 1966), p. 138.

30. *Ibid.*, p. 137.

31. Robert N. Bellah, *Tokugawa Religion* (New York: The Free Press, 1957), p. 45.

32. Andrzej Malewski, "The Degree of Status Incongruence and Its Effects," in Bendix and Lipset, *Class, Status, and Power*, pp. 306–307.

33. Daniel Lerner with Ithiel de Sola Pool and George K. Schueller, "The Nazi Elite," in *World Revolutionary Elites: Studies in Coercive Ideological Movements*, ed. Harold D. Lasswell and Daniel Lerner (Cambridge: The M.I.T. Press, 1965), p. 288.

34. Bert F. Hoselitz, "A Sociological Approach to Economic Development," in *Development and Society*, ed. David E. Novack and Robert Lekachman (New York: St. Martin's Press, 1964), pp. 157–58.

CHAPTER 10

Structural Sources: Elites
and Youth

The Western mind seems fond of thinking in dichotomies — something is *either* this *or* that. But a moment's reflection shows how inadequate this approach may be. Suppose we ask the question, is our Western level of life due to science or to religion? Although science and religion have often been dichotomous spheres, the question is obviously simplistic. Not only may we point to humane values that derive from religion and technological advances that derive from science, but we can also show how the two spheres overlap. And sometimes they overlap in the same person; the geneticist Mendel, the chemist Boyle, the astronomer Kepler, and the physicist Arthur Holly Compton are but a few of the scientists who have also been devoutly religious. Science and religion are not segregated spheres, but interacting ones.

Likewise, the categories that we are dealing with in this and the previous chapter are not necessarily independent. We have already noted that in Japan the government that implemented modernization was composed of a group that had experienced status anguish. In this chapter we shall examine two other groups that help compose the social structures — elites and youth. Elites and government may overlap. Youth have sometimes been characterized as marginal. Nonpolitical elites and youth may exert pressures that ultimately lead to change through the mediating agency of government. And so forth. Our categories are interacting and overlapping. We focus on each in turn, but we do not mean to suggest thereby that they are separable in reality.

CHANGE FROM THE TOP: ELITES

Although much elitist thought and writing has focussed on political elites, the category is much broader than that. In a democratic society in the modern world, argued Mannheim, there are a variety of elites; among the most important are "the political, the organizing, the intellectual, the artistic, the moral, and the religious." [1] Mannheim also believed that liberal-democratic society faced a crisis because of forces at work eroding these elite groups and their prestige. And in this latter assertion he agreed with many thinkers who have seen the course of change primarily in terms of the activities of elites.

Theories of Elites and Change

We have already examined one theory of change that rested heavily on the activities of elites — that of Toynbee. According to Toynbee, the development of a civilization is crucially linked to the work of creative minorities, who must devise appropriate responses to societal challenges and also lead the society to opt for that response. When the elites no longer fulfill this function, decline and death result.

But to many students of elites, the concept most immediately brings to mind the names of Pareto and Mosca. We shall look briefly at Pareto's ideas as representative (and probably more influential).[2] Pareto viewed society as a system of forces in a state of equilibrium. The major categories of any society are two — the elite and the nonelite. Elitist position is maintained by power, so a principal task of the social scientist is to account for the acquisition, exercise, and loss of power.

Pareto explains power by employing psychological variables, the so-called "residues" and "derivations." There is some dispute about the exact meaning of these variables, particularly of the residues. Pareto himself distinguished between them in the context of his effort to analyze ideas that are associated with behavior. Ideas and systems of ideas contain both scientific and nonscientific elements. The latter, in turn, have constant (the residues) and variable (the derivations) facets. Thus, residues are manifestations of sentiments which are associated with stable or recurrent patterns. Derivations are similar to rationalization and are associated with variation.

Throughout history, men have employed numberless derivations to rationalize their behavior. But certain kinds of residues have remained constant. To be sure, the residues are not distributed in the same proportion among all individuals or between various societies, and this accounts for shifts in the possession of power. Two residues which are of particular importance are the "instinct of combinations" and the "persistence of aggregates." These residues impel men to behave in particular ways.

Thus, depending upon which of the residues is predominant, we have differing types of men who compose the elite (and the nonelite). It is important here to note that Pareto divides the elite itself into two groups — the governing and the nongoverning elite. When the governing elite is composed of men who are predominantly characterized by the "instinct of combinations," change is rapid; when those rule who are predominantly characterized by the "persistence of aggregates," stability tends to prevail.

Pareto applied these ideas to more than the political realm. Men who have the persistence of aggregates as a dominant trait are called lions in government, rentiers in the economy, and prophets in the field of ideology. Those who have the instinct of combinations as a dominant trait are called foxes in government, speculators in the economy, and theorists in the field of ideology. In each case, the former act in a stabilizing fashion, while the latter act in a way that impels change.

Pareto felt that an effective elite would require men of both types. As Coser put it, a "judicious mixture in top elites" of men with the two types of residues "makes for the most stable economic structure, as well as for the most enduring political structure." [3] But there is a tendency for elites of the two types to alternate in possessing power. And this occurs because there is also a tendency for shifts to occur in the quality of the elite. To some extent, the deficiencies caused in the governing elite by a shift in quality may be remedied by "circulation of the elite," that is, by the inferior men's being replaced by others from the nongoverning elite who are capable of exercising power.

But there may also come a time when the judicious balance is no longer maintained. The quality of the governing elite diminishes, and the circulation between the governing and nongoverning elites cannot compensate adequately for it. Then "regimes either degenerate into hidebound and ossified bureaucracies incapable of renewal and adaptation, or into weak regimes of squabbling lawyers and rhetoricians incapable of decisive and forceful action." [4] And at that point, the governed will rebel and replace the effete rulers with a more effective group.[5]

More recent theories of elites and change tend to focus on the developing nations. Again, we have already noted two of these in the social-psychological theories of Hagen and McClelland; both emphasized the role of entrepreneurs in the economic development of a society. A more sociological approach is offered by Shils, who identifies the intellectual as the primary initiator of change in Asia and Africa.[6] Intellectuals, according to Shils, have been responsible in large measure for the genesis and development of the new nations in Asia and Africa.

We shall examine below some evidence relating to elites and change, but we should note one other approach, namely, that of C. Wright Mills. According to Mills, the United States has witnessed a historical development that involves

> . . . the rise of an elite of power; that the men of the circles composing this elite, severally and collectively, now make such key decisions as are made; and that, given the enlargement and the centralization of the means of power now available, the decisions that they make and fail to make carry more consequence for more people than has ever been the case in the world history of mankind.[7]

In other words, Mills saw the American elite as essentially a powerful group maintaining its own power and advantages. This power elite is composed of overlapping cliques of political, economic, and military circles. The elite is a self-serving conglomerate that controls its own destiny and that of the masses. Members of the elite enjoy the full fruits of an affluent society, while the man in the mass simply feels "pointless."

Thus, we have the idea that elites direct change and also that they retard change. There is little significant change in Pareto's scheme; the social structure is not transformed but only experiences cycles of change in personnel. And in Mills' thought, very little changes unless it is to the advantage of the elite. With Shils and modernization theorists, on the other hand, the elite becomes extraordinarily important in societal development. One might conclude that elites impel change in developing nations and inhibit it in those that are already developed. But, as we shall see below, the matter is more complex than that.

Studies of Elites and Change

One of the most extensive historical studies of elites and change, which also offers a theory of change, is that of Martindale. The theory of change that he sets forth is social-behavioristic, and its basic tenets include the following:

1. All social and cultural change is the work of individuals;
2. The major events in human history consist of the formation and destruction of societies and civilizations;
3. Because of their role in forming and justifying communities and civilizations, the intellectuals represent a strategic reference point for the study of these processes.[8]

Specifically, Martindale examines China, India, Israel, and Greece during the Axial period (900–200 B.C.) and the modern West. In each case, he finds, intellectuals were prime movers of change. The social role of the intellectual has varied widely across these societies. In the Axial period, the primary intellectual roles were the mandarin bureaucrat in China, the Brahman purohita in India, the rabbi in Palestine, and the "moral counselor and jurist" in the Graeco-Roman world. But in each case, the intellectuals were highly creative and guided the formation of more complex social orders. In the West, social development has been linked up with the humanists and scientists, who have tended to "establish a sphere of pure expediency"; in particular, the scientific mentality "liquidates every traditional configuration of value with which it comes in contact." [9]

Other historical studies support Martindale's thesis that the intellectuals have been crucial sources of change, or at least important sources of pressure towards change (the change agent may be thwarted by opposing forces). In a study of education in nineteenth-century India, China, and Japan, Tangri concluded that there were a number of differences in the educational systems of the three societies, but that "in all three cases the intellectual was (and is) an activist, deeply committed to the processes of social change, and not an objective bystander." [10]

We pointed out in the last chapter that the Nazi elite included considerable numbers of those suffering from status anguish. Nazi propagandists were identified as marginal men. More specifically, they were identified as alienated intellectuals. Their intellectual identity was established on the basis of their fathers' occupations, the number of their own publications, and the kind of publications they produced. Alienation was measured by unemployment rates. The data lead to the conclusion that Nazi propagandists were typically "a class of intellectuals born and raised within the *elite* of Imperial and Weimar Germany who became *alienated* from the prevailing structure of symbols and sanctions of the elite that nurtured them." [11]

A great many studies of elites have focussed on their role in the underdeveloped and developing nations of the contemporary world. And that role has been a varied one. In some traditional societies, the ruling elite has offered strong resistance to change. In many traditional nations, landowners have linked themselves with political rulers and certain other elites to form a powerful upper stratum.

As nations embark upon the process of modernization, however, we find certain elites actively leading the development, but they are not often the same elites as those who held sway in the traditional society. In West Africa, for example, the elites in the traditional society included chiefs, priests, and wealthy traders. But the nationalist movements were led by Western-educated elites, who "accused their elders of too great an accommodation with European rule, of being 'Uncle Toms.' " [12]

Still other elites may exercise little influence on change; rather, they basically engage in the task of adapting to whatever change occurs. Lawyers in Colombia occupied a position of high status during the traditional days of that nation. But their status became problematic during the process of modernization, because they sought to retain traditional values. Those values, however, did not mesh with the modernization process, which offered new opportunities but also demanded such things as a revised curriculum for law students and a changed perspective about being practical with people and things. By 1970, the lawyers found themselves in an ambivalent position with respect to their status; there were too many lawyers for a traditional type of practice and too few lawyers willing to strike out on a new course. Colombian lawyers, therefore, were struggling to adapt to a social order that was changing far more rapidly than they were.[13]

Some sense can be made out of the diverse patterns of behavior of elites by recognizing two important points: one, there are different kinds of elites, and, two, the consequences of change for the elites are complex and sometimes contradictory. As to the first point, we have already noted the two different types of elites involved in African development. A more complex typology has been offered by Pye, who identified six roles crucial to development: administrators, agitators, amalgamates, transmitters, ideological propagandists, and political brokers.[14] The varied courses of development in different societies, according to Pye, depend upon which combination of the above roles direct the development.

Briefly, the roles may be characterized as follows. The administrators direct the transition from traditional to bureaucratic modes of functioning, often incurring thereby hostility towards themselves. The agitators strive to destroy authoritative systems and increase general participation in political life. The amalgamates function well in both traditional and modern contexts; their ability to make use of traditional sources of power has made them quite effective in economic development in nations like Japan and Turkey. The transmitters communicate knowledge and values, facilitating the transition of others from the traditional to the modern context. Ideological propagandists strive to integrate the traditional and modern on some common ideological ground. And political brokers differentiate various special interests and relate them to the system of government.

Other typologies, of course, have been offered.[15] But however the elites are classified, there seems to be little doubt that modernization, and the particular course taken by modernization in a nation, is crucially linked up with elitist activity. Typologies are important because they direct our attention to the diverse interests and goals and behavior of elites. This, in turn, can help us understand why elites sometimes retard change, sometimes accelerate it, and sometimes simply adapt to it.

And these considerations confront us with the second point made above — the complex and sometimes contradictory consequences of change for elites. Eisenstadt has stressed this in his concept of "split-level" modernization.[16] Split-level modernization is directed by elites — in some cases, foreign elites. But the elites are a diverse group, and strive for various kinds of modernization. Even the governing elite may have contradictory aims with respect to modernization. For example, it may desire the enhanced power and affluence that come from modernization but may wish to avoid certain social and political consequences such as the erosion of its own power within the nation. Thus, elites sometimes act to counter the effects of their own previous actions, with the result that modernization has often been a spastic process of advance, decline, and turbulence.

Elites and Change: Conclusions

Certain important conclusions can be drawn from existing studies to guide future investigations of the relationship of elites to change. Among them are the following:

1. The elites of any society are a heterogeneous group. As Bottomore pointed out, the term is now generally used to identify "functional, mainly occupational, groups which have high status (for whatever reason) in a society." [17] We may try to understand their behavior with respect to change by analyzing their varied social roles,[18] by identifying their position on the problem of tradition vs. modernity,[19] by identifying their social origins,[20] and so on. But the important point is that we cannot understand the relationship between elites and change unless we also understand the heterogeneity of the elites of any society.

2. Elites may inhibit as well as impel, and adapt to as well as lead in, change. An important consideration here is the anticipated consequences of the change for elitist positions. As pointed out above, however, there may also be unanticipated consequences, with the result that the elites may act ambivalently about change. Furthermore, the elites do not exercise absolute control. They themselves may be swept along by currents not of their own making, currents created by technological developments, mass movements, or emergent ideologies, for example. Or the elites may

simply be incapable of coping with the demands presented by the social process. One of the reasons Eisenstadt gives for the breakdown of modernization in a number of countries is the inability of political elites effectively to meet the challenges of rapid change.[21] Only where political elites could accomplish their own will in the face of numerous demands from self-seeking, antagonistic interest groups has modernization continued steadily.

3. Different kinds of leaders may be required for different kinds of change and different types of situations. For example, many nationalistic movements have been led by charismatic individuals. But whereas charisma may be quite effective in attaining independence, it is not necessarily effective in building a nation. The people themselves may react against the charismatic leader when they realize that independence has not brought the good life they anticipated. Indeed, charismatic leadership may contradict the demands of nation building when the latter involves the development of citizenship and participation in the political process.[22]

Furthermore, various stages of nation building may also require different kinds of leaders. As economic development proceeds, there is need for the specialist rather than for the "polyvalent" leader.[23] In other words, the social context may demand particular kinds of elites, with the result that there is a circulation of elites with respect to both type and personnel over time. This dependence of elites upon the social context is illustrated by shifts in the elites in Russia following the Revolution. Those with expertise in persuasion were replaced by those with expertise in coercion:

> . . . the old Bolshevik intellectuals were executed, assassinated, or "disappeared" . . . In their place came the specialists skilled in violence rather than symbols, the administrators of coercion rather than persuasive ideology. The big change is well characterized by the transition from loquacious Lenin to silent Stalin.[24]

4. Different kinds of elites may be effective in different cultural and socio-historical settings. The third point dealt with elites and change in the same society over time; this one deals with different societies. In other words, the same basic kind of change in differing societies may require different kinds of elites. In the United States, for example, we associate effective change at local levels with democratic procedures. But an experiment in land reform in India yielded different results.[25] It was found that the program worked primarily in villages that had a tradition of landlessness. But it did not work even in all of those villages; rather,

it was effective when the social workers who directed the program were authoritarian rather than democratic!

Another example is provided by the argument of some Western economists that economic development — at least of the capitalist variety — hinges upon the activities of entrepreneurs.[26] But elites in the developing nations argue that this is too slow a process for their countries. Furthermore, the world in which a nation must develop today is enormously different from the world in which the West experienced development. If we contrast the Western experience with the problems facing a contemporary peasant society, we find the peasant societies in a frustrating situation; they "have no room for major territorial expansion; no technical advantage over competitors; a much higher rate of population growth; and a less differentiated economy, with around 80 percent of population in the agricultural sector." [27] The entrepreneurial elite that effectively led Western development is simply inappropriate for developing nations today.

CHANGE FROM THE BOTTOM: YOUTH

"Our civilization is doomed if the unheard-of actions of our younger generations are allowed to continue." These are not the words of a contemporary prophet of doom; they were discovered on an ancient tablet uncovered in Ur. They reflect an opinion of youth which seems rather common in every age, namely, that youth is the vanguard of change and that change is all for the worse. Youth, on the other hand, has often conceived of itself as the vanguard of change, and has believed that change is all for the better. More than one student has told me that the hope of the world — the *only* hope of the world — lies in the action of youth. How realistic are these contrary views on youth's role in change? As we shall see, the role of youth in change, like that of other groups we have examined, is a varied one.

The Conservatism of Youth

Although the older generation has often looked upon young people as though significant numbers of them were exponents of radical change, there is considerable conservatism among youth. Studies made by Remmers and Radler of high-school students during the 1950's found that the students, like adults, tended to be intolerant of divergent viewpoints. They were found to be rather traditional "in the sense that they continue a habit of disrespect for traditional American liberties of conscience, free speech, and the press." [28]

Among college-age young people, there is considerable diversity of perspective. In the first place, there is a great deal of variation among those within the university, and in the second place there is a large gap between the college and noncollege young person. Young people who go directly into some kind of work after high school have been found to be strikingly more conservative than those who go to college or a university. Among the evidence for this is the disproportionate number of younger voters who supported George Wallace in 1968. And in a series of polls conducted among 1400 young people in Massachusetts, employed youth were consistently more conservative than their college and university peers. In fact, 43 percent identified themselves as conservative, whereas only 22 percent of college students chose that classification.[29]

Even within the college or university, radicalism is not nearly so widespread as the public has sometimes tended to believe. A 1971 Gallup poll of 1063 students in 61 colleges and universities found minimal support for extremist groups. Only 6 percent of the students rated SDS as highly favorable (compared to 7 percent of the general public sampled), and 8 percent rated the Black Panthers as highly favorable (compared to 2 percent of the general public). Right-wing organizations had even less support, but it is obvious that students were not infatuated with leftist organizations.[30]

Thus, it is clear that differences among young people themselves are as great as those between the young and the old.[31] If the student uprisings and campus turmoil of the 1960's seemed to point to a generation of radicals, we might remind ourselves that universities in the contemporary world are quite placid compared with those of the past.[32] There is little or no evidence of a generational political revolt, either in the United States[33] or in the developing nations.[34] There is, on the contrary, evidence of a continuing sense of solidarity with the family,[35] a considerable amount of traditionalism among young people, and a degree of continuity between generations that indicates continuing and significant parental influence.[36]

In sum, much of the youth both in the United States and elsewhere is quite conservative. The majority of students in the United States have always been preparing to fulfill elite positions in society rather than training to transform their society. Nevertheless, college-educated youth are far less conservative than the young who go directly to work. After studying generational differences in attitudes among both blacks and whites, Brunswick concluded that without question "education is at least as important a divider, or determiner of generations, as age." [37]   Education is a liberalizing and, to a small degree, radicalizing force; but conservatism is strong among youth.   There is always change between the generations, of course; but the average youth is no flaming radical bent on destroying and recreating the social order at any cost.

Radicalism in Youth

While the majority of youth is either conservative or moderate in outlook, there are probably more extremists among the young than in the adult population.   Youth tends to be extreme, but the extremism may be either to the right or to the left.   The Weathermen, advocate of violent revolution, was a youth organization; but so is the Young Americans for Freedom, which presses for the conservative or reactionary viewpoint.

Our concern in this section, however, is not with extremism but with radicalism, in the sense of commitment to fundamental changes in the social structure.   Again, both leftists and rightists may call themselves radicals; an example of the latter are the rational anarchists who define themselves as radicals because of their commitment to institute a system of pure laissez-faire capitalism.   But our interest here is with the radicalism of the left and the extent of its presence or absence among youth in the United States.

In the decades prior to the 1960's, radicalism tended to be located in a few large, urban universities.   It is not a new phenomenon, but one which has existed more or less for the greater part of our history.[38]   The Intercollegiate Socialism Society dates back to 1905.   By 1921, Calvin Coolidge was deploring radicalism in colleges.   Nevertheless, by the 1930's, when the student radical movement reached the peak of intensity — at least until its resurgence in the 1960's, it still included only a relatively small number of adherents.   The American Student Union, a leftist-pacifist organization, claimed twenty thousand members in 1939, a time when it had reached the pinnacles of its strength.   There were other youth organizations, but the total number of students who participated in radical groups was only a small fraction of the total soaring college population, which reached nearly one and one-half million by 1940.

Student radicalism emerged anew in the 1960's.   The roots of this radicalism are to be found in a number of movements that began to crystallize in the late 1950's.[39]   In England, university intellectuals began to publish two new journals, which merged into the *New Left Review* in 1959. There were also a number of leftist political clubs that arose, composed of both college and working-class youth. In the United States, concern with the racial problem and international peace gained intensity; a number of journals and organizations emerged that reflected leftist concern with the problems.

The mood of student radicals in the 1960's is caught by "An American Student Manifesto," a document compiled from interviews with some 500 students:[40]

> We accuse the present society of a perverted frame of mind. A frame of mind that tolerates injustice, insensitivity, lack of candor, and inhumanity . . . The world's wealthiest nation, America, finds a large part of its population living in poverty. A nation founded on the belief that all men are created equal, it systematically denies civil rights and economic opportunity to its black citizen . . . The Viet Nam war, since we were the ones who were called to fight it, led us to make our first moral judgments. We are destroying more than we could possibly reconstruct.

The resolution of these problems, of course, depended upon fundamental changes in the social structure, and since the adult generation was seen the defender of that structure, adults were also seen as enemies of change towards a humane and fully human existence. As Flacks observed regarding the 1960's, "the relations between young people and the society at large have been qualitatively transformed." [41]

To some observers, the youth of the nation were forging ahead into the new era and there was cause for celebration. The extent of alienation of youth from the existing social order was seen as so intense that young people could only be understood in terms of a "counter culture." Roszak defined the latter as a culture that had become "so radically disaffiliated from the mainstream assumptions of our society that it scarcely looks to many as a culture at all, but takes on the alarming appearance of a barbaric intrusion." [42]

A number of events aided the disaffiliation of youth and the growth of radicalism. Skolnick has suggested that eight events were particularly important.[43] One was the nonviolent Southern civil rights movement. Considerable disillusionment followed upon the brutal treatment of civil rights workers and blacks who were only attempting to exercise their rights as citizens. A second event was the war on poverty, which promised much and delivered very little. Third were the events at Berkeley which cast university administrators in a new light and reshaped the image of the actual functions of the university in the society. The university and its administrators were seen to reflect the same corruption that pervaded the larger society.

Fourth, the escalation of the Vietnam War and the attendant credibility gap regarding governmental policies were blatantly counter to the will of the people which supposedly was sovereign. Fifth, the involvement of the universities with the Vietnam War and with the military establishment in general clearly destroyed the claim of academic neutrality and corroborated the belief in academic corruption.

The draft was the sixth factor. Student deferments were restricted, and many students faced the possibility of being called to participate in a war which they believed was immoral. Moreover, the draft was perceived as violating basic rights of individualism and voluntarism. A seventh factor was the continuing inability of the government to resolve problems of race, poverty, and urban decline. And, finally, the eighth factor was confrontation with police on campus. Police violence radicalized a number of students who had been either moderate or uncommitted.

Once radicalized, what were the students like? Many became activists, but not all. However, radicalization always involves new beliefs, the commitment to new ideologies. Radical ideologies vary, but there are some common elements. As pointed out above, all radicals are committed to fundamental changes in the social structure. In addition, Matza has noted three themes that have characterized modern student radicalism — a "vision of the apocalypse," populism, and evangelism.[44] The first refers to a belief in a better world that will replace the evil world of the present. The second is a belief in the creativity and worth of the common people, so that the new and better world may involve the liberation of these people. And the third refers to efforts to gain members and supporters of the movement.

But while radicals may have shared these broad beliefs, they differed considerably on other points and particularly on the point of how to effect the change into the new world. Some advocated violent revolution, while others insisted on nonviolent change. Some looked to separatism, such as that offered by communes, while others persisted in efforts at large-scale societal change. One of the reasons for the splintering of SDS was disagreement over means to effect the transition to the new social order.

In sum, student radicals have been, even in the 1960's, a heterogeneous and relatively small proportion of the total student population. The impact made by the youth of the 1960's has yet to be determined, but at least a few points seem clear. One is that the young have not emerged as the counter culture ushering in the new age. Only a few years after Roszak had celebrated the new generation, newspapers were remarking about the new, quiet atmosphere on the campuses and about the changed mood regarding violence and the possibility of effectively working for change within the system rather than challenging it from without. It seems that those who write about radical youth tend to ignore the existence of large numbers of conservative and moderate youth as well as the historical fluctuations of radicalism.

On the other hand, those who stress the conservatism of the young tend to ignore the radicals and their potential impact. Future historians may identify a number of ways in which the youth of the 1960's and 1970's affected the course of American history, including the influence of the young in illegitimating war, demanding equality of rights for all citizens in fact as well as in ideology, and reordering national priorities so that human existence becomes a humane existence.

Youth and Change

The effects of contemporary American youth on the course of history are not yet clear, but we may point to a variety of instances in which youth played a decided role in change. In this section, we shall examine the role of the young in a number of nations around the world, paying particular attention to some activities of Chinese youth.

One question we have not yet answered, of course, is what is meant by youth. And the answer is not easy to give. To a teenager, the 25-year-old may be an older adult. To the philosopher, his thoughts as a 40-year-old are part of his young thoughts. In the political realm, anyone in his thirties is considered a young politician. As a rule of thumb, therefore, I will be talking about youth in terms of those who are 35 or less.

What impact has this age group made? So far we have been discussing political change and politically directed change. But we must not ignore the contributions to change that the young have made by virtue of their work in science, technology, and ideology. Blaise Pascal was 19 when he invented the adding machine. Einstein was 26 when he started working on his theory of relativity. Whitney invented the cotton gin when he was 28, and Watt had obtained a patent for the first practical steam engine by the time he was 33. The list is long, and includes many writers and artists who produced major works in their youth.[45]

Sometimes the young have made significant contributions which differ in some respects from their later ones. During the 1960's, great interest developed in the writings of the "young

Marx." Before he was 30 years old, Karl Marx had produced a number of writings that were pervaded by a humanitarian social concern. Rediscovery of these early writings provided an ideological basis for a number of purposes, including revisions of the relationship between democracy and socialism, and defense of workers' rights against Stalinist bureaucracy.[46]

Youth has been prominent in many social movements and revolutions. The Protestant Reformation and revolutions in England, France, the United States, Cuba, China, and other nations have all been marked by significant participation of youth. Abolitionism in the United States was "a revolt of the young," with the median age of the antislavery leadership of the 1930's being 29.[47] In Meiji Japan, the course of modernization was impelled to a considerable extent by young men. In fact, Japanese youth felt that their elders were little more than an impediment to needed change. As a magazine published by youth in the latter part of the nineteenth century put it, "Today's elders are already useless to society. In a progressive age they are unfortunately a troublesome burden." [48]

Young people were also prominent in Germany prior to World War II, and tended to see themselves as alone being sufficiently pure to create society anew. More recently, studies of youth in a variety of nations show considerable political activity. Numerous governments have been overthrown following major student protests, including those of Venezuela (1958), Japan (1960), South Korea (1960), Turkey (1960), South Viet-Nam (1963), Bolivia (1964), the Sudan (1964), and Indonesia (1966).[49] But numerous others successfully withstood student opposition, and those that fell did so because of additional factors. Among the additional factors, intervention of the military ranks high.

Of course, the overthrow of the government *may* be nothing more than a change of the palace guard, while the government *may* remain in power yet initiate important changes in response to youth pressures. That is, the fall or persistence of a particular regime does not in itself indicate a significant change. Rather, we need to examine the course of events that occur in a society after the rebellion of young activists.

Among the many historical examples of significant change effected through the political action of youth is the case of China. In a society that traditionally assigned great respect and deference to the aged, the young have become prominent. A case in point is the Red Guard during the Great Proletarian Cultural Revolution. Here we shall focus on events that preceded the Communist revolution.

China was subservient to and exploited by the West through

most of the nineteenth century. It was not until the ideology of nationalism — a "prickly, touchy, demanding kind of nationalism" which grew out of China's humiliation by the West — that the Chinese were roused to change their situation.[50] This nationalistic ideology took hold in the student movement in the first years of the twentieth century. The young opposed everything that appeared reactionary, and were determined to liberate themselves and their nation from every form of bondage.

Student activity reached a peak of intensity in the famous May Fourth Movement of 1919, which gave birth to modern China.[51] In order to understand that Movement, we must emphasize again the intense interest in national affairs held by Chinese students as the twentieth century dawned. Because of China's repeated humiliation by the West, whom she had previously considered inferior, and because of continuing internal corruption, war, and economic disaster, Chinese students possessed a strong political and social consciousness. In addition, the traditional examination system was abolished in 1905, making professional careers problematic. The road to achievement and power seemed to lie through the organization of mass action rather than through the pursuit of a professional career.

The student leaders were young — in their twenties; and so were their professors, many of whom were in their twenties or thirties. This group confronted the older scholars and warlord leaders with the vision of a new China. And the contrast in composition between the two groups was as striking as the contrasts in their visions of the nation; in age, education, and ideology, the gap between the new intellectuals and their opposition was unbridgeable.

A number of factors encouraged mass activities. The students lived in very crowded dormitories. Their study and recreation was highly structured by their superiors. They possessed a collective rather than an individualistic perspective. And public opinion indicated an acceptance of the idea of student intervention in political affairs. Finally, the students were already grouped in a number of organizations.

The event that finally triggered mass action was the news from the Paris Conference; this news reached Peking at the end of April, 1919. China had expected that some of the inequities of the past would be rectified at the Conference. But President Wilson's ideas of self-determination and a war without victory were not to apply to the Chinese. Germany's holdings in Shantung, including Tsingtao, were to be given to Japan, who had seized them in 1914.

The Chinese students felt that both the West and their own government had sold them out. The student organizations met and declared May 7 as a day for mass demonstration. But the news from Paris grew worse and public feelings became increasingly bitter.   Efforts of the Peking government to mollify the populace and discourage dissent only intensified the anger.   Finally, students in Peking felt that the mass demonstration could not wait until May 7 and moved the time up to May 4.

It was to be a day of orderly protest.   Efforts of the Peking government to stop the rally failed.   By 1:30 in the afternoon, over 3000 had gathered.   Students distributed a "Manifesto of All the Students of Peking" which called on all of the people to join their protest.   The Manifesto left little doubt about either the severity of the crisis or the depth of commitment of the young:

> This is the last chance for China in her life and death struggle.   Today we swear two solemn oaths with all our fellow countrymen: (1) China's territory may be conquered, but it cannot be given away; (2) the Chinese people may be massacred, but they will not surrender. Our country is about to be annihilated.   Up, brethren! [52]

The day was significant not only because of the demonstration itself, but because it marked the beginning of organized efforts to gain mass support for radical change.   The ideas of the students were disseminated throughout China, and the students themselves made contact with the common people.   The incident of May 4 and the subsequent activities of youth were a prophetic microcosm of the new China as well as an important step in attaining the new order.

The continuing influence of youth in development in China is illustrated by the average age of members of the Communist Politburo, which remained at approximately twenty-nine from 1921 through 1931.[53]   And, interestingly enough, as the Chinese leaders have aged they have continued to emphasize and encourage the youth role in China's development.   The young created a new China.   And now that those young people are old, many of them continue to stress the work of youth in making China a great nation.

Youth and Change: Speculative Conclusions

How can we account for the role of youth in change?   As we have seen, the majority of youth in the United States have been more concerned with securing their own place in the social order than with effecting basic changes in that order.   Yet there are many young people who commit themselves to the task of change.

What kind of context is likely to generate that commitment?   I would offer a number of suggestions.

First, the general status of the young will bear upon their interest in effecting change.   It has been argued that youth in America are in a position of "structural marginality," with no socially significant roles available to them.[54]   This would mean that the young fall into the category of status anguish discussed in the last chapter, and to the extent that they do, they will be amenable to a commitment to change.

A similar argument has been advanced by Musgrove, who says that where the status of adolescents and young adults is high the rate of change will be slow, while a low status will tend to generate a commitment to change.[55]   According to Musgrove, high status seems to lead to conservatism even when the young are segregated from the adult world — as they were among the Plains Indians and the Nuer of Africa.   When segregation is combined with low status, the young are likely to be leaders in change — as they were among the Tiv of Nigeria and the Manus of New Guinea.

Second, the young are likely to lead in change when there is a clear contradiction between ideology and reality.   The events of the 1950's and 1960's which led to the radicalization of many American youth were all clearly contradictory to American ideals. The young radicals did not reject those ideals; they rejected the society that both praised and betrayed the ideals.   The young of any society do not generally have economic and psychological commitments to the existing social order; they are, therefore, a potent source of change when ideology and reality conflict.

Third, youth's willingness to engage in change will be a function of certain sociocultural factors.   In the United States, "the apex of rebelliousness is reached during the period of youth, before and after which rates of rebelliousness seem considerably lower." [56] At least two factors can help account for this.   One is the expectation of rebelliousness during adolescence.   Any number of books on parent-child relationships remind us that children advance from the dependence of infancy, to the independence of adolescence, to the interdependence of adulthood.   The adolescent rebels only to establish a more mature relationship; under such conditions, that rebellion is to be expected from any healthy youth.   As the anthropologists remind us, however, adolescent rebellion is peculiar to certain cultures.   Its frequent occurrence in the United States is due to, among other things, the expectation that it will happen.

A second factor in youthful rebellion in America is the influence of the university.   The emphasis on universal education means that more and more young people are subjected to more and more education.   And while that education often serves only to socialize the young into a mindless acceptance of their culture, it sometimes liberalizes and even radicalizes them. The latter effect may be an unwitting byproduct of the contradiction between reality and university ideology, but education, nevertheless, is instrumental in transmitting the ideology.

A fourth type of context likely to generate youth commitment to change is a society undergoing rapid change. Historically, revolutionary student movements have arisen in transitional societies.[57] And in the contemporary world, student revolt is particularly characteristic of modernizing nations. A number of reasons can account for this, including inevitable and intense conflict between the generations, a high degree of ideological polarization, inadequate employment of educated youth, inferior universities, and the fact that the young may be the only group willing and able to lead in change.[58]

One theme runs throughout the above — generational conflict. We saw this in the case of Meiji Japan, China, and the United States. It is not clear whether change leads to the conflict, or the conflict leads to change, or whether (which I think is more likely) this is a chicken-and-egg question, with conflict and change perpetuating each other. Mannheim argued that rapid change is of particular importance in intensifying generational differences.[59] On the other hand, Flacks has asserted that "the emergence of sharp generational conflict and the mass uprising of privileged youth signify that a certain stage of social development is coming to an end and a new one is taking form." [60] Both are correct; change tends to intensify generational conflict and generational conflict leads to change. The young may effect change in collaboration with adults through their contribution to scientific and other kinds of innovation, but they do not seem to effect significant political change without generational conflict.

ENDNOTES TO CHAPTER 10

1. Karl Mannheim, *Man and Society in an Age of Reconstruction,* trans. Edward A. Shils (New York: Harcourt, Brace, & World, 1940), p. 68.
2. Pareto's thought is elaborated in his massive work, *The Mind and Society.* For a concise introduction to Pareto, see Lewis A. Coser, *Masters of Sociological Thought* (New York: Harcourt Brace Jovanovich, Inc., 1971), pp. 387–426.
3. Coser, *Masters of Sociological Thought,* p. 400.
4. *Ibid.,* p. 399.

5. In addition to problems of conceptual definition which we noted, Pareto's thought presents certain difficulties. See T. B. Bottomore, *Elites and Society* (Middlesex: Penguin Books, 1964), pp. 48–54.

6. Edward A. Shils, "The Intellectuals in the Political Development of the New States," *World Politics*, XII (April, 1960), 329–68.

7. C. Wright Mills, *The Power Elite* (New York: Oxford University Press, 1956), p. 28.

8. Don Martindale, *Social Life and Cultural Change* (Princeton: D. Van Nostrand Company, Inc., 1962), p. 60.

9. *Ibid.,* p. 503.

10. Shanti S. Tangri, "Intellectuals and Society in Nineteenth-Century India," *Comparative Studies in Society and History*, III (July, 1961), 393.

11. Daniel Lerner, with Ithiel de Sola Pool and George K. Schueller, "The Nazi Elite," in *World Revolutionary Elites: Studies in Coercive Ideological Movements*, ed. Harold D. Lasswell and Daniel Lerner (Cambridge, Mass.: The M.I.T. Press, 1965), p. 222.

12. P. C. Lloyd, *Africa in Social Change* (Middlesex: Penguin Books, 1969), p. 127.

13. Judith Granich Goode, "Responses of a Traditional Elite to Modernization: Lawyers in Colombia," *Human Organization*, XXIX (Spring, 1970), 70–80.

14. Lucian W. Pye, "Administrators, Agitators, and Brokers," *Public Opinion Quarterly*, XXII (Fall, 1958), 342–48.

15. See, for example, Clark Kerr, John T. Dunlop, Frederick H. Harbison, and Charles A. Myers, *Industrialism and Industrial Man* (Cambridge, Mass.: Harvard University Press, 1960), pp. 50ff. The authors identify five ideal types: the dynastic elite, the middle class, the revolutionary intellectuals, the colonial administrators, and the nationalist leaders. These types are differentiated along a number of dimensions, including their strategies, various cultural factors, and implications of their policies.

16. S. N. Eisenstadt, *Modernization: Protest and Change* (Englewood Cliffs: Prentice-Hall, Inc., 1966), pp. 67–75.

17. Bottomore, *Elites and Society,* p. 14.

18. Pye, "Administrators, Agitators, and Brokers."

19. Paul E. Sigmund, ed., *The Ideologies of the Developing Nations*, revised edition (New York: Frederick A. Praeger, 1967), pp. 7–8.

20. C. E. Black, *The Dynamics of Modernization* (New York: Harper & Row, 1966), pp. 62–67.

21. S. N. Eisenstadt, "Breakdowns of Modernization," in *Readings in Social Evolution and Development*, ed. S. N. Eisenstadt (Oxford: Pergamon Press, 1970), pp. 421–52.

22. Thomas E. Dow, Jr., "The Role of Charisma in Modern African Developments," *Social Forces*, XLVI (March, 1968), 328–38.

23. See the articles on "leadership and economic growth" in the *International Social Science Journal*, XVI (1964), 185–274.

24. Daniel Lerner, "The Coercive Ideologists in Perspective," in *World Revolutionary Elites*, ed. Lasswell and Lerner, p. 461.

25. Partha Nath Mukherji, "Study in Induced Social Change: An Indian Experiment," *Human Organization*, XXIX (Fall, 1970), 169–77.

26. See, for example, Joseph Schumpeter, *Capitalism, Socialism, and Democracy* (New York: Harper & Row, 1950).

27. Guy Hunter, *Modernizing Peasant Societies* (New York: Oxford University Press, 1969), pp. 98–99.

28. Reuel Denney, "American Youth Today: A Bigger Cast, a Wider Screen," in *The Challenge of Youth*, ed. Erik H. Erikson (Garden City: Anchor Books, 1965), p. 166.

29. See "New Left Reconsidered," *Trans-Action*, June, 1970, pp. 6, 8.

30. *St. Louis Post-Dispatch*, February 7, 1971, p. 3F.

31. S. M. Lipset and E. Raab, "The Non-Generation Gap," *Commentary*, L (Aug., 1970), 35–39.

32. Walter Laquer, "Reflections on Youth Movements," *Commentary*, XLVII (June, 1969), 33–41.

33. Vern L. Bengtson, "The Generation Gap: a Review and Typology of Social-Psychological Perspectives," *Youth & Society*, II (Sept., 1970), 20–21.

34. Donald K. Emmerson, ed., *Students and Politics in Developing Nations* (New York: Frederick A. Praeger, 1968), pp. 396–97.

35. Editors of *Fortune*, *Youth in Turmoil* (New York: Time-Life Books, 1969), p. 38.

36. Samuel Lubell, "That 'Generation Gap'," in *Confrontation: The Student Rebellion and the Universities*, ed. Daniel Bell and Irving Kristol (New York: Basic Books, 1968), pp. 58–59.

37. Ann F. Brunswick, "What Generation Gap?" *Social Problems*, XVII (Winter, 1970), 369.

38. Much of the material in this paragraph is drawn from David Matza, "Subterranean Traditions of Youth," *Annals of the American Academy of Political and Social Science*, CCCXXXVIII (Nov., 1961), p. 109, and Lewis S. Feuer, *The Conflict of Generations* (New York: Basic Books, Inc., 1969), p. 318.

39. Paul Jacobs and Saul Landau, *The New Radicals* (New York: Vintage Books, 1966), pp. 8–14.

40. Editors of *Fortune*, *Youth in Turmoil*, pp. 47–55.

41. Richard Flacks, *Youth and Social Change* (Chicago: Markham Publishing Company, 1971), p. 17.

42. Theodore Roszak, *The Making of a Counter Culture* (Garden City: Anchor Books, 1969), p. 42.

43. Jerome H. Skolnick, *The Politics of Protest* (New York: Ballantine Books, 1969), pp. 100–105.

44. Matza, "Subterranean Traditions of Youth," pp. 109–11.

45. Don Fabun, *The Dynamics of Change* (Englewood Cliffs: Prentice-Hall, Inc., 1967), p. 21.

46. Loyd D. Easton and Kurt H. Guddat, eds., *Writings of the Young Marx on Philosophy and Society* (Garden City: Anchor Books, 1967), p. 1.

47. David Donald, *Lincoln Reconsidered*, 2nd edition (New York: Vintage Books, 1961), pp. 26–27.

48. Kenneth B. Pyle, *The New Generation in Meiji Japan* (Stanford: Stanford University Press, 1969), pp. 6–7.

49. Emmerson, *Students and Politics in Developing Nations*, p. 390.

50. Etienne Balazs, *Chinese Civilization and Bureaucracy*, trans. H. M. Wright, ed. Arthur F. Wright (New Haven: Yale University Press, 1964), p. 164.

51. Material on the May Fourth Movement is drawn from Chow Tse-tung, *The May Fourth Movement* (Cambridge, Mass.: Harvard University Press, 1960), pp. 92–120.

52. *Ibid.*, p. 108.

53. Robert C. North, "Kuomintang and Chinese Communist Elites," in *World Revolutionary Elites*, ed. Lasswell and Lerner, p. 383.

54. Tamme Wittermans and Irving Krauss, "Structural Marginality and Social Worth," *Sociology and Social Research*, XLVIII (April, 1964), 348–60.

55. F. Musgrove, *Youth and the Social Order* (Bloomington: Indiana University Press, 1964), pp. 126–41.

56. Matza, "Subterranean Traditions of Youth," p. 104.

57. Skolnick, *The Politics of Protest*, p. 82.

58. Seymour Martin Lipset, ed., *Student Politics* (New York: Basic Books, 1967), pp. 3–53, 239–245.

59. Karl Mannheim, *Essays on the Sociology of Knowledge*, ed. Paul Kecskemeti (London: Routledge & Kegan Paul, 1952), pp. 309–10.

60. Flacks, *Youth and Social Change*, p. 14.

PART IV

Patterns of Change

In Part I we tried to clear away some of the haze surrounding our understanding of change by identifying and rejecting certain false assumptions. In Part II we were concerned with various answers to the question, how can we understand the course of change? Part III dealt with specific factors that seem to impel change. And in this part, we shall look at some views about the "how" of change, that is, the form or pattern taken by change.

Some patterns have already appeared in Part II, where we considered the evolutionary pattern proposed by Comte, Spencer, and Durkheim, and the dialectical pattern worked out by Marx. Obviously, the form of the pattern is separable from its content. That is, the actual content of Spencerian evolution differs considerably from that of Durkheimian evolution. The Hegelian dialectic is quite contrary to the Marxist dialectic. And both differ from Whitehead, who argued that the essence of the universe is an ongoing creation of unity out of disjunctive multiplicity. But that conjunctive unity itself is a disjunctive multiplicity, so that the process continues indefinitely.

In this part, therefore, we want to look at some of the patterns of change that have been proposed, patterns that can have diverse contents. Many more have been suggested than we shall have space to examine. For example, there have been a number of efforts to identify forms of change mathematically.[1] Hart has shown how aspects of culture have changed over time in accordance with two patterns which he calls "cultural acceleration" and "logistic surges." [2]   In the former, man's ability to control his environment has been enhanced at an accelerating rate, and the rate of acceleration itself has accelerated.   Thus, if we plot such things as world speed records, cutting tool efficiency, and expectation of life over time (generally, over thousands or even hundreds of thousands of years), we get a curve that rises up at an increasing rate.

The "logistic surge," on the other hand, refers to changes that begin slowly, speed up quickly, then slow again or even stop. Examples of this kind of change are developments of particular inventions, like birth control clinics, and the growth of particular social entities, like the British Empire.   Thus, cultural acceleration tends to characterize "the long-time development of basic capacities (such as the use of power, speed in travel, expectation of life, and power of destruction)," whereas the logistic surge tends to characterize particular inventions or social organizations. [3]

Hart has provided us with algebraic patterns of change. Moore notes ten geometric forms of change that may be found in various theories. [4]   These include rising straight lines (ongoing progress theories), rising cyclical curves (progress with fluctuations), and level cyclical or sinusoidal curves (fluctuations with neither progress nor regress over long spans of time), among others.

Of the various patterns, however, three seem to be particularly important: those identified by anthropologists, including evolution, diffusion, and acculturation; dialetic patterns; and the contemporary pattern of industrialization and modernization.   The dialectic was treated both in the section on Marx and that on conflict.   In this part, we shall attend to the work of anthropologists and some views and insights about industrialization and modernization.

ENDNOTES TO PART IV

1. For a readable and interesting example, see Boulding's distinction between simple, populational, and structural patterns of growth: Kenneth E. Boulding, "Toward a General Theory of Growth," *The Canadian Journal of Economics and Political Science*, XIX (Aug., 1953), 326–40.   For a more mathematically complex approach, see James S. Coleman, "The Mathematical Study of Change," in *Methodology in Social Research*, ed. Hubert M. Blalock, Jr. and Ann B. Blalock (New York: McGraw-Hill Book Company, 1968), pp. 428–78.
2. Hornell Hart, "Social Theory and Social Change," in *Symposium on Sociological Theory*, ed. Llewellyn Gross (Evanston, Ill.: Row, Peterson & Co., 1959), p. 201.
3. *Ibid.*, pp. 218–19.
4. Wilbert E. Moore, *Social Change* (Englewood Cliffs: Prentice-Hall, Inc., 1963), pp. 34–39.

CHAPTER 11

Cultural Patterns: Some Anthropological Views

Among anthropologists, three patterns are considered of particular importance — evolution, diffusion, and acculturation. But underlying these three is another factor — invention, or innovation. "The most incisive form of cultural addition is invention, the finding things out, or, etymologically, 'coming into' something new." [1] According to Kroeber, while necessity and accident both account for a few inventions, the most common source is the "play impulse." The innovations of both science and art are "adult sublimations . . . of the sensorily exploratory and kinaesthetic activities that constitute play in children and mammals." [2]

A more detailed treatment of innovation has been offered by Barnett, who treats innovation as commonplace among humans. Every individual is innovative, though "individuals differ in their propensities and abilities to veer across the normal boundaries of acceptable deviation." [3] The materials used by the innovator come from two sources, his culture and the "nonartificial" aspects of his experience such as nature and his own physical and mental characteristics. Thus both external and internal factors help explain differences among individuals with respect to innovative activity. Barnett himself laid particular stress on the psychological aspects of innovation and treated the cultural context as a framework within which the psychological factors would be operative. The important point for our purposes, however, is that, as the title of his book asserts, innovation is the basis for cultural change.

The point is important because it not only identifies a typical anthropological approach but also shows an area of difference between some anthropologists and some sociologists. That is, certain changes that may be significant to the sociologist are identified by the anthropologist as only a prelude to change. A sociologist would normally view demographic changes and economic developments as significant in themselves as well as consequential for other change. But, according to Murdock, these processes are likely to lead to cultural innovations, and "cultural change begins with the process of *innovation*, the formation of a new habit by a single individual which is subsequently accepted or learned by other members of his society." [4]

The emphasis on innovation highlights certain other differences between anthropological and sociological approaches. The former has often been a micro approach, identifying specific items or traits which have been incorporated into a culture and have, thereby, changed that culture.[5] Sociologists have dealt with the effects of innovation, particularly technological innovation, but generally in the context of its implications for intergroup and interpersonal relations rather than for its impact on the pattern of culture. Furthermore, sociologists have often taken a more macro approach by studying such phenomena as broad sweeps of history or institutional changes over time.

Finally, sociologists have tended to stress intergroup conflict as a factor in change. Innovation may generate conflict, but it can also set off a cumulative process, with the culture growing by addition and integration of the novel elements. Nor does all innovation involve change from a sociological point of view; novelties in the way of children's toys or styles of automobiles may mean changed patterns of culture, but they have little or no effect upon patterns of interaction or structures of relationships.

In spite of the differences, however, anthropological and sociological approaches tend to blend into each other. Both have employed such concepts as evolution, diffusion, invention, and social structure. What we shall discuss next, therefore, is not the anthropological approach as distinct from the sociological, but the typical fashion in which anthropologists have described the pattern of change.

EVOLUTION

Evolutionary thought in anthropology, as in sociology, has had a checkered career. Early anthropologists were infatuated with the idea of evolution. But it was almost fanatically rejected by a succeeding generation, to be cautiously rediscovered by a still later group. During the course of all this, some rather diverse meanings have been attached to the notion of evolution.

In the latter part of the nineteenth century, social anthropologists identified evolution in terms of a pattern of development from lower to higher forms of cultural life. This pattern was marked by a series of successive stages, and the task of the anthropologist was to identify the stages. For example, Lewis H. Morgan traced the evolution of human culture through the successive stages of savagery, barbarism, and civilization. His basic concern was with categorizing societies according to "distinguishing social characteristics that people shared at certain levels of social organization" and with "noting the sequences in the development of these types." [6]   And unlike some others, Morgan realized that diffusion of elements from other cultures may intrude upon the sequence and alter it.

At the heart of the writings of these early evolutionists was the idea that the most primitive form of social organization was the matrilineal sib.[7]   This form eventually yielded to patrilineal and patriarchal forms as males gained dominance. Finally, bilateral descent and the nuclear family emerged only in late stages of evolution. This aspect of cultural evolution was "so logical, so closely reasoned, and so apparently in accord with all known facts" that it was accepted by virtually all social scientists until the end of the nineteenth century.[8]

All aspects of culture, however, evolved, and different writers paid particular attention to varied aspects of culture. Edward Tylor traced the evolution of religion from animism through polytheism to monotheism. A. C. Haddon said of art that in its early stages it was characterized by "realistic representation," while in later stages it was characterized by "geometric, symbolic, or abstract representation." [9]   Religion, art, language, technology, and any other facet of culture, then, could be shown to have developed through successive and higher stages.

This early, unilinear idea of evolution broke down as the twentieth century dawned, however. It was attacked at a number of points, most of which involved the disparity between the theory and the accumulating knowledge of primitive societies. Some, if not most, of the studies upon which the theory was based were inadequate and inaccurate, and the theorists themselves did not generally engage in intensive field studies. Furthermore, evolutionary theory tended to minimize the importance of cultural borrowing, and the new anthropologists tended to see that borrowing as of crucial importance. Finally, unilinear evolution reinforced ethnocentric attitudes and led to the disparagement of the "less advanced" societies.

The new evolutionary thought, which has emerged after apparently being done to death by strident critical attack, lacks the myth of unidirectionality. It is an effort to synthesize some of the insights of the early evolutionists with the later diffusionist and functionalist thought. Diffusionist thought, as we shall see in the next section, emphasized the mobility of various cultural traits and tried to ascertain how the traits that comprise any given culture came together. Functionalist thought stressed the interdependence of traits, the linkage of traits into a meaningful whole; this perspective, like sociological functionalism, seems incapable of adequately treating the problem of change.

The new evolutionism includes diverse ideas, however. Some contemporary anthropologists equate evolution with change, while others conceive of it as growth, development, or progress. Wolf conceives of evolution in terms of cumulative development that is both quantitative and qualitative.[10]   The quantitative aspect implies a ranking along a numerical scale; cultures might be differentiated, for example, according to the amount of energy harnessed or demographic characteristics or intensity of communication. The qualitative aspect means "the emergence of new cultural components which subsume and integrate pre-existing components in a new way."[11]   Most inventions are the integration in a new way of previously existing parts. The state is a social invention which results in a qualitative change in organization of the culture. And a major qualitative change has been the transition from unspecialized cultures to those which function on the basis of specialization of parts, that is, the transition from hunting-and-gathering societies to more complex forms.

A number of anthropologists have paid more detailed attention to developing evolutionary thought. We shall examine briefly three of them: Leslie White, Julian Steward, and the team of Sahlins and Service. Each represents a modern variant of evolutionary thought, and each presents us with a distinctive approach.

Leslie White claims to deal with culture as a whole rather than with particular cultures.[12] Like Durkheim, White rejects the role of psychological factors and the "great man" theory of development. Man's behavior must be understood in terms of culture. If man is competitive, for example, it is not because he is by nature that way, but because he exists in a competitive culture. How, then, can we account for culture?

According to White, culture is "a symbolic, continuous, cumulative, and progressive process."[13]   It is symbolic in the sense that man is a symbolic animal (and, especially, an animal who uses language). It is continuous because the symbolic nature of culture enables it to be easily transmitted from one individual to another and one generation to another. It is cumulative in that new elements are constantly being added. And it is progressive in the sense of attaining increasing control over nature and more security of life for man.

In other words, culture is a self-generating phenomenon that enfolds the existence of every individual and, thereby, explains all of man's behavior.

White's argument is clear in his treatment of invention. No invention or innovation (and, consequently, no change) will emerge until cultural development has reached a point that will admit a novel element. More importantly, when the development of culture has reached that point, the novel element will emerge independently of people's desires. A primary support for this latter argument is the occurrence throughout history of the simultaneous and independent discovery or invention. And, indeed, the list of such inventions and discoveries is quite impressive, and includes among others technological inventions like the telegraph, mathematical breakthroughs like the calculus, and the formulation of scientific laws such as those pertaining to the behavior of gases.

Thus, while man has remained basically the same in terms of his intelligence and biological makeup, culture has grown at an exponential rate. And this growth must be understood in terms of the nature of culture itself, not in terms of the activities of particular men. Cultural evolution is a phenomenon sui generis. It is like an overarching process that engulfs man and carries him along, willingly or unwillingly, into the future.

A different approach to evolution is offered by Julian Steward, who created the idea of multilinear evolution. According to Steward, there have been three main approaches to understanding cultural development. One was that of the early evolutionists and their theory of unilinear evolution. The second was that of the cultural relativists, who saw development as "essentially divergent," and who tried to identify characteristics that distinguished societies from each other. And the third approach is multilinear evolution.[14]

Multilinear evolution is "an affirmation that significant cross-cultural regularities exist but a denial that such regularities must pertain to all human societies." [15] Culture has evolved along a number of different lines; we might picture it as a branching tree. At the same time, there are some cross-cultural regularities, or parallels in cultural history. These parallels arise from the fact that culture change results from adaptation to environment; similar adaptive processes in similar environments result in the cross-cultural regularities.

Steward calls the process of adaptation "cultural ecology." The problem presented to us by cultural ecology is the determination of "whether the adjustments of human societies to their environments require particular modes of behavior or whether they permit latitude for a certain range of possible behavior patterns." [16] This, of course, means ascertaining the extent to which behavior is determined by environmental factors.   The method of cultural ecology involves: 1. an analysis of the interrelationship of technology and environment; 2. analysis of "behavior patterns involved in the exploitation of a particular area by means of a particular technology"; and 3. determination of the extent to which those behavior patterns affect various other facets of the culture.[17]

In comparing cultures, in searching for cross-cultural regularities, the analysis focusses on "cultural cores," which are the facets of the cultures involved in subsistence activities and economic patterns.   The societies whose cultural cores are being compared must be at the same level of sociocultural integration and be of the same cultural type.   But even when we find regularities, they will pertain to limited aspects of the cultures rather than to each culture as a whole; we could expect to find cross-cultural kinship types, religious types, or government types, for example.

Thus, Steward has tried to avoid the mistakes of the early evolutionists and provide a theory of evolution that incorporates both the generalizing and the historical approach to social anthropology.   Unfortunately, he makes very modest claims for a rather complex theory and method, and we are not encouraged to regard his work as more than an interesting effort to affirm evolution while discarding the mistakes of the early evolutionists.

The final effort we shall examine is that of Sahlins and Service, who give the basic pattern of evolution as the inverse of inorganic evolution (increasing disorder that ends in homogeneity): cultural evolution is marked by an "increase in organization, higher energy concentration, and . . . increased heterogeneity." [18]   Furthermore, that evolution involves both advance and divergence, progress and variation.   These two facets are called General Evolution and Specific Evolution.

In other words, evolution is a process marked by simultaneous movement in two directions: "On one side, it creates diversity through adaptive modification: new forms differentiate from old. On the other side, evolution generates progress: higher forms arise from, and surpass, lower." [19]   Although the two processes occur simultaneously, it is important to recognize that cultural change must be viewed from one or the other of the two perspectives; we can analyze change *either* in terms of adaptation *or* in terms of general progress.

For from the perspective of adaptation, the two authors argue, "we are cultural relativists."   Adaptive advances are relative, each being suited to its own situation and none being any better than any in other cultures.   The authors acknowledge their indebtedness to Steward for his pioneer work in adaptation. But they argue that there is also general progress in culture which "can be absolutely, objectively, and nonmoralistically ascertained." [20] This general cultural evolution involves the successive appearance of new levels of "all-round development."

An example of general evolutionary analysis is provided by the authors with respect to warfare. In terms of specific evolution, we would try to explain differing types of warfare among diverse groups, such as the differences between the Plains Indians and the Iroquois. It would be found that the types are adaptive forms to specific contexts. But from the perspective of general evolution, we would search for stages in the overall development of warfare. We would then discover increases in the scale of war, in the number of men fighting and dying, in the duration of the war, and in the consequences of warfare for human societies. As the authors point out, then, "progress" is not to be equated with "good" but with development.

To sum up the distinction between the two aspects:

> General cultural evolution . . . is passage from less to greater energy transformation, lower to higher levels of integration, and less to greater all-round adaptability. Specific evolution is the phylogenetic, ramifying, historic passage of culture along its many lines, the adaptive modification of particular cultures. [21]

Sahlins and Service make a number of additional points about their theory, such as the "phylogenetic discontinuity of progress," which says that advanced forms of culture do not usually generate the next stage of advance; adaptation at one stage tends to mean the inability to be adaptive at a higher stage.

But we need not delve into the details of any of the above theorists in order to see that they clearly are trying to reaffirm evolution and just as clearly are rejecting the unilinear type. Stages of evolution can be identified for culture as a whole. Specific cultures, however, show diverse lines of development. The new evolutionists recognize the errors of their intellectual forebears, but they continue the search for patterns of development that can be scientifically identified and analyzed.

DIFFUSION

In spite of the revival of interest in evolution, a more common approach to cultural change is to focus on the processes of diffusion or acculturation. We shall examine each of these in turn in the remainder of this chapter.

Diffusion is simply the spread of elements or traits from one culture to another. Some anthropologists would dispute this, however; Malinowski argued that diffusion cannot even be studied unless we take organized systems or institutions as the units that are diffused rather than traits or even trait complexes.[22] A more general definition, then, would assert that diffusion is the spread of some facet of one culture to another.

The theory of diffusion arose as an alternative to evolution. But some of the early diffusionists were as extravagant in their claims as were the early evolutionists. During the 1920's G. Elliott Smith and W. J. Perry claimed that all the early civilizations arose as a result of diffusion from Egypt. A flowering of culture had occurred in Egypt about 3000 B.C., with developments in such fields as agriculture, mathematics, technology, and the polity. These innovations spread throughout the Mediterranean and, eventually, throughout the world.

This theory was supported by such evidence as cultural similarities between the early Egyptians and peoples in the Western hemisphere. Even the totemism of the Australian aborigines was said to have been a degenerate form of culture that derived from Egypt. In other words, these diffusionists were able to support their theory by arguing that the diffused culture was altered in the course of its spread. On that basis, however, one could argue that virtually anything came from anywhere else; for if, as Smith argued, the pyramid-shaped sacrificial altars of the Mayans derived from the Egyptian habit of constructing pyramids for their mummified dead, it would seem possible to link all sorts of cultural features by the exercise of one's imagination. In addition to the impossible connections between cultures that the theory entails, it also falls before the fact of the multiple, simultaneous invention of ideas and techniques.

Nevertheless, the diffusionists provided a necessary corrective to the evolutionists. The pattern of cultural development could not be understood as a series of stages through which each culture passed as though it existed in isolation. Cultures interacted, and that interaction was of critical importance for change.

Later anthropologists laid great stress on the importance of diffusion as the pattern of change. As Kroeber put it, "whatever else diffusion does or does not involve, it does always involve change for the receiving culture. The total part played by diffusion in human culture is almost incredibly great." [23] This, argued Kroeber, is clear in part because of the "retarded" nature of marginal cultures. That is, those cultures that were farthest from the "higher centers" of civilization and, consequently, less likely to benefit from diffusion, fell farther and farther behind in terms of development. Societies that are relatively isolated are never as culturally rich and complex as those that interact with other societies.

Some anthropologists would argue that as much as 90 percent of known cultures is the result of diffusion. This is perhaps most evident in modern, complex societies. In a famed and often quoted passage, Linton detailed the foreign origin of numberless facets of the average American life: the pattern of his bed, his pajamas, his soap, his umbrella, his money, his coffee, and so forth. And, concludes Linton, if he is a conservative, he will "thank a Hebrew deity in an Indo-European language that he is 100 percent American." [24]

But the process of diffusion clearly affects primitive peoples also. Kroeber offers the example of pipe smoking.[25] Smoking originated in tropical America, where tobacco is an indigenous plant. It spread by diffusion throughout Central and North America, with both "cigar" and "pipe" smoking appearing among various peoples. But the Eskimos apparently did not smoke until recent centuries. They borrowed the habit from traders who came across the Bering Strait. The traders had acquired it from the diffusion across Europe and Asia; the source of that diffusion was Spain, where it had arrived as a result of contact with the Indians of tropical America by Spanish explorers. In other words, pipe smoking reached the Eskimos after a process of diffusion around the entire world.

Obviously, diffusion is an important pattern of change. The problem, then, becomes one of how to use the concept as an analytical tool. That is, what are the problems of theory and method involved in the study of diffusion? One problem, of course, is how to determine whether a particular aspect of culture is the result of diffusion or of innovation within the culture. Some facets of culture are easier to trace back than others. And the problem is compounded by the fact that diffusion very often involves modification as well as transfer. The Japanese, for example, have been noted for their willingness to borrow freely from other cultures and also for their propensity to give their borrowings a distinctive Japanese cast.

A number of examples of this modification are given by Malinowski, who notes that "the clash and interplay of the two cultures produce new things. Even a material object, a tool or an instrument like money, changes in the very process of culture contact." [26] Thus, in Africa, townships, mining componds, and agricultural cooperatives are neither pure imports nor mixtures of African and European elements, but are "entirely new products" that have resulted from "the impact of European civilization on archaic Africa." [27]

Other problems of diffusion theory include the rate of diffusion and factors that bear upon rates and sociocultural variables that impede or facilitate diffusion. The problems of diffusion have been of interest to sociologists as well as anthropologists, so that both disciplines have contributed to our understanding of the diffusion of innovations and other aspects of culture.

Early American diffusionists, unlike the Britishers Smith and Perry, made less grandiose claims for diffusion. Sapir and Wissler tried to come to terms with the problem of identifying and tracing the diffusion of some aspect of culture in their "age-area" theory.[28] This theory gave a basis for determining the chronological status of varied features of culture. It indicated, for example, that culture traits become more complex as they become older; generally, therefore, the simpler the form of the trait the older that form is. Furthermore, traits diffuse from the center of the culture outwardly; the more widely diffused the trait, the older it is. While this approach is reasonable, it has evident limitations. Diffusion from the center outward implies the most direct route; as Kroeber's example of the pipe among the Eskimos shows, sometimes aspects of culture take a very circuitous route. Nor will the sequence of simplicity to complexity always hold up. Nevertheless, this was an effort that led in much more fruitful directions than that of Smith and Perry.

Among contemporary diffusionists, a notable and extensive effort is offered by Rogers in his study of the diffusion of innovations.[29] Rogers bases his analysis and conclusions upon a massive number of studies of diffusion: he summarizes his study in the form of 52 generalizations. Some of Rogers' work is not relevant to our immediate purpose here, e.g., his discussion of traditions of diffusion research. But much of what he has done bears upon the study of diffusion as a pattern of change.

Rogers provides a considerable amount of information related to one of the problems mentioned earlier — sociocultural variables that impede or facilitate diffusion. He discusses the role of norms; the characteristics of the innovation, the innovators, and the adopters; the role of opinion leaders; and the role of the change agent. All of these, of course, bear upon the problem of whether and the extent to which diffusion will occur.

When diffusion does occur, the patterns of change will vary. The older idea of expanding concentric circles is too simple. For example, the pattern of change with respect to the adoption of 2,4-D weed spray was found to resemble a logistic curve.[30] Awareness of the spray spread more rapidly than adoption; later adopters took longer between the period of awareness and adoption than did earlier adopters. And the rate of adoption increased between the slower initial rate and the final leveling-off rate.

As the above suggests, diffusion seems to lend itself particularly to a more formalized approach. And, in fact, more recent efforts have employed mapping techniques, Monte Carlo simulation models, and complex mathematical equations to describe the pattern of change involved in diffusion.[31] Even with hundreds of studies already published, the analysis of diffusion is still in its infancy; sociologists and anthropologists, among others, are employing the most sophisticated techniques available to study this important pattern of change.

ACCULTURATION

Acculturation refers to the influence exercised by one culture on another, or the mutual influence of two cultures, that results in cultural change.   As with diffusion, no definition satisfies every anthropologist.   The one we have just given, however, is similar to the classic formulation of Redfield, Linton and Herskovits: "Acculturation comprehends those phenomena which result when groups of individuals having different cultures come into continuous first-hand contact, with subsequent changes in the original cultural patterns of either or both groups." [32]   In this definition, acculturation is only one aspect of cultural change, while diffusion is only one aspect of acculturation.   Also, diffusion always occurs in the process of acculturation, but it can occur without the "continuous first-hand contact" necessary for acculturation.

Acculturation implies, then, a greater degree of influence than does diffusion, at least in the sense of one culture's influencing another to become more like itself.   Kroeber specifically defines acculturation as a process of change in which there is an "increased similarity" between two cultures.[33]   Diffusion is a more microscopic idea; for in spite of Malinowski's insistence that institutions rather than traits are the units of diffusion, most studies of diffusion focus on specific items.   And even if we study the diffusion of an institution, the study is still more microscopic than that of acculturation, which involves "two cultures bombarding each other with hundreds or thousands of diffusing traits." [34]

Thus, acculturation is a pattern of change in which there is a convergence between two cultures.   And this convergence is the result of continuing contact.   The contact may come about in a number of ways.   Colonization, war, military conquest and occupation, migration, missionary work, trade, travel by businessmen or tourists, and contiguous boundaries are among the means whereby two cultures could have more or less continuing contact.   In addition, the mass media — particularly printed materials and the radio — link peoples throughout the world.

Early acculturation studies focused on a particular kind of contact.[35]   Acculturation was assumed to occur as a result of the impact of a powerful and prestigious culture upon a weaker and backward culture.   Furthermore, acculturation resulted not from the mere fact of interaction, but from the deliberate plan of the powerful. The Colonial Office, for example, tried to "civilize" the Africans; the Bureau of Indian Affairs has tried to "civilize" the American Indians. In this kind of situation, "convergence" is misleading; the two cultures did not converge towards a synthesis, but the weaker became more like the stronger. This meant, of course, that the final outcome of acculturation was the disappearance of the weak and backward culture.

But acculturation is more complex than this. As Redfield, Linton and Herskovits pointed out, a number of factors must be considered in any analysis of acculturation. One is the *type* of contact between two cultures. How many people are involved in the contact, and who are the people involved? Is the contact friendly or hostile? How complex are the two cultures? Where does the contact take place?

In addition, we need to know the situation under which acculturation takes place — whether the process is voluntary or imposed, and the degree of social and political inequality between the two groups concerned. Finally, we need to examine the selective processes by which certain traits are included in the acculturation, and the process of integration of the traits into the accepting culture(s).

The notion that acculturation can occur other than by the integration of aspects of a stronger culture into a weaker one is basic to a more recent theory offered by Dohrenwend and Smith.[36] Pointing out that acculturation studies suffer from a lack of standardized terminology, these authors offer a perspective that will allow analysis in terms of the kind of contact between the two cultures involved and the kind of consequences likely to flow from that contact.

With respect to the first, the two cultures may be categorized as strong, weak, or equal in terms of strength (or ability of members of one culture to impose activities upon members of the other culture). A case of extreme dominance of one culture over another is that of the Afrikaner and the Bantu. Extreme dominance occurs when one culture can bring members of the other into its own activities in low status positions and exclude them from high status positions, and can at the same time gain entrance into the activities of the other in high status positions.

But acculturation can also occur when the two cultures are relatively equal, as in the case of the Spanish-Araucanian contact from the sixteenth to the eighteenth centuries. Neither culture was dominant over the other, but acculturation still occurred. We must not, like some of the early students of acculturation, assume that the process is primarily associated with superior-subordinate relationships between cultures.

Dohrenwend and Smith note four possible directions of change that can result from the contact. One is alienation, involving the discarding by members of one culture of their traditional ways without, however, adopting the ways of the other culture.   A second is reorientation, involving change towards the normative structure of the other culture.   A third is reaffirmation, a nativist movement, in which the traditional culture is reaffirmed.   Fourth is reconstitution, the emergence of a new form such as that found in the Utopian movements.   Thus, acculturation is only one of a number of possible outcomes of culture contact.

In sum, acculturation is a pattern of change in which there is some degree of convergence between two cultures.   That convergence may involve changes in both cultures or primarily in one of the two cultures.   Convergence here does not mean that the similarities outweigh the differences, but only that the two cultures are more alike than they were prior to the contact.

ENDNOTES TO CHAPTER 11

1.   A. L. Kroeber, *Anthropology* (New York: Harcourt, Brace and Company, 1948), p. 352.
2.   *Ibid.*, p. 357.
3.   H. G. Barnett, *Innovation: The Basis of Cultural Change* (New York: McGraw-Hill, 1953), p. 20.
4.   George P. Murdock, "How Culture Changes," in *Man, Culture, and Society*, ed. Harry L. Shapiro (New York: Oxford University Press, 1956), p. 250.
5.   For a different approach taken by anthropologists, see Robert F. Murphy, "Culture Change," in *Biennial Review of Anthropology*, ed. Bernard J. Siegel (Stanford: Stanford University Press, 1967), pp. 1–45.   Murphy examines four studies that "are all mainly concerned with social institutions rather than with the pattern components of culture" (p. 2).
6.   Melville Jacobs and Bernhard J. Stern, *General Anthropology* (New York: Barnes & Noble, Inc., 1952), p. 122.
7.   In a matrilineal sib, the "members of a consanguineal kin group acknowledge a traditional bond of common descent" in the maternal line, but cannot necessarily "trace the actual genealogical connections between individuals." George Peter Murdock, *Social Structure* (New York: The Free Press, 1949), p. 47.
8.   Murdock, *Social Structure*, p. 185.
9.   Jacobs and Stern, *General Anthropology*, p. 122.
10.   E. R. Wolf, "The Study of Evolution," in *Readings in Social Evolution and Development*, ed. S. N. Eisenstadt (Oxford: Pergamon Press, 1970), pp. 181–90.
11.   *Ibid.*, pp. 182–83.
12.   White's thought may be found in two books: Leslie A. White, *The Science of Culture* (New York: Farrar, Straus & Giroux,

Inc., 1949), and *The Evolution of Culture* (New York: McGraw-Hill, 1959).

13. White, *The Science of Culture*, p. 140.

14. Julian H. Steward, *Theory of Culture Change: The Methodology of Multilinear Evolution* (Urbana: University of Illinois Press, 1955), p. 4.

15. *Ibid.*, p. 5.

16. *Ibid.*, p. 36.

17. *Ibid.*, pp. 40–42.

18. Marshall D. Sahlins and Elman R. Service, eds., *Evolution and Culture* (Ann Arbor: The University of Michigan Press, 1960), p. 8.

19. *Ibid.*, pp. 12–13.

20. *Ibid.*, p. 27.

21. *Ibid.*, p. 38.

22. Bronislaw Malinowski, *The Dynamics of Culture Change*, ed. Phyllis M. Kaberry (New Haven: Yale University Press, 1945), p. 19.

23. Kroeber, *Anthropology*, p. 412.

24. Ralph Linton, *The Study of Man* (New York: Appleton-Century Co., 1936), p. 327.

25. Kroeber, *Anthropology*, pp. 478–80.

26. Malinowski, *The Dynamics of Culture Change*, p. 25.

27. *Ibid.*

28. Melville J. Herskovits, *Man and His Works* (New York: Alfred A. Knopf, Inc., 1947), pp. 517ff.

29. Everett M. Rogers, *Diffusion of Innovations* (New York: The Free Press).

30. *Ibid.*, p. 109.

31. See, for example, Torsten Hagerstrand, "On the Monte Carlo Simulation of Diffusion," *European Journal of Sociology*, VI (1965), 43–67; and Robert Mason and Albert N. Halter, "The Application of a System of Simultaneous Equations to an Innovation Diffusion Model," *Social Forces*, XLVII (Dec., 1968), 182–95.

32. Robert Redfield, Ralph Linton, and Melville J. Herskovits, "Memorandum for the Study of Acculturation," in *Beyond the Frontier: Social Process and Cultural Change*, ed. Paul Bohannan and Fred Plog (Garden City: The Natural History Press, 1967), p. 182. The article was originally published in the *American Anthropologist* in 1936.

33. Kroeber, *Anthropology*, p. 425.

34. *Ibid.*

35. *Ibid.*, p. 428.

36. Bruce P. Dohrenwend and Robert J. Smith, "Toward a Theory of Acculturation," *Southwestern Journal of Anthropology*, XVIII (Spring, 1968), 30–39.

CHAPTER 12

Societal Patterns:
Industrialization and Modernization

"The mass of men lead lives of quiet desperation," wrote Thoreau. There may be many in the contemporary world who are struggling with desperation, but not many appear to be doing so quietly. Rather, the whole world is caught up in that quest that drove Thoreau into the wilderness: "I wanted to live deep and suck out all the marrow of life. . . ." Peoples throughout the world are no longer content — if they ever were — to live in quiet desperation; a passion for bread and freedom has swept over the world.[1]

A primary reason for this passion is that peoples of the world are no longer willing to be paupers, to eke out a wretched existence on crumbs that fall from the well-filled tables of the affluent few. The situation is dramatized in the Indian untouchable who picks undigested pieces of grain out of cow dung in order that he and his family may eat, and in the thousands of Latin American children dying for lack of water, and the hundreds of millions throughout the world who exist at every moment on the edge of starvation or disease.[2]

In more quantitative terms, we may note the gross inequalities among the world's nations.[3] If we divide up the nations into five groups according to their level of economic and political development, there are striking differences in valued goods and services. For example, the gross national product in recent times has ranged from $45 per capita to $2577 per capita; the average of eleven traditional nations was $56 per capita, while the average of fourteen high-mass-consumption nations was $1330 per capita.

Other figures show the same disparities. Among the nations at the lowest level, adult literacy averaged 12.9 percent of the adult population, while the figure was 98.0 percent for the nations at the highest level. Again, there was an average of 46,073 citizens for every physician among the eleven lowest nations, while in the fourteen highest nations the average was 875 inhabitants per physician.

Because of such disparities, and because of their unwillingness to tolerate them any longer, the peoples of the world are avidly pursuing the pattern of change called modernization. As noted in the first chapter, this does not mean that they are pursuing a course that will lead them to an American type of social order or economic structure. It is a pursuit of bread and freedom rather than of Americanization or Westernization. We have dealt with various facets of this quest at a number of points throughout the book; in this chapter, we shall focus on it as a pattern of change. What is involved in modernization? We must begin by trying to clarify the meaning of the term and of another that is often associated with it — industrialization.

MODERNIZATION AND INDUSTRIALIZATION: CLARIFICATIONS

Historically, modernization and industrialization have been closely associated, but they are not equivalent terms. Modernization is a more inclusive term, for modernization can occur apart from industrialization. As Apter has noted, in the West modernization proceeded by commercialization and industrialization, while in some non-Western areas modernization has proceeded by commercialization and bureaucracy. Thus, "modernization can . . . be seen as something apart from industrialization — caused by it in the West but causing it in other areas." [4] Obviously, both modernization and industrialization involve the crucial element of economic growth, but that growth can occur apart from industrialization, while it is always integral to modernization.

Industrialization and Economic Growth

Industrialization, in simple terms, is economic development through a transformation of the sources and quantities of energy employed.[5] In the agrarian society, for the most part, man and animal power were the sources of energy. It has been estimated that in 1850 65 percent of the energy used in American work was supplied by man and animals. By 1950, 65 percent of the energy was supplied by fossil fuels and hydroelectric power, and energy consumption had soared from 435 horsepower-hours per person in 1850 to 4470 horsepower-hours per person in 1950.[6]

A number of scholars have wrestled with the problem of defining stages of industrial and economic development. Perhaps one of the best known efforts is that of Rostow, who has identified five stages of economic growth.[7] These stages include the traditional setting, preconditions for "take-off," the take-off itself, the thrust towards maturity, and the stage of high mass consumption. Since these five stages, at least in their general outline, have been received with some degree of approval among many economists, we shall briefly characterize them.

The traditional setting is characterized by limited potential for productivity; science, technology, and attitudes that prevail in the society all function to put a ceiling on development. Furthermore, agriculture is predominant but not highly productive, little capital is available, few people have any savings, and illiteracy is common.

In the second stage, conditions necessary for industrialization begin to take shape. The people become convinced that economic progress is possible and that it will bring them numerous desirable benefits. Certain changes in the economic structure begin, such as the formation of banks. The content of education shifts so as to prepare people for the coming economic change and to equip them to participate in it. And most importantly, the polity takes the form of a centralized authority for the nation; it is difficult if not impossible for the next stage to be attained without a strong government.

In the third, or take-off, stage, rapid growth is achieved through the application of modern industrial techniques in a limited number of sectors of the economy. Moreover, this growth becomes self-sustaining. One necessary condition for take-off to occur is the rise of the proportion of net investment to national income to something over 10 percent, "definitely outstripping the likely population pressure . . . and yielding a distinct rise in real output per capita."[8] The noneconomic facets of take-off include the social and political triumph of those committed to modernization over those who tend either to cleave to traditionalism or to pursue other goals.

The fourth stage, the drive to maturity, involves the application of modern technology over the whole range of the economy. In this way, new sectors may supplant older ones as the driving mechanism that sustains growth. In the United States, for example, railways, coal, iron, and heavy engineering dominated the economy and sustained its growth after the middle of the nineteenth century; then steel, ships, chemicals, electricity, and varied manufactured products served the same purpose. During this stage about 10 to 20 percent of national income is invested. As a rule of thumb, maturity is achieved somewhere around sixty years after take-off in the developed nations.

Finally, there is the fifth stage, the age of high mass consumption. Actually, once the stage of maturity has been reached and the commitment made to extend technology into all spheres of life, a number of directions are available. A society might focus on welfare for its people, or expand consumption, or strive for enhanced power in the international arena. The United States, according to Rostow, opted for the second of the three in the 1920's. It was then that the movement to suburbia began, the automobile was made available to the masses of people, a proliferation of household gadgets appeared on the market, and a number of other consumption-encouraging trends were started.

As a general outline of economic development that is tied up with industrialization, Rostow's stages apply to a number of nations, though not to all.[9] The important point for our purposes is that industrialization is not simply an economic and technological pattern of change, but a social and cultural one also. We shall examine some of these social and cultural implications after we clarify the meaning of modernization as a process distinct from industrialization.

Modernization and Economic Growth

As pointed out above, modernization also involves economic growth, and that growth may or may not be based upon industrialization. Thus, we shall refer to industrialization as economic growth that occurs through the application of technology to industrial development and to modernization as a general process involving economic growth along with social and cultural development.

Most efforts to define modernization recognize it as a more inclusive term. Bendix defines industrialization along the lines of our definition, and defines modernization as "all those *social* and *political* changes that accompanied industrialization in many countries of Western civilization."[10]   This is congruent with my own idea, if we substitute economic development for industrialization and omit the specific reference to Western nations.

Many scholars have tried to capture what could be called the essence of modernization. To some, this has meant the kind of social order that is modern or in the process of becoming modern. Economists, political scientists, sociologists and others will see that social order, of course, in differing terms. To others, the essence of modernization is to be found in individual personalities

— modernization demands and results in a particular kind of individual: recall, for example, the theories of McClelland and Hagen.

To still others, modernization seems to involve choice, and the choice has been made possible by other developments. Apter emphasizes the importance of choice:

> In my view, modernization as a non-economic process originates when a culture embodies an attitude of inquiry and questioning about how men make choices — moral (or normative), social (or structural), and personal (or behavioral). The problem of choice is central for modern man.[11]

According to Pool, modernization is "very largely, the process of acquiring new images" — such as the image of directed change or of the possibility of development.[12] The process of acquiring new images is made possible by the mass media; people, therefore, are confronted with new alternatives and the necessity for choice.

Although, then, there are numerous differences, there is also a considerable area of agreement about the meaning of modernization. Among the characteristics of modernity upon which there is considerable consensus are the following:

> (1) a degree of self-sustaining growth in the economy — or at least growth sufficient to increase both production and consumption regularly; (2) a measure of public participation in the polity . . .; (3) a diffusion of secular-rational norms in the culture . . .; (4) an increment of mobility in the society . . .; (5) a corresponding transformation in the modal personality that equips individuals to function effectively in a social order that operates according to the foregoing characteristics. . . .[13]

Obviously, modernization entails the problem of bread and freedom mentioned earlier. And, like industrialization, it involves not only economic growth but a number of social and cultural changes. But, again, we must not leap to the erroneous conclusion that there is only one path to modernization or that the process itself leads to a single end. Indeed, since the social context in which modernization occurs has been quite diverse for various nations, we would expect differences both among nations which have already modernized and among those in the process or yet to begin the process.[14]

In the following sections, we shall try to identify the social and cultural changes that have been associated with modernization. I shall use the term modernization rather than industrialization, recognizing that most often the latter was a part of the former. The latter term will be used whenever the material applies specifically to that techno-economic process rather than to the larger process of modernization.

CONDITIONS OF MODERNIZATION

What is necessary for modernization to occur? From the list of characteristics of modernity given in the last section, we should expect certain economic, social, and social-psychological factors to be involved. Some of the most important of these factors will be identified below. At least two problems remain unresolved, however. One is how many of the factors are actually necessary, and the second is the extent to which a particular factor is a conditon, a concomitant, or a result of modernization.

The latter point has been discussed by Weiner, who notes that while there is general agreement that values and attitudes must change in order for modernization to occur, there are two diverse positions on sequence.[15] Some scholars argue that the values and attitudes must change *prior* to the creation of a modern social order. Others argue that values, attitudes, and behavior will all follow when opportunities and incentives are offered to people.

A more realistic approach would be to recognize the interaction between values, attitudes, and institutional arrangements. That is, institutional arrangements must at least be sufficiently flexible to allow some beginnings of development. And values and attitudes must at least be favorably disposed to change. Once modernization begins, whether in one or the other of the two areas, there will be a process of interaction in which attitudes, values, behavior, and institutional arrangements will all change.

While causal or interactive relationships are not clear, certain factors do seem to be necessary for modernization to proceed. We shall leave the problem of economic conditions to the economists for the most part. Where modernization involves industrialization, sustained economic growth demands three preconditions according to Rostow:

> First, a build-up of social overhead capital, notably in transport. This build-up was necessary not merely to permit an economical national market to be created and to allow natural resources to be productively exploited, but also to permit the national government effectively to rule. Second, a technological revolution in agriculture . . . Third, an expansion in imports financed by the more efficient production and marketing of some natural resources plus, where possible, capital imports.[16]

While many economists would agree with Rostow's position, others would differ at one or more points. There are debates both about the conditions necessary for growth and about the appropriate path towards a modern economy. Examples of arguments regarding the latter are whether a nation should opt for light or heavy industry and whether growth can be achieved through balanced or unbalanced change in various economic sectors.

A particularly important aspect of the economic situation of developing nations today is the socioeconomic environment. Habakkuk has pointed out a number of ways in which the socioeconomic climate of England greatly facilitated that nation's development. English trade was favored by geography and by the lack of destructive wars and political disarray. The size and nature of the market were also "exceptionally favorable. The geographical size of the market available to English manufacturers was wide — transport costs were lower, marketing facilities better, internal tariffs, tolls, etc. . . . were absent" in comparison to continental countries.[17]

In contrast to England and to other European nations, peasant societies of today face agonizing problems. They do not have the opportunity for significant territorial expansion. They are at a technological disadvantage with respect to competitors. They have a far greater rate of increase of population. And their economy is less differentiated; about 80 percent of the population is engaged in agriculture. Thus, "there is no real analogy with the European past; and the labour-saving capital-intensive methods of the European present are even less applicable." [18]

Consequently, it is difficult at best to identify the economic conditions that are necessary for the development of contemporary peasant societies. But clearly the developed nations play a crucial role in contemporary efforts at modernization. The developed nations were literally subsidized in their growth by the territorial and market expansion and the supply of resources afforded by the less developed and underdeveloped nations of today. The fact that some nations have modernized means that the situation in which modernization must occur has completely altered. Recognizing this fact, the Commission on International Development recommended that the industrialized countries each transfer a minimum of 1 percent of their GNP to low-income countries in order to facilitate development.[19] As of 1968, France and Portugal each provided aid that amounted to 0.68 percent of their respective GNPs; other nations fell even further below the 1 percent recommendation (the United States ranked ninth, with 0.41 percent).[20]

The economic factors are both perplexing and greatly important. Noneconomic factors, however, are equally important, although there seems to be somewhat more agreement on the kinds of noneconomic factors necessary for development. Rostow mentioned a modernizing elite, a raising of the "horizon of expectations" among the masses, and political factors as important noneconomic conditions of modernization.[21] Thus, he has touched upon the two categories of noneconomic factors that we shall consider — structural and social-psychological.

Economic growth is unlikely under certain structural conditions. The system of land tenure can preclude the agricultural development which is crucial to modernization. Popular participation in the affairs of the nation may be minimal and the increase of that participation precluded by a tyrannical government locked in with a rigid system of stratification. Associated with this, there is often little in the way of voluntary associations. Finally, the government and its bureaucracy may be unstable, inefficient, ineffective (except in the area of securing benefits for its own members), and corrupt.

These flaws in the institutional arrangements are likely to be interrelated and, therefore, self-sustaining. Moreover, they are likely to be supported by social-psychological factors. Values and attitudes support the institutions, and vice versa. This is why I argued above that an effort to determine causal priority is fruitless: there is interaction and mutual support rather than a cause-and-effect relationship.

Among the social-psychological factors that are important for modernization, one stands out as particularly urgent — a commitment of the people, or at least a willingness of the people, to modernize. Political leaders, therefore, may find that a considerable amount of their time and energy must be devoted to securing that commitment or willingness. An example of this is Indonesia, where the government allotted "immense resources to creating and maintaining particular attitudes and states of mind" in the post-1958 period.[22] In particular, the government invested heavily in "symbolic activity" — various ceremonial and ritual activities as well as propaganda and indoctrination. The results of this effort are ambiguous. On the one hand, certain economic and administrative problems were resolved; nationalist ideas impelled men to accept undesirable work that needed to be done.

But on the other hand, the overall administrative and economic effectiveness of the nation may have suffered. For an atmosphere was created in which "economic tasks are seen as of secondary importance, ideological truth and political enthusiasm being seen as the highest needs of the state." [23] The overall effects of using a nationalist ideology to secure commitment to modernization are problematic in other nations also. Nevertheless, the commitment is an imperative, and securing it may involve a nation in one of those many dilemmas of society in which a course must be pursued that makes the end towards which it seemingly leads more difficult to attain.

One reason why the commitment may be difficult to obtain is that people are called upon to disrupt old ways and, more importantly, old relationships. Men and their families may have to break away from traditional kin relationships and kin responsibilities. A second reason is that the people are normally called upon to make personal sacrifices in behalf of overall development and economic growth. Their commitment, in other words, is more likely to be in terms of securing for themselves the fruits of modernization rather than in terms of the long-range growth of the economy. In economic terms, the demand for services and consumer goods contradicts the demand for capital accumulation and growth.

A third reason that commitment is difficult to secure is that people may be called upon to work at tasks that for one reason or another involve psychic strain. Industrialization can require individuals to work at jobs that exact heavy psychic costs.[24] Yet commitment to such jobs is important. In fact, labor commitment in general is important for a number of reasons, including the lesser degree of supervision required, the greater predictability of behavior, and the reliability of behavior in crisis situations.[25]

Finally, the commitment may be difficult to secure because the leaders who are calling upon their people for sacrifice do not themselves appear to make any sacrifices. When the modernizing elite gains the immediate benefits of economic growth, the people are less likely to be willing to forego those benefits until some indeterminate future.

The extent to which commitment has been gained among the developing nations varies. Perhaps China has been singularly successful in this respect. Maoist ideology and the refusal of the elite to indulge itself in a way not possible to the rest of the nation have helped both to unify the people and to secure a remarkable degree of commitment to the task of building China.

A variety of values and attitudes have been noted as important to attaining modernization, but for the most part they bear upon the problem of commitment. Acceptance of nationalist ideology, willingness to be mobile, approval of secular-rational norms — all ultimately are tied to the commitment to modernization and the kinds of behavior conducive to modernization. Different methods may be employed to secure the commitment, such as ideology, structural change (in addition to other factors, decentralization has been important in China), and symbolic activities. But without the commitment, modernization will probably prove to be abortive.

Nevertheless, having said all this, we cannot conclude that

a committed people will modernize. Modernization is not simply "out there" waiting for the willing to seize it. In addition to problems of resources, capital accumulation, commitment, and so on, there are three critical problem areas that work against the modernization of nations today.

First, there is the problem of a model of modernization. I have said that modernization can and must follow diverse paths. But what paths? Social scientists themselves differ on what is necessary for modernization in the contemporary world. And some nations have tried to model their development partly on the West: the results have been counter-productive in many cases. This problem has been well summarized:

> The pioneer nations were trebly fortunate. On the whole, their trends of population growth, urbanization, and mechanization helped and reinforced each other. For present day developers the opposite is the case. All the various elements — population, patterns of technology, urban expansion — contradict and impede the others.[26]

A good example of this problem area is education, which many developing nations have associated with the affluence of the West (along with industrialization). Undoubtedly, a literate population is an integral part of a modern society. But some developing nations have expanded their educational systems too rapidly, with the result that they have a double problem. On the one hand, they are forced to support an expensive system at a time when capital is desperately needed for economic expansion. And on the other hand, the populace is achieving an education for which there is little use; the economic opportunities do not match the available educated population. Moreover, all these problems are compounded when the education is geared towards "aristocratic tastes and philosophic concerns," a situation which Horowitz calls "mis-education":

> This produces an anti-industrial bias; education too is not geared for industrial concepts of professional training, still harkening back to educating a conversationally stimulating, cultivating leisure class. This deepens the crisis of using "manpower" with advanced degrees.[27]

A second problem that works against contemporary modernization is the advantageous position of the developed nations, a point noted above in our discussion of the socioeconomic environment of peasant nations. The enormous advantage that the developed nations have in terms of their control of resources, research, and capital makes the task of modernization awesome for developing nations. Furthermore, modernization means that these nations will have to break into the world market, and in some cases that is a little like a man deciding to start a new automobile corporation to compete with General Motors. As noted before, apart from a sense of responsibility on the part of developed nations, the plight of the developing nations is grim indeed.

But even if the developed nations have a commitment to world-wide modernization, a third problem area intrudes: is world-wide modernization technically possible? A number of observers have recently claimed that the resources of the earth are insufficient to bring the world's population up to the standard of living enjoyed by much of the West. Furthermore, it is probable that our own standards necessarily will be lowered within the next few decades. And this prediction is not based upon a "prophet of doom" mentality, but upon a computer simulation model of the relationships between earth's population, natural resources, pollution, capital, and food production.[28]

I think that the warning regarding problems of resources is well taken, but unanticipated technological developments have nullified similar warnings in the past. We must be aware of the consequences of trying to thrust all of mankind into a Western affluence; at the same time, I am not as pessimistic regarding the possibility of such a development as are some others. If, however, technology does not advance rapidly enough to permit developing nations to satisfy their expectations at least minimally, the world situation will be explosive indeed.

In sum, while we can identify some of the conditions that are necessary for modernization, we can hardly overstress the enormous problems facing the developing nations. Nor can we overstress the significant role of the developed nations. The future of peace may well hinge upon our understanding of this critical area and upon our willingness to assume our own share of responsibility for the modernization of nations. The nature of that responsibility is not entirely clear; certainly, it cannot sink into the imperialism of past ages. But the future will be perilous and violent if the developed nations have an attitude towards the developing nations that says: "You can modernize if only you want to. If you're willing to work for it, you can get it. After all, we did."

CONSEQUENCES OF MODERNIZATION

When we deal with the "consequences" of modernization, we are referring to those changes which have commonly been found to occur along with modernization. By definition, modernization involves change in numerous areas. The changes we shall discuss are typical.[29] This does not mean that they are necessary or determined. Future modernization may well take paths that do not involve the kind of changes described in the following paragraphs. In fact, those familiar with China will recognize that that nation is pursuing a path of modernization that diverges from some of the following.

Keeping in mind, then, that these changes are typical, though not always necessary, we shall outline changes in six broad areas: demography, the stratification system, the polity, education, the family, and values, attitudes, and personality. We shall then give some attention to changes that have at times been associated — wrongly — with modernization. The remainder of the chapter will focus on three types of processes which have been, and are, of particular importance: urbanization, secularization, and bureaucratization.

Demographic changes that typically have occurred along with modernization include the population growth (intensified by a lowered death rate) and a shift from rural to urban areas. In the traditional society, 70 percent or more of the people are involved in agriculture, but a modern society is an urban society.

Numerous changes occur in the stratification system during modernization. Tumin has described nine general changes in stratification as a society moves towards industrialization[30]:

1. The division of labor becomes more complex, with increasing numbers of specialists;
2. Status tends to be based upon achievement instead of ascription;
3. An adequate means of measuring performance of those engaged in production becomes a central concern;
4. Work shifts from an intrinsically gratifying activity to one that is instrumental, a means to reward rather than the reward itself;
5. The rewards available for distribution increase;
6. Rewards are distributed on a somewhat more equal basis;
7. Some shifts occur in the life chances of those in various social strata;
8. Some shifts occur in the distribution of social prestige, though the advantage of the modern society over the traditional is problematic in this area.
9. Similar shifts and similar problems are to be found in the distribution of power.

As the above implies, the middle and upper classes expand during modernization. This expansion is a function of the changing occupational structure, and it means that there is a high rate of mobility. Modernization, then, involves a reversal of the usual trend in traditional societies, which is towards increasing inequality. That is, as we go from hunting and gathering to horticultural to agrarian societies, we find ever-increasing inequality; the modern society represents the historical reversal of that trend.[31]

Along with these changes in stratification, there is also a tendency for the status of females to rise, for adolescents to gain new positions of status, and for the aged to lose high status. Finally, an associated change is the proliferation of organizations, both formal and voluntary associations. These organizations reflect occupational interests, status problems, status achievement, and so forth.

Modernization brings changes in the polity also. Local interests and loyalties give way to some extent to nationalism. The economy itself demands this shift insofar as it requires an extensive market and modern methods of communication and transportation. Local isolation and purely parochial interests contravene large-scale economic development.

There is also a tendency towards a greater democratization of the political process; political power tends to be more widely distributed (though by no means equalized) among various segments of the modernizing or modern nation. The state also greatly expands its functions. The enormous increase in size and complexity of government which we have previously noted is associated with proliferation of governmental functions. Some indication of this change may be seen in the data on the number of employees of the federal government. In the United States, federal employees increased nearly five hundredfold from 1816 to 1961 — from 5000 to 2,436,000 — while the population increased only a little over twentyfold.[32]

Among other typical changes in the polity, we might mention the following: the locus of national politics is the urban area, and particularly the capital city; there is a tendency towards over-urbanization, creating a source of anomic activity; and intergroup interaction is as often marked by conflict as by integration.[33] The latter point has been stressed by Eisenstadt, who has argued that modernization necessarily involves disorganization and, consequently, protest movements. The protest tends to revolve about three basic themes: 1. a search for integrative principles of order and justice; 2. a search for "new common symbols" to provide both personal and collective identity; and 3. a search for meaning and the possibility of self-actualization within the emerging social structure.[34]

In other words, just as we must not minimize the extraordinary difficulty of modernizing for contemporary nations, neither must we slight the human agony and social disruption that

219

has been and seemingly will be a part of modernization. Internal political violence (as mentioned in Chapter 8), repressive reactions on the part of governments, and mass movements of various kinds are some of the political problems that have accompanied modernization. Whether developing nations of the present can avoid these remains to be seen.

The fourth area in which significant change occurs in modernization is education. Education changes both quantitatively and qualitatively. Quantitatively, there is often considerable growth of educational organizations and enrollment in schools. One of the initial steps in nations committed to modernization is the establishment of universal primary education. And efforts are made to rapidly expand secondary and university education. Sometimes this expansion is linked with efforts by local areas to enhance their own status by having their own schools.[35]

Qualitatively, education changes because the complex division of labor of the modernizing society "demands a system of formal education to prepare men for their jobs — apprenticeship is too conservative, too slow, too clumsy." [36] In other words, education is geared towards preparing individuals to function in a new type of social structure. And that means that the curriculum is modernized, a significant part of the education is of a technical nature, and education is secular rather than sacred.[37]

The family is a fifth area of change. The shift from rural to urban areas puts great strains on extended kinship relations. The nuclear family has often become prominent as the nation modernizes. Nevertheless, there has not been any kind of universal breakdown of traditional kinship relations. And as we noted in the first chapter, a variety of family forms seem to be compatible with modernization.

One reason why changes in the family are diverse in differing societies is that relationships are not severed by mere physical separation. In education, government, or the system of stratification the new structure may simply displace the old. But physical distance among kin does not necessarily mean emotional separation. The family may be important to the mobile individual, either in aiding him and supporting him in his mobility, or by depending upon him to use his enhanced status to help others in the family become mobile.

One change in the family that is apparently universal is a considerable transfer of functions to other social units. It has often been pointed out that in primitive or traditional settings, economic, educational, religious, and emotional needs all tended to be provided for in the family; but with modernization, much of this responsibility is transferred to other social units, such as the government, the schools, and business.

Finally, modernization brings considerable change in the area of values, attitudes, and personality. For the most part, these are summed up in the concept of the "modern man." The modern man, according to Lerner, is one whose personality has been transformed to include "an increment of self-things seeking . . . and 'need-achievement' . . . and an increment of self-others seeking." [38] The latter is what Lerner termed empathy in an earlier work. Empathy is "the capacity to see oneself in the other fellow's situation" and is "an indispensable skill for people moving out of traditional settings." [39] It is the ability to identify with the new and to cope with new demands. Such an ability enables the individual to implement his commitment to modernization.

This ability to cope with the new is also reflected in Inkeles' portrait of the modern man. Inkeles identifies nine elements of the modern personality: readiness for the new and for innovation; ability to formulate opinions over a wide range of matters, with a tendency to be democratic in those opinions; an orientation to the present or future rather than to the past; an orientation towards planning; a belief in man's ability to control his own destiny; a belief in man's capacity for understanding and for accurately anticipating the behavior of others; a sense of the dignity of humans; a faith in science and technology; and a belief in distributive justice (rewards should correlate with contributions).[40]

Obviously, a modern man is one who is capable of functioning effectively in a nation that is experiencing economic growth, of participating in political development and political decisions, and of ordering his behavior and his decisions by secular-rational norms. Nevertheless, Inkeles' portrait of the modern man is general enough that it does not imply uniform human beings. For the most part, the nine characteristics described by Inkeles would apply to the modern man in China, in Japan, in Nigeria, in Argentina, and elsewhere. Obviously, there are significant differences in both the people and the course of development in these nations. For instance, a most important facet of the personality of the modern man is his commitment to change, to a future that is different from the past and present. But the particular future to which he is committed can vary considerably while still requiring the same basic elements of personality.

Thus, I am stressing again a point made earlier — that there are some changes that have sometimes been wrongly associated with modernization. For whatever else modernization means, it does not mean or require uniformity; it does not mean that the whole world will someday be a modern West.

Two other changes which have been wrongly identified — implicitly or explicitly — as inevitable consequences of modernization are the obliteration of the traditional and the disruption of valued relationships. There are, of course, clear differences between the traditional and the modern, but modernization does not demand a shedding of the traditional with each forward step towards the modern.[41] Some people in a society may opt for that course — for severing themselves from all tradition. But others may opt for a different course, as exemplified by Neyl, a peasant village near Cologne. For at least seventy years, the villagers maintained their cultural identity in the midst of an industrial civilization and, in fact, used industrial wage-earnings to preserve the basic elements of their peasant culture.[42]

In sum, the consequences of modernization are diverse. And although modernization took a particular form in the West, it does not follow that other societies will take that course. Nor does modernization obliterate the traditional. Elements of tradition and pockets of traditional culture may be maintained within the modernizing society. And in some cases, traditional elements may provide a firm base upon which to modernize. This occurred in Japan, where, among other things, the traditional kinship system greatly aided modernization.[43]

MODERNIZATION AND URBANIZATION

We are living in an increasingly urban world. From 1750 to 1960 the population of the world increased by about 300 percent, from 728 million to almost 3 billion. But the number of people living in towns of 5000 or more increased about 1400 percent, from 22 million to over 900 million. In 1800, one city had a population of 1 million or more — London. By 1960, the number of such cities was approaching 100.[44]

While urbanization has not always meant modernization, the latter process has been marked by urbanization wherever it has occurred. In short, "the association of urbanization, industrialization, and per capita income is definitely positive and marked."[45] There are, of course, instances of economic development in local communities; factories have been located in essentially rural areas. But all modern societies are highly urbanized, and modernizing societies are generally characterized by a process of urbanization.

There are clear reasons for the relationship of modernization and urbanization. Most importantly, modernization has typically involved industrialization; and industries have typically been located in urban areas, with a consequent influx of population seeking to take advantage of the economic opportunities. But not all people in contemporary societies have come to the cities to

exploit economic opportunities. A study of Indonesian cities re-
vealed that some of the urban migration was a result of a search
for security, or political advancement, or other noneconomic opportunities opened up by rapid change.[46]

A more sophisticated account of the relationship between
urbanization and modernization has been formulated by Lerner.
He argues that urbanization is integral to modernization. Only
in the city do we find the "complex of skills and resources" necessary for a modern industrial economy. Furthermore, it is within
the urban setting that literacy and the mass media grow. Literacy
is necessary to performing the skills demanded by the modern
society, and the mass media accelerate the development of a
literate population. And out of this development comes the participation in the media and in political life which is characteristic
of all modern societies.[47] A sample of 54 countries shows a high
correlation among these variables — urbanism, literacy, media
participation, and political participation — and enables Lerner
to state with some confidence that "literacy and media participation
may be considered as a supply-and-demand reciprocal in a communication market whose locus, at least in its historical inception,
can only be urban." [48]

But later data require some revision of this thesis. On the
basis of 1961 data, urbanization was not found to be as essential
to the growth of literacy and the mass media. A sample of 32
nations showed that considerable growth in literacy could occur
at a quite low level of urbanization. Nor were the rates of growth
of literacy and urbanization found to increase together to the
25 percent level (as Lerner had found) to a significant degree.
Another of Lerner's hypotheses, however, still held: once a society
is about 25 percent urban, literacy and media consumption are
strongly correlated.[49]

Thus, the relationship between urbanization and modernization is not a simple one. Moreover, some scholars have argued
that urbanization is neither necessary nor sufficient for economic
development in the contemporary world.[50] Urbanization can facilitate that development; but under certain circumstances it can
impede economic development also. The latter occurs when
urbanization proceeds too rapidly, creating serious economic, political, and social problems that divert time, energy, and resources
away from development. A number of nations face these problems of overurbanization, but apparently only China has ever
actively tried to resolve them by sending some of the urban dwel-
lers out into the countryside.[51]

Whether modernization can indeed occur apart from urbanization is perhaps a moot question. With the exception of China,
the nations of the world are both modernizing and urbanizing.

The important questions, therefore, include the optimum rate of urbanization, the precise way in which urbanism facilitates modernization (and impedes it), and the consequences of urbanization for people's lives. For in addition to its role in the modernization process, urbanization has often been linked with the creation of anomie and alienation among people. It is clear both that urban life can be socially disruptive and that family and kin relations can remain strong, as we have noted in Japan, and as has been found in Lebanon and West Africa among others.[52] It is not urbanization per se that leads to one or the other of these results, but urbanization in combination with other sociocultural factors.

In sum, urbanization is generally occurring along with modernization. There are ways in which urbanism facilitates that modernization — the provision of centralized political control, the stimulus offered to literacy and education, the enhanced ease of coordination, the breaking down of localism, for example. But urbanization can occur too rapidly and become an impediment. And under certain circumstances, urbanization may be a debilitating experience to large numbers of people. Any nation committed to modernization, therefore, must deal with the serious problems presented by — and take advantage of the opportunities offered by — the process of urbanization.

MODERNIZATION AND SECULARIZATION

According to Max Weber, we live in an age that is "characterized by rationalization and intellectualization and, above all, by the 'disenchantment of the world.' "[53] The world is no longer a sacred phenomenon. Life is no longer an unfathomable mystery. The fate of humanity is no longer in the hands of some ethereal, superhuman being. Indeed, the religion which may at one time have abetted human development is no longer needed. Protestantism facilitated the rise of capitalism, but capitalism is now triumphant, rests upon "mechanical foundations," and no longer needs the support of religion.[54]

Many writers would agree with Weber that modernization is a process that slowly but surely pushes religion to the periphery of human existence. Like Dmitri in Dostoyevsky's *The Brothers Karamazov*, they see the acceptance of science as the loss of God. But while modernization does involve secularization, it does not necessarily involve the decline of religion. The polarity between modernization and religion, like that between modernization and tradition, is a distortion of reality.

What, then, do we mean by secularization? O'Dea defines it in terms of two basic changes in thinking:

There is first the *'desacralization'* of the attitude toward persons and things — the withdrawal of the kind of emotional involvement which is to be found in the religious response, in the response to the sacred. Secondly, there is the *rationalization of thought* — the withholding of emotional participation in thinking about the world.[55]

More succinctly, Cox spoke of secularization as "a historical process, almost certainly irreversible, in which society and culture are delivered from tutelage to religious control and closed metaphysical world-views." [56]

In other words, secularization is a process whereby man's response to and control of his human and natural environment are increasingly governed by social and rational considerations. But religion may still flourish, for man may continue to look to religion for a number of reasons. Religion may continue to function as a source of or justification for his morality. Religion may afford man some transcendent meaning to his existence. Or the religious community may provide support during times of crisis.

Secularization and religion, then, are not antitheses. In fact, some theologians have eulogized the secularization of Western culture. Cox called it a "liberating" development.[57] For secularization was not a process of death for religion, but only for a particular type of religion. Secularization involved the change of religion, not its disappearance.

Thus, in their survey of economic development, Buchanan and Ellis, two economists, touch upon the inhibiting function of religion. They compare the various religions in the less developed and developing nations of the world with medieval Christianity. Where Islam prevails, for example, material achievements are considered trivial: "Man is expected to disdain the relative and transitory in favor of the absolute and timeless. Acceptance, resignation, compassion, piety and reverence come close to being the proper descriptive terms." [58]

But as we saw in our discussion of the role of the ideology in change, this view is not quite accurate. Some religious systems do function to inhibit economic development. But others function to facilitate that development, including some forms of Islam, Buddhism, and Hinduism. Secularization means social and rational efforts to control and understand existence. Religion may either support that perspective, or may refrain from interfering with it by being restricted to the afterlife.

In some cases, the secularization that accompanies modernization may lead to the abandonment of religion. As McCord has argued, the urbanite who is "confronted with a society where machines have replaced the gods, where traditional incantations have no bearing on whether people find jobs" may well shed his religious affiliation and faith.[59] And a considerable number of urban migrants in the Middle East and in Africa have seemingly abandoned their faith.

But in other cases, modernization proceeds along with a continued religious faith. We have previously noted Geertz' finding in Indonesia that both a traditional Hinduism and a modernized Islam were facilitating economic development.[60] In Ceylon, Buddhism's fortunes have risen and fallen, but the religion has not declined with that nation's political and economic advance in recent times. In fact, for some of the Buddhists, their religion has ceased to be "abstract and other-worldly. It has come back into the world and it is becoming intimately concerned with the day-to-day stresses and strains of a worldly life." [61] And Western industrialism was undertaken in the Sudan without any noticeable effects on the "hard core of Islamic practice — the Pillars of the Faith, dietary regulations, family law, and the like. . . ." [62]

In sum, modernization involves secularization, which is not the demise of religion but, rather, often means a change in religion. The modern man uses his reason as a primary tool for comprehending and controlling his existence. This is the meaning of secularization, and it is a crucial aspect of modernization.

MODERNIZATION AND BUREAUCRATIZATION

For many Americans who put a premium on getting things done, bureaucracy is virtually a four-letter word. It is thought to be the pinnacle of irrationality and inefficiency. It is conceived of as a barrier and a harassment to the "go-getter." These popular connotations reflect the extent to which a bureaucratic organization can diverge from what it is in theory — the most rational and efficient form of large-scale administration.

And whether the popular or the theoretical image is more correct in actuality is quite important, for the modern world is increasingly bureaucratic as well as urban and secular. In the West, government and the merit bureaucracy evolved together: "Each is part of the other. Indeed, a mature political system needs to be partly nonpolitical so as to possess adequate managerial capacity." [63] And the bureaucracy provided that nonpolitical aspect.

Weber noted a number of reasons for the bureaucratization of the modern world.[64] One was the development of a money economy. Weber argued that if officials are paid in produce or commodities rather than money, the bureaucratic structure will gradually change. A second reason was the quantitative and qualitative increase of administrative tasks in the modern state. The technical requirements of administering a large, complex state, with all the social, political, and economic demands made upon it, are such as to demand a bureaucratic type of administration. Finally, bureaucratization has occurred because it is technically superior to any other form of administration (in terms of efficiency).

As far as the developing nations of the world are concerned, we can add a couple of reasons to this list. First, these nations are seeking to carve out a place for themselves in a world dominated by legal-rational societies; their only hope is to develop quickly a legal-rational form of state for themselves. And, second, there are pressures arising from the populace in terms of demand for services and, as importantly, demands for jobs on the part of the educated. Myrdal found increasing waste in the public sector of Asian nations due to the employment of lower civil servants in numbers greater than the need.[65] This is a real political dilemma, of course, since resistance to the pressures for employment and services would make the stability of the government extremely precarious.

Thus, in both modern and modernizing nations, there has been a process of bureaucratization. The force with which modernization seems to demand bureaucratization is reflected in the bureaucratic nature of Communist states where, theoretically, the state is withering away. When the Bolsheviks came to power in the Soviet Union, they promised a purge of the bureaucracy. Lenin even declared that "the whole inherited administrative apparatus would have to be destroyed and replaced by 'a new one, consisting of the armed workers.' " [66] But as early as April, 1918, he recognized that the management of industry demanded a revision of his ideas. Socialism could not be achieved without administrative skills and the guidance of specialists in various fields.

Gradually, the Bolshevik leaders became an industrializing elite. And Lenin led the way. In 1918, he said: "The possibility of building Socialism will be determined precisely by our success in combining the Soviet government and the Soviet organization of administration with the modern achievements of capitalism." [67]

The problems of industrialization generated considerable controversy among Russian leaders. And as bureaucratization proceeded along with industrialization, theoreticians tried to account for that unanticipated outcome. Trotsky argued, for example, that the oppressive bureaucracy was due to the lack of world-wide proletarian revolution rather than to the immaturity of socialism in Russia. Socialism cannot be achieved in one country while capitalism flourishes in the others. Under such conditions, the bureaucracy will grow stronger. Nevertheless, Trotsky, like Lenin, was optimistic about the future — ultimately the bureaucracy must vanish as socialism triumphs.[68]

Since the bureaucracy is an integral part of the modern world, we must ask about the effects of bureaucratization. And it is quickly apparent that the popular image of bureaucracy as an impediment to change may hold true in some cases. Socialist or reform governments have more than once failed to effect the changes they promised because they were thwarted by an existing bureaucracy.[69] Furthermore, in the developing nations the bureaucracy may impede effective political development by expanding too rapidly and, thereby, becoming too strong while other aspects of the polity are still weak.[70]

In spite of its potential for stifling change, however, bureaucracy has been important in modernization; in fact, at this point it would appear that bureaucratization is an indispensable element in modernization. The recognition of this paradoxical nature of bureaucracy has led Mao to be somewhat ambivalent about the bureaucratization of China.[71] Mao grew up in the midst of the disintegration of the traditional bureaucracy, and he saw the corruption that pervaded the bureaucratic organization of the Kuomintang. Moreover, his own ideological commitment is anti-bureaucratic. Nevertheless, bureaucratization proceeded along with modernization following the 1949 establishment of the People's Republic; the Cultural Revolution of the late 1960's, however, seems to represent an effort to stop and even reverse the tendency towards increasing bureaucratization.

In other modernizing nations, bureaucratization has been accepted as a necessary part of development, and the problem is seen in terms of making the bureaucracy work as it ought rather than in terms of minimizing or halting its growth. In addition to the typical problems of bureaucracies, the modernizing nations find the bureaucracy to be problematic for reasons relating to their unique socio-historical situation.[72] For one thing, bureaucracies have expanded before the traditional ways have disappeared to any significant degree. This makes the bureaucracy a political and patronage system; the kinship and friendship ties which presumably are discounted in bureaucratic operations may play a dominant role.

The same traditional patterns of behavior may continue to prevail at the lower levels of the bureaucracy, frustrating governmental efforts to deal impersonally and fairly in large-scale programs that are meant to benefit the people. This is not to say that kinship and friendship ties are absent in the bureaucratic life of modern nations; the problem is the degree to which such ties affect the bureaucracy's relationships to the people.

In those cases in which a bureaucracy existed during the colonial period, other kinds of problems have to be faced during modernization. The paternalistic and authoritarian nature of bureaucratic administration has to be replaced; the bureaucrat must achieve a greater sense of identification with the people. Furthermore, the bureaucracy in the colonial phase existed for a purpose quite different from nation building: it was designed to secure law and order and to administer revenue. And bureaucracies do not easily yield to a radical change of function.

Nevertheless, as Dube has argued, the bureaucracy will play a vital role in modernization. For it contains "people with progressive motivation, wide administrative experience, and a rich store of pooled knowledge." [73] In other words, it contains the kind of people that the Bolsheviks found to be indispensable in Russia's modernization. In addition to this pool of human resources, Spengler has identified four ways in which the bureaucracy facilitates economic development:

1. The bureaucracy can provide the necessary legal and public-service preconditions for development, including law and order, money and banking organizations, and the administrative apparatus necessary for economic enterprise;

2. The bureaucracy can help to modify "the resource-structure of a country, together with its exploitation, as to make it more favorable to economic growth";

3. Where private enterprise lags, the bureaucracy can form public corporations or other types of enterprises that will furnish the initiative for economic development;

4. In more advanced countries, the bureaucracy can fashion tax, fiscal, and investment policies that will sustain and enhance economic growth.[74]

Thus, the state bureaucracy can play a vital role at every stage of economic development. Increasing growth does not diminish this role; indeed, it may root the bureaucracy more deeply into the life of the nation. There are certain countertrends within some bureaucratic organizations; that is, a certain number of nonbureaucratic elements and a certain amount of debureaucratization may be found in individual organizations.[75] But the overall trend is towards increasing bureaucratization.

How far can that trend go? As societies pass from the industrial to the so-called postindustrial stage, does the process of bureaucratization continue or does it enter a phase of reversal? It is difficult at this point to say. There is a tension between bureaucracy and professionalism, and increasing numbers of professionals are working in organizations.   And it has been argued that the bureaucracy — in the sense of a hierarchical, procedurally oriented, impersonal organization — is an inept form that is inadequate to the problems confronting organizations in contemporary modern societies.[76]

Whether this means the impending death of the bureaucratic organization, however, remains to be seen.   Perhaps China will demonstrate for us that modernization can be achieved apart from the bureaucratization that has characterized the rest of the world. Perhaps Western professionals will force the creation of a new organizational form more appropriate to the modern social order. Or perhaps the bureaucracy will emerge triumphant against all counter forces.   I would judge that new forms of administration will be forthcoming, though at some point in the future I may be writing a retraction while working in a bureaucratic maze.

ENDNOTES TO CHAPTER 12

1. For a brief description of the meaning of the hunger for bread and freedom, as well as the dilemmas involved in trying to secure both of them simultaneously, see William McCord, *The Springtime of Freedom* (New York: Oxford University Press, 1965), pp. 3–18.

2. *Ibid.*, pp. 11 and 20.

3. The data in this paragraph are taken from a table in Brigitte Berger, *Societies in Change* (New York: Basic Books, Inc., 1971), p. 52.   The data are generally from the period 1950–1960.

4. David E. Apter, *The Politics of Modernization* (Chicago: University of Chicago Press, 1965), pp. 43–44.

5. Gerhard E. Lenski, *Power and Privilege* (New York: McGraw-Hill Book Company, 1966), pp. 298–99.

6. *Ibid.*

7. Walt W. Rostow, *The Stages of Economic Growth* (New York: Cambridge University Press, 1960).

8. *Ibid.*, p. 37.

9. See, for example, John K. Fairbank, Alexander Eckstein, and L. S. Yang, "Economic Change in Early Modern China: An Analytic Framework," *Economic Development and Cultural Change*, IX (Oct., 1960), 1–26.   The authors suggest five phases of industrialization which are similar to some extent to the scheme of Rostow: traditional equilibrium, the appearance of disequilibrating forces, gestation, breakthrough (takeoff), and self-sustaining growth.   This fits China, India, and most other Far Eastern economies with the exception of Japan.   But modifications are necessary for England and

other West European countries and for Japan. In England, for example, the framework for gestation was provided by the traditional setting itself without the necessity of the "prolonged pre-industrial period of tension and gestation as in the Far Eastern case" (p. 2).

10. Reinhard Bendix, *Nation-Building and Citizenship* (Garden City: Anchor Books, 1964), p. 6.

11. Apter, *The Politics of Modernization*, pp. 9–10.

12. Ithiel de Sola Pool, "The Role of Communication in the Process of Modernization and Technological Change," in *Industrialization and Society*, ed. Bert F. Hoselitz and Wilbert E. Moore (Mouton: UNESCO, 1966), p. 291.

13. Daniel Lerner, "Modernization, Social Aspects," in *International Encyclopedia of the Social Sciences*, Vol. 10 (New York: The Free Press, 1968), p. 387.

14. For example, Black has described seven patterns of political modernization, which differ according to time, place, and social context of the modernization. See C. E. Black, *The Dynamics of Modernization* (New York: Harper & Row, 1966), pp. 106–28.

15. Myron Weiner, ed., *Modernization: The Dynamics of Growth* (New York: Basic Books, Inc., 1966), pp. 9–12.

16. W. W. Rostow, *The Process of Economic Growth*, 2nd edition, (New York: W. W. Norton & Company, Inc., 1962), p. 313.

17. H. J. Habakkuk, "The Historical Experience on the Basic Conditions of Economic Progress," in *Comparative Perspectives On Social Change*, ed. S. N. Eisenstadt (Boston: Little, Brown and Company, 1968), p. 33.

18. Guy Hunter, *Modernizing Peasant Societies* (New York: Oxford University Press, 1969), pp. 98–99.

19. See Lester B. Pearson, et al., *Partners in Development: Report of the Commission on International Development* (New York: Frederick A. Praeger, 1969).

20. See the chart in *Intercom*, January/February, 1970, p. 24. The data were compiled from AID's *Introduction to Program Presentation to the Congress: Proposed FY 1971 Program.*

21. Rostow, *Stages of Economic Growth*, p. 26.

22. Herbert Feith, "Indonesia's Political Symbols and Their Wielders," in *Political Development and Social Change*, ed. Jason L. Finkle and Richard W. Gable (New York: John Wiley & Sons, 1966), pp. 365–78.

23. *Ibid.*, p. 370.

24. For an interesting account of an almost intolerable work situation and workers' methods of coping with that situation, see Donald F. Roy, "'Banana Time': Job Satisfaction and Informal Interaction," *Human Organization*, XVIII (Winter, 1959–60), 158–68.

25. Arnold S. Feldman and Wilbert E. Moore, "Commitment of the Industrial Labor Force," in *Labor Commitment and Social Change in Developing Areas,* ed. Wilbert E. Moore and Arnold S. Feldman (New York: Social Science Research Council, 1960), p. 2.

26. Barbara Ward, Lenore D'Anjou, and J. D. Runnalls, eds., *The Widening Gap: Development in the 1970's* (New York: Columbia University Press, 1971), p. 3.

27. Irving Louis Horowitz, *Three Worlds of Development,* 2nd edition (New York: Oxford University Press, 1972), p. 470.

28. Dennis L. Meadows, "The Predicament of Mankind," *The Futurist,* August, 1971, pp. 137–44. For a popular account see *Time,* Jan. 24, 1972, pp. 32 and 37.

29. For good summaries of typical consequences of modernization, see Joseph A. Kahl, "Some Social Concomitants of Industrialization and Urbanization," *Human Organization,* XVIII (Summer, 1959), 53–74; Wilbert E. Moore, *Social Change* (Englewood Cliffs: Prentice-Hall, Inc., 1963), pp. 97–105; and Lenski, *Power and Privilege,* pp. 298–308.

30. Melvin M. Tumin, "Competing Status Systems," in *Labor Commitment and Social Change,* ed. Moore and Feldman, pp. 280–82.

31. Lenski, *Power and Privilege,* p. 308.

32. Gerhard Lenski, *Human Societies* (New York: McGraw-Hill Book Company, 1970), p. 365. Most modern societies would provide good examples of this phenomenon. In 1972, Italy was reported to have 58,019 agencies of government, or one agency for every 1000 Italians (*St. Louis Post-Dispatch,* April 20, 1972, p. 14D).

33. James S. Coleman, "Conclusion: The Political Systems of the Developing Areas," in *The Politics of the Developing Areas,* ed. Gabriel A. Almond and James S. Coleman (Princeton: Princeton University Press, 1960), pp. 536–37.

34. S. N. Eisenstadt, *Modernization: Protest and Change* (Englewood Cliffs: Prentice-Hall, Inc., 1966), pp. 32–33.

35. P. C. Lloyd, *Africa in Social Change* (Middlesex: Penguin Books, 1969), p. 88.

36. Kahl, "Some Social Concomitants," *Human Organization,* XVIII, p. 61.

37. See, for example, Andreas M. Kazamias, *Education and the Quest for Modernity in Turkey* (Chicago: The University of Chicago Press, 1966).

38. Lerner, "Modernization, Social Aspects," *International Encyclopedia of the Social Sciences,* p. 387.

39. Daniel Lerner, *The Passing of Traditional Society* (Glencoe: The Free Press, 1958), p. 50.

40. Alex Inkeles, "The Modernization of Man," in *Modernization,* ed. Myron Weiner, pp. 141–44. A refinement, a cross-cultural scale for measuring individuals on a scale of modernity, may be found in David Horton Smith and Alex

Inkeles, "The OM Scale: A Comparative Socio-Psychological Measure of Individual Modernity," *Sociometry*, XXIX (1966), 353–77.

41. An excellent statement of the argument against the notion that tradition and modernity are mutually exclusive may be found in Joseph R. Gusfield, "Tradition and Modernity: Misplaced Polarities in the Study of Social Change," *American Journal of Sociology*, LXXII (Jan., 1967), 351–62.

42. Emilio Willems, "Peasantry and City: Cultural Persistence and Change in Historical Perspective, a European Case," *American Anthropologist*, LXXII (June, 1970), 528–44.

43. Ezra F. Vogel, "Kinship Structure, Migration to the City, and Modernization," in *Aspects of Social Change in Modern Japan*, ed. R. P. Dore (Princeton: Princeton University Press, 1967), pp. 91–111.

44. Data in this paragraph were taken from *Habitat*, XII (no. 1, 1969), 4–5.

45. Simon Kuznets, "Consumption, Industrialization, and Urbanization," in *Industrialization and Society*, ed. Hoselitz and Moore, p. 102.

46. See Bert F. Hoselitz, "The City, the Factory, and Economic Growth," in *Comparative Perspectives on Industrial Society*, ed. William A. Faunce and William H. Form (Boston: Little, Brown and Company, 1969), p. 84.

47. Lerner, *The Passing of Traditional Society*, p. 60.

48. *Ibid.*

49. Wilbur Schramm and W. Lee Ruggels, "How Mass Media Systems Grow," in *Communication and Change in the Developing Countries*, ed. Daniel Lerner and Wilbur Schramm (Honolulu: East-West Center Press, 1967), pp. 64–65.

50. See, for example, Shanti Tangri, "Urbanization, Political Stability, and Economic Growth," in *Political Development and Social Change*, ed. Finkle and Gable, pp. 305–19.

51. Franz Schurmann and Orville Schell, *Communist China* (New York: Vintage Books, 1967), pp. 456–57.

52. See John Gulick, "Old Values and New Institutions in a Lebanese Arab City," *Human Organization*, XXIV (Spring, 1965), 49–52; and Lloyd, *Africa in Social Change*, pp. 115–16.

53. H. H. Gerth and C. Wright Mills, *From Max Weber: Essays in Sociology* (New York: Oxford University Press, 1946), p. 155.

54. Max Weber, *The Protestant Ethic and the Spirit of Capitalism*, trans. Talcott Parsons (New York: Charles Scribner's Sons, 1958), pp. 181–82.

55. Thomas F. O'Dea, *The Sociology of Religion* (Englewood Cliffs: Prentice-Hall, Inc., 1966), p. 81.

56. Harvey Cox, *The Secular City* (New York: The Macmillan Company, 1965), p. 20.

57. *Ibid.*

58. Norman S. Buchanan and Howard S. Ellis, *Approaches to Economic Development* (New York: The Twentieth Century Fund, 1955), p. 78.

59. McCord, *The Springtime of Freedom*, p. 37.

60. Clifford Geertz, *Peddlers and Princes* (Chicago: The University of Chicago Press, 1963), pp. 127–28.

61. Michael Ames, "Ideological and Social Change in Ceylon," *Human Organization*, XXII (Spring, 1963), 53.

62. Harold B. Barclay, "Process in the Arab Sudan," *Human Organization*, XXIV (Spring, 1965), p. 46.

63. Fritz Morstein Marx, "The Higher Civil Service as an Action Group in Western Political Development," in *Bureaucracy and Political Development*, ed. Joseph LaPalombara (Princeton: Princeton University Press, 1963), p. 74.

64. Gerth and Mills, *From Max Weber*, pp. 204–16.

65. Gunnar Myrdal, *Asian Drama* (New York: Pantheon, 1968), Vol. 1, p. 503.

66. Merle Fainsod, "Bureaucracy and Modernization: The Russian and Soviet Case," in *Bureaucracy and Political Development*, ed. LaPalombara, p. 249.

67. *Ibid.*, p. 252.

68. Nicos P. Mouzelis, *Organization and Bureaucracy* (Chicago: Aldine Publishing Company, 1967), pp. 12–15.

69. See, e.g., Seymour M. Lipset, "Bureaucracy and Social Reform," in *Complex Organizations: A Sociological Reader*, ed. Amitai Etzioni (New York: Holt, Rinehart and Winston, 1961), pp. 260–67.

70. Fred W. Riggs, "Bureaucrats and Political Development," in *Political Development and Social Change*, ed. Finkle and Gable, pp. 409–29.

71. Richard M. Pfeffer, "Mao Tse-tung and the Cultural Revolution," in *National Liberation*, ed. Norman Miller and Roderick Aya (New York: The Free Press, 1971), pp. 264–68.

72. S. C. Dube, "Bureaucracy and Nation Building in Transitional Societies," *International Social Science Journal*, XVI (1964), 233–36, and Hunter, *Modernizing Peasant Societies*, pp. 198–200.

73. Dube, "Bureaucracy and Nation Building in Transitional Societies," *International Social Science Journal*, p. 235.

74. Joseph J. Spengler, "Bureaucracy and Economic Development," in *Bureaucracy and Political Development*, ed. LaPalombara, pp. 225–27.

75. Elihu Katz and S. N. Eisenstadt, "Bureaucracy and Its Clientele — A Case Study," *Administrative Science Quarterly*, V (1960), 253–71.

76. Warren G. Bennis and Philip E. Slater, *The Temporary Society* (New York: Harper & Row, 1968), pp. 53–76.

PART V

Strategies of Change

All history, according to Spengler, is not the same kind of history. For example: "What the conspicuously historical West calls 'Indian history' achieved itself without the smallest consciousness of what it was doing . . . Western history was willed and Indian history happened." [1] In other words, there always will be a history of a people, but the people may have consciously shaped that history or merely unthinkingly adapted to it.

Spengler's estimation of the extent to which man controlled the course of change in the West is disputed by others. Harrington argues that the twentieth-century crisis of the West is the result of our "accidental revolution." We are a living paradox, for

> these most conscious and man-made of times have lurched into the unprecedented transformation of human life without thinking about it. And in a sense, this century, this scientific, technological, and utterly competent century, has happened accidentally. [2]

The transformation must continue, Harrington believes, but it must stop being an accident, and must rather result from man's intervention and control of the social process.

While their assessments differ somewhat, both Spengler and Harrington stress the fact that man can control change as well as respond to it. In fact, unless man strives to control the course of development, he will become a slave to his own history. "If men do not make history," as C. Wright Mills put it, "they tend increasingly to become the utensils of history-makers as well as the mere objects of history." [3]

Suppose, then, that you wish to make history and not simply understand it. Suppose you want to effect change rather than simply gain insight into it. Suppose you are confronted with the problem of or desire to change a society, a group, an organization, or some facet of social existence. How do you proceed? Much of the material in the preceding chapters either implicitly or explicitly bears upon this question. But in our final chapter, we shall examine the problem of history-making in a systematic fashion.

ENDNOTES TO PART 5

1. Oswald Spengler, *The Decline of the West,* Vol. 1, trans. Charles Francis Atkinson (New York: Alfred A. Knopf, 1926), p. 133.

2. Michael Harrington, *The Accidental Century* (New York: The Macmillan Company, 1965), p. 41.

3. C. Wright Mills, *Power, Politics & People,* ed. Irving Louis Horowitz (New York: Oxford University Press, 1963), p. 25.

CHAPTER 13

The Changing of Societies: Willed History

"The progress of the world is like that of a fleet horse, galloping and galloping onward. Whatever cannot skillfully change itself and progress along with the world will find itself eliminated by natural selection . . . ."[1] This 1915 plea of Ch'en Tu-hsiu to Chinese youth is thoroughly applicable to potential history-makers in the contemporary world. If you determine to make history, you must recognize that the task is complex and demanding; you will act in a context that is rapidly changing already, and you must carefully and skillfully choose your strategies.

We have already encountered ideas about strategies for changing. Various theorists assert or imply that change will be effected by revolution, by nonintervention, by elites, by the solidarity of the group effecting the change, by marginal groups or individuals, and so on. And we have seen that technology, ideas, conflict, and social structural factors may all influence the direction of change.

Obviously, there are incompatible and contradictory elements in these ideas. And that is why the task of the history-maker is difficult — there is no one strategy of change that is universally applicable. Each situation must be carefully assessed before a strategy is selected. And for many, if not most, situations, a variety of strategies may be called for. This can involve the history-maker in a dilemma, as we shall see below.

In assessing any situation in order to select appropriate strategies of change, certain crucial questions must be answered.

Three such questions will form the outline of this chapter: What is the target of the change effort?   Who will effect the change? What method will be employed?

THE TARGET OF CHANGE

Some nations have possessed "group focused" images of change, while others have possessed "ego focused" images.[2]   That is, some peoples conceive of change in group terms — whatever change occurs must affect all the members of the group — while others conceive of change in individualistic terms — an individual might benefit from change or might change his own life situation quite independently of the group or groups to which he belongs.

These two contrary images would imply differing strategies of change; for one thing, the target of change would differ.   But to the two possible targets of individual or group we shall add a third — the social structure.   In other words, a first crucial question that must be faced by the history-maker is the proximate target of his efforts: is the immediate need to change individuals, change groups, or change the social structure?   I say "immediate" because ultimately the change will affect all three.   The long-run target, therefore, may be a wholistic one; the short-run decision involves identifying which part of the whole to attack.

The Individual as Target

The choice of individuals as the proximate target of change is based upon the premise that changed people will effect changes in the social order (or the group or the organization).   That is, individuals are to be changed not simply for the benefit of the individuals themselves (except, perhaps, in the case of religious evangelism), but for some larger purpose such as the benefit of a group or organization, or the improvement of intergroup relations, or the development of an entire society.   And if the individuals are changed, they will effect the desired changes in the larger social entity.

If individuals are the target, a number of different strategies may be employed.   One might choose a psychoanalytic, social-psychological, behavior modification, or educational strategy. Each of these makes different assumptions about the nature of man.   The psychoanalytic approach assumes a Freudian man. Social-psychological approaches assume that man's nature is a function of his social environment.   The behavior modification approach assumes that man acts on the basis of reward and punishment. And the educational strategy assumes that man is rational, and that he will act logically, or at least in his own self-interest, on the basis of knowledge that he receives.[3]

While the individual may be the target of change, the medium through which the change is effected is often a group — whether the group is the family, the classroom, or some other group created for the purpose of change. In particular, the small group has been employed to make specific changes in individuals. This technique has worked successfully in "thought reform" in China,[4] in the conversion of individuals to the Pentecostal movement,[5] and in the T-group and Lewinian-type discussion groups.[6] This last method falls into the general category of "group dynamics."

The group dynamics approach to change stems from the notion that the norms governing behavior are fashioned in group interaction; the logical place to change norms, therefore, is in a group. Thus, Lewin and his colleagues used the small group to persuade housewives to purchase and use foods such as beef hearts, sweetbreads, and kidneys during World War II. Since the housewife is the "gatekeeper" who channels the food into the family, groups of housewives were brought together. It was found that group discussion and group decision were far more effective in changing norms than a lecture; a follow-up study found that 32 percent of women in the group decision context as opposed to only 3 percent in the lecture situation served one of the meats never used before.[7]

A variety of other kinds of behavior have been attacked through this method. Studies have reported change in alcoholics, in industrial productivity, in skill levels, in various attitudes, and in personality.[8] But whatever the nature of the specific change, the group itself must possess certain characteristics. Cartwright has listed five of these; it will be evident that they assume an American, if not Western, context:

1. The people who are the change agents and those who are to be changed must "have a strong sense of belonging to the same group";
2. The group will exert more influence the more attractive it is to the members;
3. The group will exert more influence when it is seeking change in those characteristics of members which underlie their attraction to the group;
4. Group members with the highest prestige will exert the most influence;
5. Members will be least likely to change in ways that make them deviants in terms of group norms.[9]

Although all of the various individual approaches have demonstrated some successes, the individual as target can be a painstakingly slow method of seeking change even if it succeeds. For example, a therapist may help an individual cope with a stressful existence, but that individual may be incapable of doing anything other than coping. Not only may he be unable to effect any changes beyond himself, but the therapist will be faced with a continuing stream of others who must exist in the same debilitating social structure. He has succeeded in helping the individual, but has not thereby effected any larger changes. This is not to demean the work of therapists; multitudes could be psychologically shredded to pieces while we wait for the creation of a new social structure. While humans suffer, all strategies are important. By the same token, no one strategy is sufficient by itself, and some are quite limited in their consequences.

The Group as Target

As Cartwright reminds us, the group can be the target as well as the medium of change.[10] When the group or the social structure becomes the target,[11] it is assumed that a changed context will effect changes in people. Individual values, attitudes, and behavior will be modified by changing the social structure or changing the group in which individuals think and act. Again, both individuals and the social entities are to be ultimately changed; but the group and social structural approaches choose the supraindividual entity as the proximate target of change, convinced that changes in individuals will follow.

Just as there are diverse ways of changing individuals, there are differing methods of changing the group. Basically, methods for changing groups may be divided into those which change the group composition and those which change the processes or structure of the group. To change the composition means to change the membership. For example, the racial composition of a group may be changed in order to change attitudes of prejudice. Or the educational level of an organization may be changed in order to enable the organization to cope with the demands of a changing environment. Or a particular individual may be removed from an industrial workgroup in order to make the group more harmonious.

There are numerous examples of the difference that composition can make. Deutsch and Collins found that living in interracial housing changed the feelings, beliefs, and behavior of white housewives toward blacks.[12] In comparing the residents of an integrated housing project with those of a segregated project, the authors found that in the interracial situation there was:

1. Considerably more neighborly interaction between the races;
2. A social atmosphere conducive to such interaction;
3. "A more closely knit project community";
4. More favorable attitudes by whites towards blacks, i.e., towards both those in the project and blacks in general;
5. More favorable attitudes towards interracial living.[13]

As a result of the study, the segregation policy of the other project was changed.

This suggests that prejudice may be diminished by controlling the racial composition of a group; any group composed of only one race is likely to perpetuate prejudice and patterns of discrimination. But we must be cautious in our conclusions. Deutsch and Collins themselves doubted that integrated housing would work in areas like the South where social norms would intensely oppose such a pattern. Furthermore, the extent to which prejudice generally is diminished by interracial interaction in a group is problematic. Men, for example, may change their attitudes about working with those of another race when they are compelled to do so; but their attitudes regarding interaction in other settings do not necessarily change. The same white man who considers a black at work his buddy may violently oppose blacks moving into his neighborhood.

Nevertheless, changes in groups may be effected by varying the composition of the groups. The other general way of changing groups is to vary their structure or processes. Again, the examples of this approach are many. Both the task efficiency and the satisfaction of a group may be changed by changing communication patterns within the group (though it appears that a choice must be made between maximizing one or the other of the two).[14] In an organization, the satisfaction of rank-and-file groups may be increased by increasing their role in decision-making processes.[15]

An interesting case of group change is provided by the introduction of new technology into the British mining industry.[16] The new technology radically changed the organization of work teams from small, self-selected groups with a high rate of interaction to large groups with less interaction, greater specialization of work, and a diminished sense of the individual worker's role in and contribution to the overall results. Management became more intensely involved in the work, and worker dissatisfaction increased greatly. Finally, the technology was retained, but the groups were broken down into small units again. Worker solidarity and satisfaction returned, absenteeism decreased, and productivity increased.

This case is interesting because it bears upon our study of the effects of technology. The new technology did effect drastic changes in the organization; but these changes, as it turned out, were not inexorable — the technology was adapted to worker needs rather than vice versa. Furthermore, the case shows how significant changes can be made in a group by varying group structure and processes. Whenever the target of change is the group itself, with no particular concern about more extensive changes, the desired change may be effected by varying group composition, structure, or processes.

But this is not to say that all desired changes can be effected in a group by making the group the target of change. Just as it may be necessary to change the group in which an individual functions in order to change the individual, it may be necessary to change the social structure in which the group is embedded in order to change the group. For example, the students at a particular university may be generally convinced that the grading system impedes learning. But it would not be feasible for that university to abolish grades while it continues to function in a competitive social milieu where grades are used for securing employment, gaining admission to graduate school, and maintaining enrolment at a manageable level. For some kinds of change, then, only the social structure itself is an appropriate target.

The Social Structure as Target

With the social structure as target we are talking about changes that are more extensive, that diffuse throughout a larger part of the society than a group or a few groups, or an organization or a few organizations. Furthermore, we are talking about changes that affect more than a single mode of interaction; that is, these changes would affect people in more than a single setting such as a particular group or organization. Examples of this kind of change include the change in patterns of land tenure and work in Vicos, Peru, which led to important overall cultural changes,[17] the sweeping changes in a number of nations following revolutions, and the slower but extensive changes that have followed legislation in the United States.

Let us look briefly at two types of change of the social structure: the transition from an agrarian to an industrial society and the changing status of a minority group in a nation. Mexico illustrates the former, and many of the characteristics we shall identify in the Mexican experience are typical of other nations. At the preindustrial level, there is a long-term trend towards increasing inequality. With rare exceptions, agricultural societies exhibit sharp inequalities. In Mexico, a very small upper class existed prior to 1910. Power derived from ownership of the land, and about 1 percent of the population owned 97 percent of the land. Around 80 percent of Mexicans were rural people living at a subsistence level; most existed as semi-serfs on large haciendas.[18]

During Mexico's transition to an industrial society following the 1910 revolution, certain trends were established that, again, are typical. First, individuals are evaluated on the basis of achievement; education, occupation, and income begin to displace ascribed memberships as criteria of evaluation. Second, the occupational structure changes; there is an upgrading, with a demand for increasing numbers of people with some skill. In Mexico, the proportion of those engaged in nonagricultural activities changed from about one-fourth in 1910 to almost one-half in 1960.

Third, individual mobility increases. The urban population in Mexico increased from 29 percent in 1910 to 51 percent in 1960, and has continued to grow much more rapidly than the rural population. Associated with this is rising income; in 1961–62, 0.5 percent of rural families and 6.3 percent of urban families were at the highest of five income levels, while 39.9 percent of rural families and only 6.6 percent of urban families were at the lowest level.

As industrialization has proceeded, education and occupation have become even more important in determining individual positions in the social strata. Mobility has increased, and the class structure has shifted to accommodate an increasingly larger middle class. In Mexico, the middle class has roughly doubled since the turn of the century.

These basic changes in the structure of the society have occurred because of a political commitment to modernization. That commitment is reflected in certain measures that have been taken to quicken the pace of progress of the people. As Gonzalez-Casanova observes: "Mexican development has been strongly influenced by political measures of redistribution and expropriation of wealth which go beyond the redistribution that has been brought about automatically, thanks to urbanization and industrialization." [19]

Such structural changes may be brought about through a commitment on the part of the polity, as happened in Japan; or through a mass movement culminating in revolution, as happened in China; or through social movements that exert sufficient pressure on those in power to effect change. This latter is illustrated by the succession of legislative reforms that have affected the situation of blacks in America.

Black protest movements in America have gone through four phases: the transition from accommodation to protest; legal protest; nonviolent direct action; and black power strategy.[20] Associated with each of these, and with the continuing work of certain organizations, is a considerable amount of legislative action.   Protest first emerged out of the context of severe oppression and deprivation which was given at least temporary legitimacy by Booker T. Washington.   A number of blacks, including W. E. B. DuBois, took strong issue with Washington.   Segregation in public accommodations and the successful disfranchisement of large numbers of blacks around the turn of the century were among the conditions that outraged the militants.

The protest quickly took the form of legal efforts and was greatly aided by the formation of the N.A.A.C.P. in 1909.   This organization won a number of cases, beginning in the early part of the century and including the noted 1954 Supreme Court decision on school segregation.   But the failure of local, state, and Federal governments to effectively implement the legal victories led to other forms of protest, including the nonviolent direct action of Martin Luther King, Jr., and the more militant black power advocates.

A series of Civil Rights Acts and the Voting Rights Act of 1965 were among the legislative consequences of the protest movements.   It would be foolish to think that such legislation has solved the problem.   The laws have been circumvented and even ignored.   Continuing legal changes have been necessitated by continuing circumvention.   Nevertheless, it would be equally foolish to think that the overall structure is unchanged, that the situation of the black is no better than it was in the nineteenth century.

By 1970, black people in America were in the process of being fully enfranchised (though not without resistance), were gaining some measure of political power, and were showing important economic achievements.   With respect to the latter, Herman Miller declared in the early 1960's that the so-called "social revolution" of the United States was a myth, that the country was not heading towards greater equalization of income.[21]   The income gap between white and nonwhite male workers, aged 14 and over, for example, fluctuated from 1939 to 1962; but by the latter year it was greater than it was 14 years earlier.   In 1948, blacks earned about 60 percent as much as whites, while in 1962 the figure had dropped to 55 percent.   But if we update these figures, we find that the black (actually, nonwhite) percentage has steadily increased since 1962, reaching an all-time high of 67 percent in 1969.[22]   Obviously, this is a large amount of inequality; but it is still less than the 41 percent figure of 1939.

Neither the Mexican peasantry nor the black Americans could have changed their situation through the individual or group approach.   It is of little use to tell an individual to work hard and be diligent if the structure of society ensures his continued deprivation.   Nor would making membership in the N.A.A.C.P. more satisfying to members alter the white-black inequality.   This may seem obvious, but the appropriate target has not always been easily identified; many Americans would still like the nation's poor to change their status by being willing to work, in spite of the fact that the great majority of the poor are not unemployed!

THE AGENTS OF CHANGE

A second crucial question to be faced for history-makers is, who makes the change? Does the change come about by one group's imposing it on others, or by the participation of all those involved? The question is a pertinent one whatever the target happens to be.

At the individual level, therapists have employed both authoritarian and participative techniques. At group and structural levels, both elitist and democratic strategies have been advocated and employed. The elites may be experts of some kind: entrepreneurs, intellectuals, or political revolutionaries, for example. In any case, the task of the elites is to effect the change with or without the willingness of others involved in the change. In democratic strategies, there may still be experts, but they work with the people, so that all those affected by the change have the opportunity to participate in the decisions.

It has been argued that effective change must be democratic. As Simon has written in the context of the organization: "Significant changes in human behavior can be brought about rapidly only if the persons who are expected to change participate in deciding what the change shall be and how it shall be made." [23] A similar argument has been advanced, however, with respect to entire societies; whatever the size of the group, some members must be included in the planning of any change. [24]

Just how much participation constitutes democratic procedures is problematic. At the very least, people must feel that the change is being effected on their behalf. Mao has correctly noted that the Chinese revolution depended upon the support of the peasants. Long before the revolution succeeded, he wrote: "Without the poor peasants there would be no revolution. To deny their role is to deny the revolution." [25] That role was a supportive one, facilitating the survival and ultimate triumph of the Red Army.

At the most, democratic procedure will involve active participation of all those involved in the change. When the size of the group concerned becomes quite large, this will obviously be impossible. But if diverse groups are involved, all or the majority of the people must sense that their interests are adequately represented if the change is to be democratic.

Most of us would probably agree that democratic change is preferable. We value participation in decisions that affect our own existence. As expressed by the Port Huron Statement, we desire a "democracy of individual participation" in which the individual will "share in those social decisions determining the quality and direction of his life" and men are both encouraged and able to be independent and participating members of the society.[26] This ideology first infiltrated government in the TVA project; more recently, it has emerged in the idea of "maximum feasible participation" of the poor in the programs designed to eliminate poverty.

In spite of the high value we place on democratic change, however, there are a number of problems involved in choosing between it and elitist-led change. One problem has to do with the relative effectiveness of the two approaches. The above statements notwithstanding, the democratic approach is not the only and not always the most rapid way to effect change. In a previous chapter, we noted changes in Indian villages which were wrought by authoritarian leaders (and which failed where democratic leaders worked). A number of studies have indicated that authoritarian regimes are particularly effective in the early stages of modernization. And others have shown that in a context where peasants expect authoritarian procedures from the government, they may ignore or resist more democratic efforts at change.

In other words, however much we may value the democratic approach, it is not necessarily the most effective in all cultures or in all situations. A second problem is the meaning of the democratic approach. In a word, has democratic change taken place or has a potential critic been coopted? People may be brought into the decision-making process only in the sense of confirming, and thereby legitimating, decisions that have already been made. And people may be given a voice in relatively trivial matters in order to allow an authority to maintain control over more significant decisions.

All participation, then, is not participatory democracy. As a minimum, democratic approaches to change should include the following:

⅀1.   An actual, not apparent, sharing in decisions relevant to the existence of those involved;
2.   Full political rights and representation for all segments of the relevant population in order to achieve the above;
3.   Action based on consensus rather than coercion;
4.   Planning that is, in Mannheim's words, "planning for freedom." [27]

A third problem in choosing a democratic strategy is posed by certain dilemmas. For one thing, "it is always easier to organize in an elitist fashion and then simply dictate to the rest." [28] Those who are impatient to get something done may find themselves strongly tempted to take an elitist approach even when they prefer the democratic.

Another dilemma is the extent to which organizations and movements tend to reflect the larger society. That is, the same inequalities that characterize the society generally will tend to appear in any group that organizes for change. High status in the larger society, for example, will tend to command a certain amount of deference within the group seeking change in spite of a commitment to democratic structure.

One other dilemma involves the need for expertise. A particular change may demand certain expert knowledge, and that expert knowledge may demand the kind of change which would not be chosen in a democratic setting. In the context of a business firm, the dilemma takes the form of a question:

> To what extent should managers rely on technical expertise to guide their decisions, in which event they limit their own influence over the outcome, and to what degree should they insist on being involved, in which case there will be a less informed decision based more on political compromise? [29]

In the context of industrialization, the dilemma means that considerable technical skills are required to initiate enterprises; only later can workers take over or participate in the management.

Because of these dilemmas, it should not surprise us that some efforts at democratic change fail.[30] But other efforts indicate very positive results.[31] Perhaps the basic problem is the first dilemma mentioned above — the elitist approach is easier. Even assuming that most changes may be effected democratically, there may be an unwillingness to expend the time and energy necessary to democratic procedures. From the point of view of human well-being, the democratic approach is superior. From the point of view of efficiency or profit, the elitist approach is superior. As a business executive once told me: "If we tried to be democratic in our corporation, we would be broke in two weeks."

THE METHOD OF CHANGE

Numerous methods may be employed in an effort to effect change. These methods are generally chosen on the basis of certain assumptions. For example, Chin and Benne identify three types of strategies, which they call the rational-empirical, the normative–re-educative, and the power-coercive.[32] The first assumes that men are rational and that they will follow their self-interest when it is shown to them. The second also assumes that men are rational but recognizes that people act on the basis of social norms as well as from knowledge and self-interest. Consequently, it endeavors to change values and attitudes as well as to give knowledge. And the third strategy assumes that man acts on the basis of power relationships — legitimate or coercive.

A simpler classification has been proposed by Walton, who suggests that all strategies may be categorized as power or attitude types.[33] This is a useful distinction, although some methods may combine power and attitude tactics. But the basic assumptions relate to the desired outcome of the change effort; with power tactics, substantive concessions are sought, while with attitude tactics, improved relationships are sought. Obviously, both outcomes may be desired, and as we shall see below, that poses some dilemmas for us.

We shall discuss methods of change by using the distinction between power and attitude approaches as well as one other distinction — that between violent and nonviolent approaches. Violence is a power strategy, but advocates of violence often anticipate new and improved relationships arising out of the new social order. In the Marxist view, for example, the violence of revolution is a necessary prelude to the building of a humane society. Nonviolence may also be a power strategy, but it tends to emphasize the creation of new relationships. In other words, violence vs. nonviolence cuts across the power vs. attitude distinction. And we deal with the issue of violence again because as Keniston puts it, "the issue of violence is to this generation what the issue of sex was to the Victorian world."[34]

Power vs. Attitude Strategies

To many students of social life, power is the name of the game. A society is a network of groups and individuals bound together in superior-subordinate relationships. Any effort to direct change, therefore, requires the mobilization and manipulation of power over others. Power strategies are simply plans for directing change that recognize this fundamental fact of social life.

Other students, notably those who lean in a social-psychological or human relations direction, see society in terms of a plexus of groups and individuals bound together by certain attitudes and values. Change efforts require a restructuring of relationships based on attitudes and values, which generally means a changing of the attitudes and values themselves.

Thus, the power strategy assumes a different view of the nature of society than that implied in the attitude strategy. Moreover, the two strategies assume different outcomes — concessions or surrender in the case of the power strategy, and qualitatively heightened relationships in the case of the attitude strategy. Obviously, there are times when both outcomes are desired. Martin Luther King, Jr., as a leader of a movement, wished to gain both substantial concessions and improved relationships from white society. Workers striving for economic gains also may want to improve, or at least not worsen, relationships with supervisors and management. Students may desire to gain some voice in university affairs and at the same time to relate more meaningfully to faculty and administration.

Can both outcomes be achieved? They can, but as Walton points out, the two strategies "place contradictory tactical demands on a leader." [35] For example, the power strategy would lead one to overstate one's aim, stressing differences between the two groups involved, while the attitude strategy would lead one to minimize differences (e.g., "you're taking more than your share of the pie" vs. "after all, we're all Americans who want the best for our country and deserve the best it has to offer"). The power strategy would emphasize the ability to coerce, while the attitude strategy would stress trust. The power strategy would involve the control of information and creation of ambiguity for the other group, while the attitude strategy would declare for openness and honest communication.

Walton suggests three ways of coping with these and other dilemmas posed by the two strategies. First, there is the "freeze-thaw" approach, in which power and attitude tactics are alternated. Thus, in East-West relationships, both sides have tended to employ power to gain concessions and to follow that with overtures of peace and friendship. Second, different persons or subgroups can use different strategies. There is little doubt, for example, that blacks who appear to be committed to an attitude approach have used the threat of more militant groups to gain concessions and also to maintain or improve relationships.

Finally, the dilemmas may be dealt with by recognizing them and carefully choosing actions that minimize them. One might pursue a power strategy in different ways, some of which are counter-productive. A group that engages in what appears to the public to be irrational violence may quickly lose its mass support and, therefore, its cause. Feuer has criticized student movements on this basis, pointing out that they have often chosen strategies which have virtually guaranteed the failure of their objectives.[36]

Once a choice of power or attitude or combined strategy is made, an enormous number of tactics are available. We shall merely give a few examples. Attitude tactics are often used when the target is the individual. In some cases, the aim may be individual self-improvement, as in certain T-groups. In other cases, the aim may be organizational improvement; T-groups have also been used in such cases.   The attitude strategy has been used widely by organizations seeking to sell their products; motivation research and advertising campaigns are used to change attitudes so that people will be inclined to buy.[37]

The attitude strategy has been employed in modernizing nations in their efforts to gain mass support for development. Tactics here include extensive use of the mass media and educational programs throughout the countryside.   Finally, this strategy is advocated by certain students of organizations.   The "human organization," according to Likert, is one that is characterized by "complete confidence and trust in all matters."   Communication is free and frank.   Interaction is extensive and widespread.   Goals result from group participation.   And the closer the organization moves towards this ideal, the higher its productivity as well as member satisfaction and growth is likely to be.[38]

A very different picture emerges from those groups that have employed tactics that are based on a power strategy.   And like the attitude strategy, power strategy has been used in diverse contexts. In some cases it may be necessary because of the pressure of time. The British used their power in Nigeria to try to eradicate sleeping sickness among the Hausa.   It was necessary to cut down brush in which the tsetse fly bred; but the Hausa believed some of the brush to be sacred, and the power of the colonial government was applied to cut the brush and control the disease.[39]

Power tactics are commonly used in the context of social movements.   Strikes, demonstrations, violence or the threat of violence, economic boycotts, and political threats have all been used to effect change.   Saul Alinsky devoted years to mobilizing people in the effective use of power.   He defines a radical as one who uses power to effect needed change.   "Liberals dream dreams; Radicals build the world of men's dreams." [40]   Alinsky conceives of power in terms of organizing and engaging in conflict:

A People's Organization is not a philanthropic plaything nor a social service's ameliorative gesture . . . It thinks and acts in terms of social surgery and not cosmetic cover-ups . . . A People's Organization is dedicated to an eternal war.   It is a war against poverty, misery, delinquency, disease, injustice, hopelessness, despair, and unhappiness . . . A war is not an intellectual debate, and in the war against social evils there are no rules of fair play.[41]

A pure power strategy could hardly be more clearly expressed than that.   And Alinsky's tactics illustrate the extent to which he disdains the attitude strategy; he did everything from organizing boycotts to dumping garbage on an alderman's driveway.   As a national magazine put it, Alinsky "has possibly antagonized more people . . . than any other living American." [42]   It is evident that Alinsky has contempt — in both his words and his actions — for the attitude strategy.   Changes are effected by power, not by trust and persuasion.

The power strategy was also the choice of student activists of the 1960's.   Tactics of resistance and confrontation became increasingly common. [43]   These tactics involved such action as disruption of organizational activities, forceful reaction to police force, speech designed to embarrass or defy, and refusal to acknowledge the authority of those in varied positions of power.   The tactics were designed to broaden the base of support (even those who oppose the tactics may come to grant the legitimacy of the demands); to educate the public; and to deepen the commitment of the activists themselves.

A final example of the power strategy is the organizational context.   Crozier's analysis of two French bureaucracies is a portrait of continuing conflict and power struggles. [44]   The lines of conflict were drawn in terms of cohesive occupational groups; these groups were isolated from each other, exerting considerable group pressure on individuals.   The focal points of conflict were areas of "uncertainty" and the control of uncertainty is the possession of power.   For example, the maintenance workers in the Industrial Monopoly solidified their power by ensuring (through removing blueprints among other things) that only they could deal with the uncertainty of machine breakdown.

At the root of all conflicts in the organizations Crozier analyzed "there is clearly some kind of fight for power." [45]   This is well illustrated by the fact that the directors, who were socially conservative with respect to the wider society, were striving for organizational change.   Their striving did not reflect a generalized liberal attitude, but a situated effort to gain more power.   Among the tactics employed was the effort to further rationalization among other groups in the organization while resisting it in one's own group.   For rationalization means predictability, and less uncertainty.   Each group, consequently, sought to maintain ambiguity within its own realm, enhancing its own power in the ongoing struggle.

Numerous other organizations exhibit similar characteristics. And if we would judge by the available studies, we shall have to conclude that efforts to change organizations are far more likely to be characterized by power strategies than by the kind of attitude strategy presented by Likert.   And certainly in the interorganizational context — the effort by one organization to effect particular change in the face of opposition from other organizations — power is indeed the name of the game.   And as the history of American corporations shows, that power can be employed with a Machiavellian ruthlessness.

Violent vs. Nonviolent Strategies

In order to "resolve old contradictions and produce new things" in a class society, Mao tells us, "revolutions and revolutionary wars are inevitable. . . ." [46]   For class societies contain "antagonistic" contradictions which must be resolved in the violence of revolution. Under socialism, there will still be contradictions, but they will be "non-antagonistic"; thus, further bloodshed will not be required.

In Mao's view, then, some kinds of change demand violence while others clearly must be effected in nonviolent ways.   In handling controversial issues among the people "we can only use democratic methods, methods of discussion, of criticism, of persuasion, and education, not coercive, high-handed methods." [47]   In fact, even certain antagonistic contradictions, such as that between the national bourgeoisie and the working class in China, "can be transformed into a non-antagonistic one and resolved in a peaceful way" if properly handled.[48]

Thus, even those with great expertise in the use of violence to effect change do not see violence as a universal prod to social evolution.   In our earlier discussion of violence, we noted that under certain conditions it was effective and in at least a few contexts it has seemed to be necessary.   But for the most part, violence is an alternative method rather than the necessary one for effecting a particular change.   And some violence — such as the indiscriminate killings by terrorists or the abuse of people trying to protest peacefully — can be counter-productive.

What, then, is the nonviolent alternative?   Can change come about through nonviolent methods?   The examples of Gandhi, Martin Luther King, Jr., and Cesar Chavez, among others, show the usefulness of the nonviolent alternative.   And this alternative tends to incorporate both power and attitude tactics.   For example, satyagraha, the method of Gandhi, means "the Force which is born of Truth and Love or non-violence." [49]   Nonviolence here means force or power, for a fundamental rule of the method is the refusal to compromise "basic principles or essential portions of valid objectives." [50]

At the same time, the attitude strategy is employed.   For another fundamental rule of satyagraha is the "persistent search for avenues of cooperation with the adversary on honorable terms," including making every effort "to win over the opponent by helping him . . . thereby demonstrating sincerity to achieve an agreement with, rather than a triumph over, the adversary." [51]

The same mixture of elements of power and attitude strategies was evident in Martin Luther King, Jr.   The enemy who had to be overcome was clearly identified: "The policy-makers of the white society have caused the darkness: they created discrimination; they created slums; they perpetuate unemployment, ignorance, and poverty." [52] At the same time, King deplored certain kinds of behavior on the part of blacks and he noted that "white man" was only a general description of the enemy. For there are "millions who have morally risen above prevailing prejudices" and who "are willing to share power and to accept structural alterations of society." [53] This kind of distinction between a group and its leaders is a common way of following both the power and the attitude strategies.

Thus, nonviolence does not imply a less forceful course of action than violence. Bondurant has outlined nine steps in a satyagraha campaign:

reverse for violent △

1. Try to resolve the conflict or grievance by negotiation and arbitration (without compromising fundamentals);
2. Prepare the group for direct action (including preparation to suffer the consequences of the action);
3. Engage in propaganda and demonstrations;
4. Try once again to persuade the opponent to accede to the demands, explaining further action to be taken if he refuses;
5. Begin economic boycotts and various kinds of strikes;
6. Initiate a program of non-cooperation with established authorities and institutions;
7. Engage in civil disobedience to selected laws;
8. Take over some of the functions of government;
9. Establish a parallel government to handle those functions. [54]

The above is a progressive type of strategy; it could stop at any point at which the opponent acceded to the demands. Obviously, many of the steps were used by Martin Luther King, Jr., who acknowledged his own indebtedness to Gandhi. In India, satyagraha has been used by various groups, including Muslims who had traditionally resorted to violence to achieve their ends.

Nonviolent methods have been successfully used to effect change in other situations also. The efforts of Cesar Chavez to organize field laborers in California during the late 1960's and early 1970's has been a nonviolent crusade. The effort began as a strike of the grape pickers — mainly Mexican-American farm workers. And in spite of harassment by the police, strikebreaking efforts by the growers, hostile and contemptuous statements by the governor, and increased purchase of grapes by the Defense Department when other Americans were pressing for a nation-wide boycott, the growers eventually agreed to negotiate and sign a union contract. [55]

Other alternatives were open to Chavez, of course. He could have tried violent tactics against growers, strikebreaking workers, or the crops. Whether this would have enabled him to gain more or to gain it more quickly is an open question; we can only speculate on the basis of other historical change efforts. But the point here is that the nonviolent method did work. The course of history may be shaped by methods other than the heavy hand of violence.

In sum, it is man who makes history. And the methods by which he makes it are many. The history-maker must analyze each situation on its own merits in order to determine the appropriate target of his change effort, who should be involved in the effort, and what method will most likely lead to the desired outcome. For we now live in the history of the future. And the way that history will be written depends upon the extent to which and the manner in which we strive to shape the future. Pascal said that man is both "'the pride and refuse of the universe." [56] Any moral commitment will demand that we select strategies that will lead future historians to write about mankind in terms of the former rather than the latter.

ENDNOTES TO CHAPTER 13

1. Ch'en Tu-hsiu, "Call to Youth," in *China's Response to the West,* ed. Ssu-yu Teng and John K. Fairbank (New York: Atheneum, 1967), p. 242.

2. Albert O. Hirschman, *The Strategy of Economic Development* (New Haven: Yale University Press, 1958), pp. 11–20.

3. For a fuller treatment of each, see Harvey A. Hornstein, Barbara Benedict Bunker, W. Warner Burke, Marion Gindes, and Roy J. Lewicki, eds., *Social Intervention: A Behavioral Science Approach* (New York: The Free Press, 1971), pp. 9–142. For applications of the individualistic approach in organizations, see Harold J. Leavitt, "Applied Organizational Change in Industry: Structural, Technological and Humanistic Approaches," in *Handbook of Organizations,* ed. James G. March (Chicago: Rand McNally & Company, 1965), pp. 1151–67.

4. Robert J. Lifton, "Brainwashing in Perspective," *New Republic,* May 13, 1957, pp. 21–25.

5. Luther P. Gerlach and Virginia H. Hine, *People, Power, Change: Movements of Social Transformation* (Indianapolis: The Bobbs-Merrill Company, Inc., 1970).

6. Examples of T-group studies may be found in Hornstein, et al., *Social Intervention,* pp. 31–90. Examples of the discussion groups may be found in Kurt Lewin, *Field Theory in Social Science,* ed. Dorwin Cartwright (New York: Harper & Brothers, 1951).

7. Kurt Lewin, "Group Decision and Social Change," in *Readings in Social Psychology*, ed. Eleanor E. Maccoby, Theodore M. Newcomb, and Eugene L. Hartley, 3rd edition (New York: Holt, Rinehart and Winston, 1958), p. 202.

8. See A. Paul Hare, *Handbook of Small Group Research* (New York: The Free Press of Glencoe, 1962), pp. 46, 59–61.

9. Dorwin Cartwright, "Achieving Change in People: Some Applications of Group Dynamics Theory," *Human Relations*, IV (1951), 388–89.

10. *Ibid.*, pp. 390–91.

11. I am roughly differentiating between group and social structure by the extensiveness of the change involved. The group could be a small gathering of the T-group or group dynamics type, or a family, or a particular organization. In any case, it is a particular, identifiable group which may change without any significant consequences for the larger society. The social structure involves more extensive change because it involves the general social context or a plexus of interacting groups. The change diffuses through much or all of the society rather than remaining within a particular group. Obviously, a group has a structure, and, obviously, the social structure has numerous groups. One might try to change the social structure by changing certain groups. But one might also have as a target only a certain group, without any plan to effect wider changes.

12. Morton Deutsch and Mary Evans Collins, "Interracial Housing," in *American Social Patterns*, ed. William Petersen (Garden City: Anchor Books, 1956), pp. 7–59.

13. *Ibid.*, pp. 50–51.

14. Harold J. Leavitt, "Some Effects of Certain Communication Patterns on Group Performance," *Journal of Abnormal and Social Psychology*, XLVI (Jan., 1951), 38–50.

15. Nancy C. Morse and Everett Reimer, "The Experimental Change of a Major Organizational Variable," *Journal of Abnormal and Social Psychology*, LII (Jan., 1956), 120–29.

16. See William Foote Whyte, *Organizational Behavior: Theory and Application* (Homewood: The Dorsey Press, 1969), pp. 561–62.

17. There is a considerable amount of material published on Vicos. See, for example, Alan Holmberg, "Land Tenure and Planned Social Change: A Case from Vicos, Peru," *Human Organization*, XVIII (Spring, 1959), 7–10; and the papers in *Human Organization*, XXI (Summer, 1962), 107–24.

18. Data about Mexico are taken from the introduction and first three chapters of Joseph A. Kahl, ed., *Comparative Perspectives on Stratification: Mexico, Great Britain, Japan* (Boston: Little, Brown and Company, 1968), pp. ix–82.

19. Pablo Gonzalez-Casanova, "Dynamics of the Class Structure," in *Comparative Perspectives on Stratification*, ed. Kahl, p. 78.

20. August Meier, Elliott Rudwick, and Francis L. Broderick, eds., *Black Protest Thought in the Twentieth Century*, 2nd edition (Indianapolis: The Bobbs-Merrill Company, Inc., 1971).

21. Herman P. Miller, *Rich Man, Poor Man* (New York: Thomas Y. Crowell Company, 1964), pp. 37–55.

22. U.S. Bureau of Census, *Current Population Reports — Consumer Income*, Series P-60.

23. Quoted by Robert T. Golembiewski, "Small Groups and Large Organizations," in *Handbook of Organizations*, ed. March, p. 117.

24. Margaret Mead, ed., *Cultural Patterns and Technical Change* (New York: Mentor Books, 1955).

25. Mao Tse-tung, *Selected Works of Mao Tse-tung*, Vol. 1 (Peking: Foreign Languages Press, 1967), p. 33.

26. Paul Jacobs and Saul Landau, *The New Radicals* (New York: Vintage Books, 1966), p. 155.

27. Some of these points are treated more fully in Richard Flacks, "On Participatory Democracy," *Dissent*, November-December, 1966, pp. 701–708.

28. C. George Benello, "Participatory Democracy and the Dilemma of Change," in *The New Left*, ed. Priscilla Long (Boston: Porter Sargent Publisher, 1969), p. 410.

29. Neil W. Chamberlain, *Enterprise and Environment: The Firm in Time and Place* (New York: McGraw-Hill, Inc., 1968), p. 155.

30. Walter Gove and Herbert Costner, "Organizing the Poor: An Evaluation of a Strategy," in *Planned Social Intervention*, ed. Louis A. Zurcher, Jr., and Charles M. Bonjean (Scranton: Chandler Publishing Company, 1970), pp. 275–88.

31. See Zurcher and Bonjean, eds., *Planned Social Intervention*, pp. 289–338.

32. Robert Chin and Kenneth D. Benne, "General Strategies for Effecting Changes in Human Systems," in *The Planning of Change*, ed. Warren G. Bennis, Kenneth D. Benne, and Robert Chin, 2nd edition (New York: Holt, Rinehart and Winston, Inc., 1969), pp. 32–59.

33. Richard E. Walton, "Two Strategies of Social Change and Their Dilemmas," *The Journal of Applied Behavioral Science*, I (1965), 167–79.

34. Kenneth Keniston, "Youth, Change and Violence," *American Scholar*, XXXVII (1968), p. 242.

35. Walton, "Two Strategies of Social Change," *The Journal of Applied Behavioral Science*, p. 171.

36. Lewis S. Feuer, *The Conflict of Generations* (New York: Basic Books, Inc., 1969), pp. 529–31.

37. Philip Zimbardo and Ebbe B. Ebbesen, *Influencing Attitudes and Changing Behavior* (Reading: Addison-Wesley Publishing Company, 1969), pp. 94–122.

38. Rensis Likert, *The Human Organization: Its Management and Value* (New York: McGraw-Hill Book Company, 1967).

39. Garth N. Jones, "Strategies and Tactics of Planned Organizational Change: Case Examples in the Modernization Process of Traditional Societies," *Human Organization*, XXIV (Fall, 1965), p. 195.

40. Saul D. Alinsky, *Reveille for Radicals* (Chicago: University of Chicago Press, 1946), p. 30.

41. *Ibid.,* p. 154.

42. *Time*, March 2, 1970, p. 56.

43. Jerome H. Skolnick, *The Politics of Protest* (New York: Ballantine Books, 1969), pp. 105–109.

44. Michel Crozier, *The Bureaucratic Phenomenon* (Chicago: The University of Chicago Press, 1963).

45. *Ibid.,* p. 139.

46. Mao Tse-tung, *Selected Works*, pp. 343–44.

47. From the essay, "On the Correct Handling of Contradictions Among the People," in *Mao Tse-tung: An Anthology of His Writings*, ed. Anne Fremantle (New York: Mentor Books, 1962), p. 269.

48. *Ibid.,* p. 266.

49. Joan V. Bondurant, *Conquest of Violence* (Berkeley and Los Angeles: University of California Press, 1969), p. 8.

50. *Ibid.,* p. 39.

51. *Ibid.*

52. Martin Luther King, Jr., *The Trumpet of Conscience* (New York: Harper & Row, 1967), p. 8.

53. *Ibid.*

54. Bondurant, *Conquest of Violence*, pp. 40–41.

55. See *Time*, July 4, 1969, pp. 16–21, and "Cesar Chavez's Triumph," *St. Louis Post-Dispatch*, July 3, 1970, p. 2B.

56. Blaise Pascal, *Pensées*, trans. W. F. Trotter (New York: The Modern Library, 1941), p. 143.

Index

DATE DUE

PRINTED IN U.S.A.